Mediatized Dramaturgy

Methuen Drama Engage offers original reflections about key practitioners, movements and genres in the fields of modern theatre and performance. Each volume in the series seeks to challenge mainstream critical thought through original and interdisciplinary perspectives on the body of work under examination. By questioning existing critical paradigms, it is hoped that each volume will open up fresh approaches and suggest avenues for further exploration.

Series Editors

Mark Taylor-Batty
University of Leeds, UK
Enoch Brater
University of Michigan, USA

Titles

Harold Pinter
Edited by Basil Chiasson and Catriona Fallow
ISBN 978-1-3501-3362-4

A Companion to British-Jewish Theatre Since the 1950s
Edited by Sarah Jane Ablett, Jeanette R. Malkin and Eckart Voigts
ISBN 978-1-3501-3596-3

Brecht and Post-1990s British Drama
Anja Hartl
ISBN 978-1-3501-7278-4

Contemporary Drag Practices and Performers: Drag in a Changing Scene
Volume 1
Edited by Mark Edward and Stephen Farrier
ISBN 978-1-3500-8294-6

Drag Histories, Herstories and Hairstories: Drag in a Changing Scene
Volume 2
Edited by Mark Edward and Stephen Farrier
ISBN 978-1-3501-0436-5

Performing the Unstageable: Success, Imagination, Failure
Karen Quigley
ISBN 978-1-3500-5545-2

Drama and Digital Arts Cultures
David Cameron, Michael Anderson and Rebecca Wotzko
ISBN 978-1-472-59219-4

Social and Political Theatre in 21st-Century Britain: Staging Crisis
Vicky Angelaki
ISBN 978-1-474-21316-5

Mediatized Dramaturgy

The Evolution of Plays in the Media Age

Seda Ilter

Series Editors: Mark Taylor-Batty and
Enoch Brater

methuen | drama
LONDON • NEW YORK • OXFORD • NEW DELHI • SYDNEY

METHUEN DRAMA
Bloomsbury Publishing Plc
50 Bedford Square, London, WC1B 3DP, UK
1385 Broadway, New York, NY 10018, USA
29 Earlsfort Terrace, Dublin 2, Ireland

BLOOMSBURY, METHUEN DRAMA and the Methuen Drama logo are trademarks of Bloomsbury Publishing Plc

First published in Great Britain 2021
This paperback edition published 2023

Copyright © Seda Ilter, 2021

Seda Ilter has asserted her right under the Copyright, Designs and Patents Act, 1988, to be identified as author of this work.

For legal purposes the Acknowledgements on p. xi constitute an extension of this copyright page.

Series design by Louise Dugdale
Cover image: © Helen Murray / ArenaPAL

All rights reserved. No part of this publication may be reproduced or transmitted in any form or by any means, electronic or mechanical, including photocopying, recording, or any information storage or retrieval system, without prior permission in writing from the publishers.

Bloomsbury Publishing Plc does not have any control over, or responsibility for, any third-party websites referred to or in this book. All internet addresses given in this book were correct at the time of going to press. The author and publisher regret any inconvenience caused if addresses have changed or sites have ceased to exist, but can accept no responsibility for any such changes.

A catalogue record for this book is available from the British Library.

A catalog record for this book is available from the Library of Congress.

ISBN: HB: 978-1-3500-3115-9
PB: 978-1-3502-5475-6
ePDF: 978-1-3500-3117-3
eBook: 978-1-3500-3116-6

Series: Methuen Drama Engage

Typeset by Deanta Global Publishing Services, Chennai, India

To find out more about our authors and books visit www.bloomsbury.com and sign up for our newsletters.

To Selma and Faruk

Contents

List of Figures	x
Acknowledgements	xi
Preface	xii
Introduction: Theatre in a mediatized age: A brief overview	1
1 Theorizing mediatized dramaturgy	13
2 Plays of discord: Mediatized thematics and traditional dramatic form	39
3 Dramaturgy of language: Tracing mediatized culture in words	63
4 'Characterizing' the mediatized subject	101
5 New designs for the mediatized world: Plot structure	147
6 Mediaturgical plays: Writing for theatre through media	173
Conclusion: Mediatized dramaturgy and beyond: Texts in progress	193
Notes	199
References	204
Index	213

Figures

1	*The Nether*	57
2	*Closer*	91
3	*Attempts on Her Life*	93
4	*Attempts on Her Life*	95
5	*This Is How We Die*	98
6	*Firefall*	142
7 & 8	*Love and Information*	168
9 &10	*The Yes/No Plays*	181
11	*The Yes/No Plays*	185

Acknowledgements

My thanks begin with those who supported and advised this project in its first version as a doctoral thesis in the Department of Drama and Theatre at Sussex University. I am extremely grateful to my supervisor Professor David Barnett for his impeccable guidance and for shaping my way of thinking in most exciting ways. I would also like to extend my deepest gratitude to Dr Sara Jane Bailes for her intellectual support and scholarly guidance, and for her heartfelt encouragement and friendship. I am so very grateful to Bloomsbury Methuen Drama Series (London) who agreed to give this book a home, and to Mark Dudgeon and Meredith Benson for their kind support. Special thanks to the playwrights and theatre directors who permitted me interviews and provided me with materials: Tim Crouch, David Greig, Douglas Maxwell, Simon Stephens, John Tiffany, Nicola Bramkamp from Das Schauspielhaus in Hamburg. For collegiality and support: Dr Molly Flynn, Dr Louise Owen, Dr Fintan Walsh, Professor Heike Bauer and my inspiring colleagues at Birkbeck College, University of London. For helpful comments and valuable suggestions on this book in its various stages and for her never-ending encouragement, my thanks are due to my wonderful friend and editor, Dr Ruth Charnock. The fruition of this book would not have been possible without the support and inspiration of my friends near and far: Özge Aktaş and Başak Candemir for reminding me not to miss life while being an academic; Seda Bilgi for patiently waiting for me to come home and always being there for me; Kelly Ann Ee for bringing adventure into my life; Aynur Mete for shining a light on my life; Clair Morrow for always empowering me; Chris Odle for being my lighthouse; and my friends – Cate, Em, Hannah, Maddie, Mhairi, Rachel, Syd and Claire – for being my powerhouses and inspiring me everyday to be a better human.

My deepest thanks go to my family for their constant support and for patiently bearing my absence. Thank you my parents – Selma and Faruk – for always believing in me and encouraging me to go far away and find my own path even if this meant an everlasting longing; to my sister Bilge for being my rock; to Oscar for bringing joy into our family, and to my dearest Damien Çınar for every smile you have put on my face. Finally, thank you to Adam for bringing more meaning, depth and excitement to my life, and for laughing, thinking and being with me.

Preface

What can plays do?

In February 2020, I went to the Unicorn Theatre (London) to see Tim Crouch's *I, Cinna (The Poet)* – one of Crouch's *I, Shakespeare* plays – which tells the story of Shakespeare's *Julius Caesar* with a focus on Cinna the poet, a minor character with only a few lines in Shakespeare's play. Cinna sits at the heart of Crouch's play; he is a struggling poet – struggling financially, but also and importantly, struggling to write, to find the words to make sense of and respond to the world outside. The world Cinna lives in is not fifth century BC Rome, but the precarious world of the twenty-first century, identified through projected images of protests, riots and police brutality, through the constant bombardment of information on our mobile phones and breaking news on our screens which may be fake or real. As Cinna explains, language in this world can be dangerous, repressive, manipulative or guilty, hinting at surveillance, censorship and big data services working through social media, scrutinizing our words. In the face of such turmoil, a sense of powerlessness and the complicated ways that language works through us, the writer questions the relationship between the artist and the world. What can art do to generate responsible and effective deeds? Asking '[w]hat can words do?', 'How can words change things?', he invites us to take responsibility for our words and write a poem together.

As I entered the auditorium, what I saw struck and enthused me not because there was something shocking or extraordinary to be seen. On the contrary, what I saw on stage was rather simple: in front of a massive hanging sheet of crumpled paper sat Crouch at a desk on which there was a notepad, a laptop and a mobile phone (besides a wrapped plastic chicken). This image, which is also on the cover of this book, gathered more meaning as the play began, and Tim and Cinna – two writers, real and fictional – acknowledged their media-saturated lives, how these technologies shaped their environment, consciousness and creative process. Phone notifications, buzzing, pinging, bombardment of information, breaking news on the laptop and the app 'Freedom' as an antidote to all define Cinna's world. Crouch's act of contextualizing the writer in the info-loaded, globally connected mediatized culture is not merely or simply about bringing Cinna into the contemporary moment. But, I contend, it is also and importantly a symbolic gesture referring to the changing social, cognitive and aesthetic conditions of writing, shaping the form and content of the texts produced. The image of the writer – particularly of the playwright – in a mediatized world is an emblematic embodiment of the root of the question I set out to explore in this book: How do playtexts evolve in relation and response to our media-saturated everyday lives, our mediatized culture and consciousness?

Drawing and expanding on this question, I also ask how plays in the mediatized age can crack open our deep-seated perceptions of the world that are profoundly affected by media culture and technologies. How can plays offer a critically engaging, transformative and dissident perspective on the contemporary – the culture of screens, short attention spans, fast-paced lives and the disempowering discourse of populist media and politics? The questions Crouch's Cinna recurrently asks – *What can words do?; How will my words change anything?* – echo my questions here about the capacity of language and what it can do in the face of a complex and uncertain world. The play is an invitation to think about the power and role of language, what words can do and undo, and how a writer (the playwright, Cinna, and the audience) can use words *responsibly* to generate an alternative, unorthodox view of the world we live in. In a similar vein, this book is an invitation to think about how playwrights write today, how the aesthetics and thematics of contemporary dramatic writing have evolved to respond to our media-driven culture and consciousness, and how plays can create space for dissident thinking about and critical resistance to the given narratives of our late capitalist, mediatized culture.

Introduction

Theatre in a mediatized age: A brief overview

At a talk that theatre-maker and playwright Tim Crouch gave to our postgraduate students at Birkbeck College (University of London, 2017), he pointed out a significant aspect of playwriting when he said that the writing is shaped always in conversation with our environments and the tools we create and use. In an age where media technologies pervade and contour almost every aspect of our lives, dramatic writing is inevitably formed and delivered in relation to this mediatized social, cultural and cognitive ecology. Increasingly since the 1990s, and especially since the digital revolution of the early 2000s, when information and communication technologies became more ubiquitous and accessible than ever before, a growing number of plays written for the stage have tackled the impact of media on society, politics, human relationships and perception. Some of these plays overtly address these themes by directly referring to them in form and/or content such as Patrick Marber's *Closer* (1997), Lucy Prebble's *The Sugar Syndrome* (2003), Sarah Ruhl's *Dead Man's Cell Phone* (2007), Jennifer Haley's *The Nether* (2013), Hannah Jane Walker and Chris Thorpe's *I Wish I was Lonely* (2013) and the Royal Court Theatre's *Bytes* (2013). A prominent example is Caryl Churchill's *Love and Information* (2012), which, with its fifty-seven short individual scenes that eschew a linear and coherent storyline, formally and thematically evokes the information bombardment we are exposed to, our fragmented society, fast-paced lives and consumerist attitudes. On the other hand, certain plays respond to media culture *implicitly* through aesthetic reflection and inquiry, namely, through their dramaturgical structure, without necessarily or straightforwardly referring to new technologies in their content. For instance, through the mode of language and characterization, Simon Stephens's *Pornography* (2007), John Jesurun's *Firefall* (2009) and Christopher Brett Bailey's *This Is How We Die* (2014; *THWD*) reflect on the changing nature of human relationships and subjectivity in our networked world without directly presenting technologies at the heart of their narratives. *Pornography*'s unidentified, fragmented mode of characterization not only resists the liberal-humanist concept of character but also speaks to our fragmented, multiple sense of subjectivity and media-driven, transitory engagements with others on platforms such as social media.

Correspondingly, the stage has become increasingly interested in using emergent technologies in theatre performance and with the ways in which rapidly evolving media technologies impact our everyday lives and society. One of the most intriguing forms to emerge has been the use of simultaneous filming of live performance on stage and its synchronized projection on screens, as seen in the works of the Wooster Group, Katie Mitchell and Robert Lepage. The shaping influence of media technologies on theatre is also in evidence in interactive theatre performances by such companies as Blast Theory, Metis Arts and Coney, and in multimedia pieces by 1927 and Complicité – among others. As audiences, we easily recognize the translation of our everyday technologies onto stage, and we grasp the structures and meanings media technologies have generated when, for example, we are asked to take part in a performance through a handheld computer in Blast Theory's *Rider Spoke* (2007) or when we have a multisensory experience through the mix of animation, film, live performance and music in 1927's *Between the Devil and the Deep Blue Sea* (2008). This media-saturated theatrical context has also introduced us to broadcast theatre: the National Theatre has live-streamed productions such as *Medea* (2014) in cinemas since 2009; Forced Entertainment broadcast some of their works such as *Quizoola!* (2013) and *Speak Bitterness* (2014) live on the internet, and Robert Wilson's *Einstein on the Beach* (2012) and Thomas Ostermeier's *Richard III* (2016), among others, have been live-streamed online.

These developments, radically and irrevocably changing the landscape of theatre practice and experience, have re-galvanized scholarly debate about the ontology and phenomenology of theatre as well as drawing attention to new categories such as intermedial theatre, digital theatre and multimedia theatre. As I will discuss in Chapter 1, the majority of critical discussion often concentrates on aesthetics and design, directing and spectatorship in performance.[1] One of the common debates, for instance, has been about the question of 'liveness',[2] namely, how the incorporation of media technologies in performances affects the ontology of theatre; its here-and-nowness, proximity and immediacy. Although these discussions are fundamental and necessary, they often focus on the *performance* aspect of theatre, on components such as the performer's body and scenographic elements without essentially reflecting on the playtext, the written component of theatre performance. This gap in the scholarship is particularly interesting when considered in relation to the historically text-oriented British theatre tradition in which the practice of writers' theatre still plays a crucial role.

There have certainly been attempts to fill this gap. Nevertheless, more often than not, the emerging literature on dramatic writing in relation to technology and media culture has often focused on the thematic content, on whether a play 'talks about' the technologies or not, focusing on 'the development of theme rather than [. . .] the exploration of form' (Lonergan 2015: 48). For example, Amy Petersen Jensen and Michael Kustow look into the explicit representation of media technologies in the narrative content of plays such as Mark Ravenhill's *Shopping and Fucking* (1996) and *Faust Is Dead* (1997). Kerstin Schmidt studies American drama, particularly Jean-Claude van Itallie's plays, and explores how they thematically address the 'trivializing power of the omnipresent media on contemporary society's ritualized behaviour patterns, and its unrestrained consumerism' (2005: 89). A similar desire for direct representation of technologies in theatre is evident in Matt Trueman's *The Guardian* piece, 'What Can Theatre Say about the Internet?', in which Trueman critiques Caryl Churchill's *Love and Information* for not directly representing the internet: 'despite scenes titled Google and Twitter, the play hardly ever mentioned the web directly – once in terms of dodgy network signals, once when an insomniac logs onto Facebook, and again when a character is sacked by email' (*The Guardian* 2013). This kind of focus on the explicit presence and portrayal of technologies in the content of plays and their performances is, to an extent, rooted in naturalism's desire for reproducing what is found in the physical world directly and with objectivity 'as it is'. However, the emphasis on the *overt* thematization of media technologies in plays' thematic content overlooks the possible, often implicit, ways in which these texts respond to the mediatized culture and consciousness.

Drawing on these observations about playtexts within the changing ontology and aesthetics of theatre, *Mediatized Dramaturgy* explores how dramatic writing has evolved in content and form, and how the emerging shifts speak to our media-saturated society, culture and consciousness. To this end, I will explore components of plays such as characterization, plot and language. In relation to this, I also examine new textual formations such as plays written through social media platforms (i.e. *mediaturgical plays*, Chapter 6) and explore the aesthetics and critical meanings of such media-based playtexts. By focusing on the dramaturgy of certain playtexts in Anglophone theatre, this study investigates contemporary plays' aesthetic evolution in an age of theatre marked by mediatization and its possibilities, and in a theatre culture that praises its plays and playwrights. In order to carry out this investigation, I propose a new critical paradigm: 'mediatized dramaturgy'. It is useful at this point to briefly outline how I use these two key terms – 'mediatization' and 'dramaturgy' – in the context of this study.

Mediatized dramaturgy

I will discuss the notion of mediatization in more detail in Chapter 1, but here it suffices to briefly introduce the term in order to delineate my concept of *mediatized dramaturgy*. The idea of mediatization emerged from and is used most often in the fields of sociology and media studies. It refers to the ubiquitous influence of media, in the form of social and cultural institutions and ideological technologies of power, on society and individuals increasingly and most influentially from the late twentieth century onwards. 'Media'[3] here refers to something more than a simple collection of individual mediums or tools. By 'media', I mean 'all institutionalized structures, forms, formats and interfaces for disseminating symbolic content' (Couldry 2012: viii). Media are 'characterized by historical, cultural, social, aesthetic and communicative facets' (Ellestrӧm 2010: 5), and they produce, shape and communicate meanings in connection with the sociocultural and political context. This definition of media denotes two important points: (1) media is profoundly intertwined with power relations and (2) media and society (the human) are connected and they co-evolve.[4] In relation to the phenomenon of mediatization, 'media' does not merely refer to the human-generated tools or technologies that determine our contemporary condition, but that, rather, '*are* our situation' (Mitchell and Hansen 2010: xxii; emphasis in original). As technologies of meaning, which are increasingly more central to our existence, media shapes and influences our everyday lives, interpersonal relations, subjectivity and consciousness. Hence, when we think about a mediatized culture, we think about the contemporary world in which we are constantly inundated with information, our attention spans are shorter, our spatio-temporal experience has transformed, our interpersonal relationships are demarcated increasingly by social media and our perception of virtual reality and physical reality as distinct states and experiences has radically changed.

The second notion, dramaturgy, which is a 'slippery, elastic and inclusive term' (Turner and Behrndt 2008: 18), has multiple meanings such as 'the ceaseless dialogue between people who are working on a play together[,] the thing that connects all the various elements of a play together [, and] the soul, the internal structure, of a production' (Van Kerkhoven cited in Eckersall 2006: 288). Dramaturgy is not restricted merely to the translation from written text to stage, to the organization of performance in close and direct connection with dramatic composition and the historical, cultural or political context. In contemporary Western theatre, dramaturgy considers performance as a whole and offers a theoretical framework that functions as a conceptual coordinator for a production's intellectual, critical, structural, compositional and contextual codes and coherence. 'With dramaturgy', Duška Radosavljević explains, 'anything goes, so long as the artwork being created – text-based or not – is crafted with rigour, intelligence, intuition and attention to detail' (2013: 103). These are all valid and effective uses of this wide-ranging term, but this book puts forward a related yet also different use of the notion. Here, I identify and use dramaturgy *solely* with reference to the fabric of the written text – namely, the organization of character, plot, theme and language, and the critical logic underpinning these elements.

Combining the two key terms, I put forward the notion of *mediatized dramaturgy* in order to refer to and explore new modes of playtext that have evolved in response to a mediatized world rather than to theatrical dramaturgies and to investigate how they incorporate media technologies within performances. Using this notion as the theoretical framework, I look into different elements of the playtext – its thematic content, language, characterization and plot structure. For example, I examine the ways in which language is mediatized through the use of medialect in *Closer*. Elsewhere, I consider how *Attempts on Her Life* and *Firefall* (2006, 2009) use fragmented language to deliver bits of information that fail to form a coherent narrative or dialogue among the characters, and as a result, evoke the sense of social disintegration in a firmly networked culture. Following the analysis of dramaturgical elements in relation to mediatization, as mentioned earlier, I will use the same theoretical framework to explore media-based playtexts, which I call *mediaturgical plays*. This new category is not necessarily or hugely different from the playtexts as we know them: they still contain the same elements such as plot structure and characterization, yet they are created via media platforms and shaped in relation to the aesthetics and contexts of these media technologies. David Greig's *The Yes/No Plays* (2013–14), for instance, is formed via the news and social network site Twitter and structured as short, 140-character dialogues culminating in micro-scenes.

What is a playtext?

In this study, playtext (sometimes used interchangeably with 'play') refers to dramatic writing, namely, to the playscript written by a playwright for an audience. Dramatic writing 'is linked to performance, to the action grasped in its tension, to an action performed by *actants* (acting forces), generally characters' (Pavis 2016: 55). I will elaborate on certain aspects of contemporary playtexts in relation to dramatic and postdramatic theatre, particularly in terms of *no-longer-dramatic theatre texts* in Chapter 1. But suffice it to say that the no-longer-dramatic texts under examination herein are often the basis or outline for a performance without being the primary element or absolute centre of the performance that the director firmly adheres to and translates to the stage.

In addition, a playtext is, more often than not, a published, material text that one can hold in one's hands. However, as shall be examined in Chapter 6 with reference to mediaturgical plays, this new mode of dramatic writing can sometimes be documented without being published. This is mainly because these playtexts are written entirely or mostly by using the platform and aesthetic design of media technologies such as Twitter, Facebook and weblogs. Therefore, perhaps in line with the visual and transitory qualities of these digital platforms and due to the fact that publishers might not consider these scripts as *proper* plays in the traditional sense, these texts are not often published. Yet I argue that this does not change their status as plays, for they are written by a playwright for an audience and performance, and they display and exercise elements of dramaturgical design such as characterization, plot structure and so on. These playtexts are a part of current theatre practice and therefore require further critical attention.

This categorization and analysis of playtexts exclude some other forms of writing for performance such as 'theatre texts', which are 'braided, knotted, threaded, sewn, patched together, edited, *montaged* [and] *evolve in the process of making performance*' (Furse 2011: 5). Theatre texts are often produced *collectively* by devised theatre companies, artist groups or theatre-makers. Companies such as Forced Entertainment, the Builders Association and Suspect Culture work collaboratively with texts – found, new, montaged – and other material that often emerges not only prior to but also during rehearsals and performance process. Theatre texts also comprise what I preliminarily call *techno-texts* which are formed collectively by theatre-makers and, sometimes, along with participants via digital platforms such as Blast Theory's *Karen* (2015). In *Karen*, an app-based virtual theatre piece about the big data culture we live in and our indifference to the invasion of privacy, there are layers of text: the framing story written by the artists while building the app; the interactive narrative formed through the responses of the participant-audience; and the personality analysis report produced at the end by the artists' algorithmic system in response to the participants' responses. These theatre texts emerge as original textual constituents of mediatized theatre with similarities to playtexts such as character presentation, dramatic dialogue and episodic plot structure.[5]

The discussion of theatre texts is beyond the focus of this study. Here, I investigate the evolution of playtexts in the Anglophone theatre context, predominantly within the historically text-oriented British theatre tradition since the 1990s. The focus on British theatre mainly originates from the question I pose above: In a theatre culture, where the idea and trend for writers' theatre have flourished and where a theatre event is often considered in connection with a dramatic text, what has happened to the playtext in the current mediatized cultural ecology? It is important to consider not only how plays have evolved but also how or whether they offer innovative aesthetic forms and strategies to grasp and critically engage with the social, political and cognitive environment we live in. Throughout this study, I will enrich my focus on British theatre by studying and referring to North American plays such as John Jesurun's *Firefall*, Jeremy Gable's *The 15th Line*, and Jennifer Haley's *The Nether*. Additionally, I have chosen to consider original[6] English-language playtexts written since the 1990s because it is predominantly since then that the 'transformation of culture into e-culture, of computers into universal carriers, of media into new media' (Manovich 2001: 6) has escalated along with the prevalent use of social media, information and geo-location technologies, which has been picked up on the British theatre scene as well as in Irish and North American theatres. This does not mean that theatre in text and performance did not engage with emerging technologies and media culture prior to this moment. Productions by the Wooster Group or some of the plays by Jean-Claude van Itallie since the 1970s, to name a few, engage with media technologies and the cultural shift they had generated. Nevertheless, as I will elaborate in Chapter 1, the extent of media's influence on society and consciousness has never been as pervasive and rapidly evolving as it has been since the digital revolution of the 1990s–2000s.

In addition, with the fall of the Berlin Wall in 1989 and the collapse of the Communist East thereafter, political discourse lost the tension between capitalism and socialism. Instead, finance capitalism, technological advances and globalization have dominated societies. Developments in media, particularly in information and communication technologies, have reinforced the expansion of capitalist economy, values and social relationships on a global scale, challenging traditional concepts of nationhood, subjectivity, social relations and class. This shift became manifest in Anglophone theatre as state-of-the-nation-plays gradually went out of fashion, and new modes of dramaturgical and theatrical expression emerged in response to the virtual erasure of an alternative discourse to discussing capitalism due to the seeming inevitability of its triumph. As I will explore, certain plays have rethought their dramaturgical conception and ideological groundings in relation to this change in sociocultural and political circumstance, and sublimated overt and direct political discussion to a discourse on or critique of mediatized culture. That is, plays have become interested in media technologies and mediatization as a political–critical phenomenon and thus present a new way of discussing the dominant, late capitalist order. This critical interest is evident not necessarily in 'the direct thematization of the political' (Lehmann [1999] 2006: 178) and of what it means to live in a mediatized culture, but, significantly and primarily, in the dramaturgical structure,[7] in 'the implicit substance and critical value of *mode of representation*' (Lehmann [1999] 2006: 178). In other words, the critical potential of plays and theatre lies predominantly in their form. Text and stage have reconfigured form in response to the dominant narratives of late capitalist society, which are profoundly structured and disseminated through media technologies, shaping our perceptions, subjectivity and relationships. Accordingly, I will investigate how certain modes of mediatized dramaturgy offer the possibility for resistant aesthetics and dissident thinking that can challenge these narratives.

From text to stage: Mediatized dramaturgy in action

The focus on playtexts does not suggest restoring textual autonomy and primacy – the idea that has traditionally treated the text separately from performance and its elements. Instead, I follow the idea that dramatic writing 'is always in motion, thinking about and with performance, not in place of performance, and without predetermining performance' (Worthen 2010: 81). Hence, this book considers playtexts as one of the components and tools of theatre and as incomplete and latent without or outside performance that 'resurrects it and brings it to completion' (Badiou 2008: 212). My analysis here always takes in the text–performance relationship and examines how a play, as a form, shapes performance materials and is interpreted on stage in order to appreciate the possibilities that the new dramaturgical modes offer. For instance, when I discuss characterization in texts, this is accompanied by the analysis of character presentation in performance through the performer's body. Likewise, when I think about plot structure, I am also considering the mechanics and meanings of scenography and spatio-temporal action. For example, in *Firefall* the use of screens, live filming of stage action, pre-recorded material and rapidly changing images draws on and works in tandem with the text's plot structure and language. In *The Nether*, the scenography created through mirrors, projected images and lighting completes the double reality the plot is based on. However, it is important to note here that as mediatization can be implicit in playtexts, it can also be covert in performance. Or, when it is obvious in a playtext, it may not be tangible in a performance. For instance, despite the fact that there are direct references to the internet, television and social media in Churchill's *Love and Information*, in James Macdonald's production at the

Royal Court Theatre, we do not overtly experience the mediatization of our lives through the materials of performance such as props, but through our aesthetic engagement with the play's plot structure in short, abrupt scenes that bombard us with information.

The performances in question are often the playtexts' first productions. I am aware that first productions may offer a restricted view because they might easily be raw or naive rather than critical and may take the plays at 'face value'. Nevertheless, since the engagement with the plays is without prior examples, first productions represent important and fresh perspectives on directorial tendencies in relation to dramaturgical trends. Where access to the first productions is not possible or easy, I have chosen to examine the best-known productions of the playtexts; this allows for the consideration of predominant and popular fashions in dramaturgy of performance as well as of text.

Summary

Chapter 1 sets the theoretical background for the discussion of rapidly evolving media–theatre relations and explains the phenomenon and notion of mediatization. Drawing on the given theoretical foundations, I demonstrate some of the context and trends in contemporary Anglophone theatre in relation to mediatized culture, and then inquire about the place of the playtext within current theatre practice, scholarship and culture. After setting the theoretical foundations, Chapter 2 examines the ways in which certain plays engage with mediatization directly in terms of their thematic content and by adhering to the vision and aesthetics of dramatic theatre tradition. In this chapter, I investigate what the critical and formal implications of *dramatic mediatized dramaturgy* are and to what extent these plays critically map and engage with contemporary mediatized society. To this end, I examine Mark Ravenhill's *Faust Is Dead* (1996) and Jennifer Haley's *The Nether* (2013), which belong to different periods of our rapidly changing mediatized culture, and discuss how their timely thematic reflections accommodate and respond to the experiential and perceptual conditions of contemporary mediatized culture.

Drawing on the argument set in Chapter 2, Chapters 3, 4 and 5 move the analysis of mediatized plays further from thematic content towards the study of the fabric of playtexts by focusing on three dramaturgical components – language, characterization and plot. Chapter 3 focuses on the dramaturgy of language, exploring how the form of language in plays changes in response to mediatization. It considers direct and indirect expressions of mediatization through language. The former consists of new modes of linguistic styles, directly originating from specific media (*medialect*). The latter refers to more implicit manifestations of mediatization in relation to other social processes, which cause the linguistic medium to be an increasingly ideological, fragmented and Anglicized construct. The chapter explores these ideas through Patrick Marber's *Closer* (1997), Martin Crimp's *Attempts on Her Life* (1997) and Christopher Brett Bailey's *THWD* (2014).

Following the analysis of language, Chapter 4 focuses on the mode of characterization and examines the ways in which character presentation accommodates our changing sense of self and other, our subjectivity and intersubjective relations in a mediatized context. Drawing links specifically with poststructuralist and posthumanist views on subjectivity as well as with debates about the mediatization of the subject and human relationships in the late capitalist era, this chapter explores how playtexts consider mediatized subjectivity and engages with the question of what it means to 'be' in contemporary culture. The chapter studies Simon Stephens's *Pornography* (2007) and John Jesurun's *Firefall* (2009), and the ways in which they destabilize the liberal-humanist view of the human subject and the traditional form of dramatic character in a bid to grasp how new configurations of subjectivity encourage dissident perspectives on our idea and experience of subjectivity, profoundly shaped by media culture.

As the last section of the book that focuses on dramaturgical components, Chapter 5 explores the form and workings of the plot structure of playtexts. In this chapter, I further investigate mediatized dramaturgical patterns in plays and discuss whether and how new approaches in plot composition directly or implicitly accommodate media aesthetics and aspects of a mediatized culture. The chapter examines Douglas Maxwell's *Helmet* (2002) and its use of a computer game format as the basis for its dramaturgical framework, and the unidentified, fragmented, multi-sketch form of Caryl Churchill's *Love and Information* (2012). The analysis of these plays demonstrates the fundamentally different mechanics and critical implications of these forms of mediatized plot composition and shows how the no-longer-dramatic mode of plot composition opens new vistas for critical thinking and engagement with our mediatized existence. This chapter concludes the part of the study focusing on the playtext as a form written solely by playwrights and published in the traditional sense either before or after their stage productions.

Chapter 6 offers a different and significant remark on mediatized theatre and plays by exploring the playtexts, which place media technologies and aesthetics at the heart of their formation process and dramaturgical composition. Here, I draw on Bonnie Marranca's term 'mediaturgy', which suggests a shift from a text-centred performance dramaturgy into a media-inspired composition that embeds media forms in the performance. Extending her focus on performance to the written component of theatre, I propose to identify the playtexts in question as 'mediaturgical plays'. This subcategory of mediatized plays highlights the central role of media in the formation process, structure and presentation of these plays and, relatedly, distinguishes them from the ones examined in the previous four chapters. The chapter explores the creation, composition and the performance of mediaturgical plays to question how they engage with contemporary culture and consciousness. To this end, the chapter considers David Greig's Twitter plays *The Yes/No Plays*, formed via Twitter and edited for live performance, and also refers to Jeremy Gable's Twitter drama *The 15th Line* and Chris Goode's *Hippo World Guest Book*, which is based on participants' edited inputs on an online blog for a year. While considering the new category of plays in terms of form, content and authorship, I also examine how these technologically generated playtexts are put on stage.

The final chapter demonstrates that the capacity of a playtext's mediatized dramaturgy to relate and respond to sociocultural and perceptual conditions of the mediatized age varies according to its approach to the mode of representation. In relation to this, I conclude my argument that 'no-longer-dramatic theatre texts' with mediatized dramaturgical patterns engender and work through resistant aesthetics that subvert the dominating modes of perception, values and behaviours in society and invite the critical questioning of media's role in these modes. I also highlight how the evolution of playtexts in response to mediatization generates new aesthetic trends inviting critical thinking and demonstrate how these texts challenge the dominant idea that the written component of theatre in an age of audiovisual, digital forms is less relevant or capable of relating to this culture. This chapter also briefly mentions other forms emerging in mediatized theatre practice and concludes that it is crucial to recognize and examine various forms of and approaches to texts with mediatized dramaturgies within and in relation to the Anglophone theatre tradition, which has historically privileged writing.

1

Theorizing mediatized dramaturgy

We live in a media-saturated culture: we shop online; track our nutrition, movements and sleep with wearable tech; communicate ideas and opinions on global social media networks; consent to our privacy being violated by multinational corporations and political actors, while, at the same time, participating in social activism against dataveillance on media platforms funded or owned by these same corporations. Theorizing this culture, Neil Postman puts forward an important argument:

> [T]echnological change is neither additive nor subtractive. It is ecological. [. . .] One significant change generates total change. If you remove the caterpillars from a given habitat, you are not left with the same environment minus caterpillars: you have a new environment, and you have reconstituted the conditions of survival; the same is true if you add caterpillars to an environment that has had none. (1992: 18)

Media's ecology is deeply connected to sociocultural and political ecology: as new technologies emerge and enter our lives, a consequential change occurs in the social, cultural, economic and political spheres of society. As Postman illustrates, fifty years after the invention of the printing press, 'we did not have old Europe plus the printing press. We had a different Europe' (1992: 18). Likewise, in today's fast, hyper-connected and digitized world, everything has changed: from our everyday lives and relationships to our sense of reality and self-expression. We now live, as Zygmunt Bauman argues, 'in the insubstantial, instantaneous time of the software world' (2012: 118). New realities such as the global capitalist culture industry characterized by data mining and information manipulation prevail.

Playtexts, stamped with the structures and circumstances of the culture that they are produced in, have undergone intriguing changes. As with the stage, which is populated by current technologies and aesthetically and conceptually influenced by the changing media ecology, playtexts speak of a world and consciousness shaped by media technologies and the societal, cultural transformation they have engendered. However, when we consider the relationship between the theatre and media, we often focus on the audio, visual, tactile and virtual aspects. We think about the use of multiple projections or screens on stage as shrewdly deployed in Tonnelgroep Amsterdam's *Roman Tragedies* (2007) and the Builders Association's *Super Vision* (2005–6), or the inventive use of sound technology in such works as the Fuel Theatre's *Ring* (2015) and Complicité's *The Encounter* (2015). Considering the increasing influence and presence of technologies and media culture in theatre, one wonders where playtexts sit. How has dramatic writing evolved, and how does it make meaning in relation to a media-saturated world and theatre landscape? How do playtexts accommodate, speak to and raise critical awareness about the impact of media on our lives?

This chapter provides the theoretical background for the analysis of these questions throughout *Mediatized Dramaturgy*. To this end, first I define and outline the notion of mediatization – the sociocultural backdrop that generates media-derived structures, language and meaning in contemporary theatre and dramatic writing. Second, I present an overview of how the increasing presence of media technologies in everyday life has affected the theatre scene, and relatedly, how critical interest in this subject, which has often separated media and text, has left the question of dramatic writing under-examined.

Mediatization: Background

The technological has always been at the core of the human evolutionary process. Technology and media are not 'something external and contingent, but rather an essential – indeed, *the* essential – dimension of the human' (Hansen 2010: 65; emphasis in original). Media has never been a neutral force: specific technologies have long-shaped social organization, cognitive patterning, and cultural interaction and values. Today, we live in an age and culture where media is increasingly prevalent, affecting aspects of our lives, consciousness, selfhood, social relations and sociopolitical institutions. We have instant access to information via search engines; we record and digitize our memories on Instagram; we follow news and, at least to a certain extent, affect sociopolitical dynamics by releasing news via social networking services such as Twitter. In this sociocultural setting, 'characterized by diverse, intersecting, and still-evolving forms of multimodal, interactive, networked forms of communication' (Livingstone 2009b: ix), media is not an accumulation of different technological mediums, separate from cultural and other social institutions; nor is it supplemental to the content it carries and communicates. Instead, media is a cultural technology, a social institution and an ideological mechanism that operates in its own right and affects the workings of society, individuals' lives and consciousness. It is not merely and narrowly a technical body or system, but the perceptual and ontological condition and the sociocultural and epistemological environment we live in. Media technologies do not merely determine our situation, as Friedrich Kittler initially suggested, but rather, as Mark Hansen and William J. T. Mitchell put it, they '*are* our situation' (Mitchell and Hansen 2010: xxii). The changing social and cognitive landscape since the late twentieth century and predominantly since the early twenty-first century – a process that marks the emergence and widespread use of digital media technologies and platforms such as personal computers, the internet and social media – has led to the search for frameworks through which to understand the contemporary world and the changes media has exerted on society. The concept of mediatization can be usefully applied to the theatre and dramaturgy in order to tackle the question of how contemporary plays have evolved in our media-saturated culture and theatre.

Let's briefly consider the Germanic roots of the term *Mediatisierung* to clarify its complex meaning in English. The German use of 'mediatization' dates back to the nineteenth century when 'the states of the Holy Roman Empire were "mediatized" by Napoleon [as] Napoleon interposed between the miscellany of independent cities, the princes and the archbishops who previously answered only to the Emperor, an intermediate level of territorial authorities' (Livingstone 2009a: 6). The term, used in a governmental context, may appear irrelevant to its current use. However, Sonia Livingstone argues that, similar to the way 'the rule of the annexed state keeps his title' (Livingstone 2009a: 6), the media 'not only get between any and all participants in society but also, crucially, annex a sizeable part of their power by mediatizing – subordinating – the previously powerful authorities of government, education, the church, the family' (Livingstone 2009a: 6). The increasing power of media over other societal and cultural institutions is an important aspect of mediatization.

The contemporary use of the term *Mediatisierung* simply refers to social change in relation to media's prevalent influence and presence, as well as to the interconnections between media and other social systems and institutions. Some media scholars and sociologists use terms such as 'medialization'[1] and 'mediazation'[2] to denote the influence of media on social and cultural conditions. However, alongside mediatization, 'mediation' is the most commonly used notion to characterize media influence in the contemporary world. These two notions can be confused or considered to be the same. Nevertheless, media theorists such as Stig Hjarvard, Sonia Livingstone, Gianpietro Mazzoleni and Winfried Schulz suggest mediatization differs from, though overlaps with, the broader concept of mediation. Briefly, mediation refers to 'any acts of intervening, conveying, or reconciling between different actors, collectives, or institutions' (Mazzoleni and Schulz 2010: 249). By contrast, mediatization refers to a process whereby media move beyond simply mediating in the sense of 'getting in between' (Livingstone 2009b: ix–x); instead, they 'alter the historical possibilities for human communication by reshaping relations not just among media organizations and their publics but among all social institutions – government, commerce, family, church, and so forth' (Livingstone 2009b). Mediatization, therefore, implies a social phenomenon exerted on contemporary society and individuals by media.

It is also important to touch on the idea of 'media logic' at this point since it is fundamental to our understanding of mediatization as a current social, cultural and cognitive experience. David Altheide and Robert Snow's understanding of media as a social force proposes that media has a unique logic of its own which shapes social life and other social institutions (1979: 9, 12). Media logic, they argue, is 'a way of "seeing" and of interpreting social affairs' (1979: 9); it suggests a framework or process through which media presents and shares information and, accordingly, influences the sociocultural organization and perceptual and cognitive patterning. 'Form' in Altheide and Snow's sense, borrowing from Georg Simmel's definition of form – 'a process through which reality is rendered *intelligible*' (1979: 15) – is not a structure per se, but 'a processual framework *through which* social action occurs' (1979: 15). Media logic, in this regard, comprises a single, coherent framework underpinning all media forms and the social and cultural institutions that are revolutionized through media. In response to Altheide and Snow's idea, modern sociologists and media theorists such as Knut Lundby, Stig Hjarvard and Friedrich Krotz argue that 'it is not viable to speak of an overall media logic [and] it is necessary to specify how various media capabilities are applied in various patterns of social interaction' (Lundby 2009a: 117). Critiquing the idea of a unified, singular mechanism structuring all media, Nick Couldry, among others, argues that the roles the media take on to transform social and cultural spheres are 'too heterogeneous to be reduced to a single "media logic"' (2008: 378) and should not be treated 'as if they all operated in one direction, at the same speed, through a parallel mechanism and according to the same calculus of probability' (2008: 378). There is no *single* media logic independent of various cultural and societal contexts and history.

For example, if we consider the workings of mass media such as national newspapers or television in Turkey, where there has been an increasing filtering of news due to state censorship, as opposed to how mass media operates in the UK, we would see that the idea of a single stable media logic is unconvincing. Thus, there are diverse instances of media logic at work in different societies and times. This, however, does not mean that there is no *shared* media logic at all. In contemporary late capitalist societies, the current media logic often abides by and works through capitalist ideological discourse and perspective. This common logic is important while considering contemporary plays since it emerges as a significant element in their thematic and aesthetic compositions. For example, in Martin Crimp's *Attempts on Her Life*, we hear the neoliberal voice of advertisements. In Christopher Brett Bailey's *THWD* and Caryl Churchill's *Love and Information* the aesthetics of speed speak to the fast-paced consumer culture. Building on the origins and some important foundational aspects of mediatization that I introduced here, the following section defines the notion in detail.

Mediatization: Theorizing the contemporary

Technogenesis – the idea that human beings co-evolve with the tools and technologies they have created – is a processual story. Media theorists and sociologists such as Friedrich Krotz, John B. Thompson and Stig Hjarvard claim that mediatization points to a 'long-lasting process, whereby social and cultural institutions and modes of interaction are changed as a consequence of the growth of the media's influence' (Hjarvard 2013: 19). Thompson argues that the origins of *mediasation* (similar to the processes of mediatization) date back to early modernity, to the printing press and the media organizations founded after Gutenberg's invention in the second half of the fifteenth century (1995: 46). The invention of the printing press rendered it possible to circulate information to society, over long distances and among large numbers of people, as well as institutionalizing mass media as influential forces in society. This technological revolution led to an increase in literacy, undermining the domination of the elite in education, and led to the emergence of a middle class, to the Reformation and the destabilization of political and religious authorities, as well as of the feudal society. This view on mediatization identifies it *as* a long historical process.

Undoubtedly, the human–machine interaction and the societal changes occurring as a result of our technological creations and how we use them have a long history. Besides the example of printing press, we can think of the use of mass communication and information technologies as propaganda machines in Nazi Germany, and how these mass media forms such as film and radio started to be used also for commercial purposes in the post-war era. However, the influence of media on society and consciousness has attained a different degree since the late twentieth century as a result of a drastic increase in the media saturation of everyday lives in highly industrialized, late capitalist, mainly Western[3] societies.

Mediatization *as a part of* the long history of our interaction with technology refers to this radical shift that has happened more predominantly since the late twentieth century, and to sociocultural transformations that media has generated in contemporary high-modern societies. Although the influence of media has been in play for a long time, the phenomenon of mediatization does not characterize *every* process through which media affects society and culture. Rather, it suggests a process in high or late modernity in which media has become an autonomous body that majorly influences other social entities such as politics and education. As a result of the independent position and increasingly prevalent presence of media in society, other social, cultural and political institutions have adapted to its logic and workings. For example, we cannot deny that the invention of the printing press transformed individuals' lives and perception of the universe and profoundly influenced religion and knowledge. Nevertheless, this medium did not revolutionize the form or content of social organizations such as politics, education and the family. Also, the printing press did not operate as an independent medium but was an instrument in the hands of other institutions such as religion, science, politics and commerce, and was used in relation to their ideological logic. It is mainly through the expansion and wide accessibility of media in the twentieth century that it has started to have a major influence on other social institutions, individuals' everyday lives, knowledge and perception. These are the markers of mediatization and a mediatized society. Yet again, it is important to stress that mediatization does not suggest a single historic event or an entirely new singularity that creates a rupture in our long co-evolutionary process. Rather, it presents an interesting leap in this course.

The operations of media as a social institution, with its technological and ideological modus operandi in high-modern societies, are directly and deeply connected to late capitalism and its other processes such as globalization, commercialization, dataveillance and individualization. Mediatization is therefore a *metaprocess* that contains 'long-term and culture-crossing changes, processes of processes in a certain sense, which influence the social and cultural development of humankind in the long run' (Krotz in Hepp 2012: 9). For example, mediatization is associated with globalization in various ways. On the one hand, it means going beyond physical borders between countries, cultures, languages and viewpoints as media technologies extend communication and enable people to connect with others from different places and cultures, and share information in an instant. On the other hand, it operates through the late capitalist logic underlying most media structures, and reinforces cultural imperialism on a global scale. The relationship of mediatization to commercialization is evidently based on the fact that mediatization as a social phenomenon and media as its working structures are ideologically loaded and related to the discourses and machinery of late capitalism. In this regard, mediatization, more often than not, supports global emergence and the dissemination of consumer culture through cultural products and commercial images and discourses presented by different media platforms. For example, the language of 'free service' or 'free access' that big media corporations such as Google and Facebook use is mainly a marketing strategy through which they attain more subscribers and, relatedly, attract more advertising revenue. Moreover, through such strategies, the international media conglomerates acquire access to one of the most important assets today: information. As we agree to the terms and conditions of social media platforms among other media structures, we give away personal information and allow our data to be mined and used. The operation of data mining and dataveillance is one of the fundamental social phenomena that mediatization as a concept encompasses. In relation to this, mediatization also relates to the 'societies of control' (Deleuze 1992: 3–7) in which our lives are turned into data to be tracked, regulated and manipulated by governments and corporations.

Through its connection with commercialization, mediatization is also linked to the processes of individualization. Our consciousness and experiences are constantly exposed to and synchronized with capitalist ideology as a result of being bombarded by media and cultural industries. We are continually inundated with images, information and self-interest discourse that impose an *ideal* lifestyle, body, relationship and so on. Media operates through the guise of individual autonomy and self-gain – making us believe that it is our decision to share a selfie or to choose a certain anti-ageing product. This is surely not a new phenomenon, yet it is increasingly more prevalent than before. T. W. Adorno predicted the deceptive attribute of media technologies in relation to capitalism as he argued that media turned individuals into 'dupes of mass deception' (Bernstein 1991: 21), and obstructed the development of autonomous individuals who decide and act consciously for themselves. As a result, today we are encouraged to consent to the machinery of consumerist media which leaves us with a sense of selfhood that we think is autonomous while regulating our decisions, subjectivity and behaviours. Furthermore, as we are more *subjected* to this illusory state that media subtly inundates our lives with, we find it harder to interrupt it or imagine an alternative to it.[4]

That said, it would be wrong to consider mediatization merely as a phenomenon denoting 'change for the worse' (Livingstone 2009a: 5) as a result of its deep connection with the capitalist order. Although the ideological role of the media is fundamental and the advantages of its impact on society are sometimes questionable, media as a cultural technology and social institution also brings about change for the better and has positive effects on society and the individual. Media can serve society as interactive, unifying instruments, rather than as totalitarian or manipulative tools for ideological communication. There is a potential in media for a 'dialogical, telematics society of image producers and image collectors' (Flusser 2011: 4), which allows democratic communication among all members of society. Let me give a short example. During the Arab Spring across parts of the Arab world and the Gezi Protests in Turkey, it was mainly through news and social networking platforms such as Facebook and Twitter that people were able to access information and call for help because mass media agencies were often censored by repressive states. Numerous examples of how social media, particularly Twitter, facilitated communication and access to information during such events can be listed here, and, at the same time, one can question whether media technologies actually enable social mobility, activism and resistance.[5] However, mediatization is a social process that accommodates both the liberating and the repressive, manipulative impacts of media on society. Hence, a technophobic viewpoint would be as misleading as a technophilic one when considering the contemporary moment and the meanings mediatization as a social phenomenon contains. Nevertheless, we should remember that mediatization as a metaprocess is always already related to other social phenomena and that we should treat it with these aspects of contemporary culture. In relation to this, despite operating as a social institution in its own right, media is not an entirely independent organism within society. It is in conversation with other societal processes and is subject to political and economic manipulation, ideological discourses and usage, and cultural trends.

While identifying mediatization as a concept, I have highlighted that it is a part of technogenesis, our co-evolution with our technologies. Therefore, when we consider mediatization, we defy technological determinism, which considers media as the principal motor of social, cultural, political and economic changes. Although mediatization focuses on how media generates societal and cultural transformations, it acknowledges the fact that media technologies are human-made and their use, content and development are based on our needs and goals.

The sociocultural and cognitive changes in our lived experience in these mediatized times have certainly influenced the ways in which we artistically address the changing realities of our world. In theatre, both text and performance engage with new technologies and the conditions of our mediatized existence, consciousness and society. In what follows, I consider the mediatization of theatre and the ways in which meaning-making practices, particularly in performance, have been influenced by a media-saturated environment.

Mediatized theatre: The focus on performance

I didn't think of media as a different thing from theatre.
(Elizabeth LeCompte on *The Southbank Show*, 1987)

Theatre has always been in close conversation with emerging technologies, whether this was the lifting machine in ancient Greek theatre (for the deus ex machina), electric lighting technology on the nineteenth-century stage, or the use of film and photography in the twentieth century by such theatre-makers as Bertolt Brecht and Erwin Piscator, who deployed film and photography as critical tools. Therefore, *media in theatre*, by which I chiefly mean the use of technologies in theatre performance as well as the impact of technologies on theatre language, aesthetics and themes, is certainly not a new phenomenon. However, it is undeniable that the media–theatre relation has intensified since the late twentieth century with the pervasiveness of digital technologies in our everyday lives and culture. Theatre today has become *mediatized*, responding to our media-saturated sociocultural ecology through the explicit and/or implicit use of technology and media aesthetics not only as a scenographic or narrative element but also as a critical-aesthetic tool. This leap in the continuum of theatre–media relation, which I identify as the *mediatization of theatre* (or *mediatized theatre*), has manifested itself in interesting and innovative ways.

A pioneer in multimedia theatre, the New York-based Wooster Group has explored and critically engaged with mediatized culture through works that speak to an age 'where we can talk on the phone, look out the window, watch TV, and be typing a letter at the same time' (The Wooster Group 1981). The Wooster Group experiments with media forms such as film and television overtly through the content and composition of their work while, at the same time, investigating how media influences our everyday existence, subjectivity and perception of reality as well as our sociocultural patterns. In the 1984 production *L.S.D. (. . . Just the High Points . . .)* – an appropriation of Arthur Miller's *The Crucible* – the group used various media forms. For example, the actor Michael Kirby's pre-recorded video image was played in the early stages of the production when he was not able to attend the performances, which later became a part of the piece even when Kirby was physically present on stage. The actor interacted with his own image throughout the performance, while, at times, other performers recreated behaviour and patterns from videotape. The Wooster Group has always used media as a critical device that questions the historical texts while contemporizing them. Besides using multimedia aesthetics in the composition of their work, the group thematically engages with the impacts of media on society to demonstrate to its audience 'the voiding of historical and political discourses under mediatization' (Auslander 1992: 171).

The Wooster Group often uses classic texts as found material which they treat as a source and a part of the composition that can be redesigned, deconstructed, fragmented and quoted yet which is never the primary centre of their work. For example, the group did not appropriate Miller's text in *L.S.D.* for its narrative content, but for what it culturally symbolized, namely, for its iconic position that suggests a grid of associations. The Wooster Group's approach to playtexts has often exemplified a postmodern aesthetics of intertextuality, pastiche and self-reflexivity located in a multimedia aesthetic context. In so doing, the Wooster Group destabilizes the source text and its narrative cohesion and redesigns it in a neo-Brechtian manner for a mediatized society.

Katie Mitchell, whose experiments with media tend to involve the marriage of live filming with live performance, has been a prominent figure in the UK and continental Europe. *Fräulein Julie* (2010) – directed by Mitchell for Berlin's Schaubühne theatre – offers an adaptation and reinterpretation of August Strindberg's play through a technologically enhanced narrative that shifts the text's focus from Julie to her maid Kristin. Throughout the performance, the stage accommodated not only the actors but also the filming crew and technicians who constructed the narrative on screen through close-ups and background images simultaneously with the stage action. Mitchell's use of technology in the composition of this piece serves both as an aesthetic and critical tool through which she asks the audience to question the problematic discourse of the 1888 play, and also proposes an inventive perspective on naturalism in relation to our mediatized perception, namely, on how we see and understand reality through the camera's eye that saturates our everyday lives in the contemporary.

Besides these examples, which epitomize some key aspects of mediatized theatre, there are numerous other theatre-makers whose works incorporate media technologies and aesthetics *overtly* in their formation and composition process. For example, companies such as Forced Entertainment, Builders' Association, Robert Lepage/Ex Machina and Imitating the Dog produce multimedia performances using digital and virtual technologies on stage. They sometimes incorporate emerging media as narrative tools to reinforce theatrical representation (e.g. Lepage/Ex Machina's *887*), and other times as critical devices to challenge representational structures (e.g. the Wooster Group's *Brace Up!*, Nature Theater of Oklohoma's *Rambo Solo*). Companies such as Blast Theory (*I'd Hide You*, 2012) and New Paradise Laboratories (*Fatebook*, 2009) use interactive and social media to involve audiences as participants and performers to collaboratively explore and question aspects of mediatized culture.

The influence of media on theatre manifests itself not only through the direct or explicit use of media technologies on stage, but also, in the *absence* of hi-tech multimedia which, as Karen Jürs-Munby explains, 'nevertheless can only be understood by being related to life in a "mediatized" society' (Jürs-Munby 2006: 10). Tim Etchells, artistic director of Forced Entertainment, identifies this less-pronounced media influence on stage by explaining that their work is 'understandable by anybody brought up in a house with the television on' (Etchells 1999: 95). This is evident in Forced Entertainment's minimalist, bare stage production *Tomorrow's Parties* (2011) in which media is not used as a scenographic and compositional element of the performance, and is not the obvious subject of discussion in the narrative. However, even when media is absent both as a scenographic and thematic tool, media-derived aesthetics and discourses can shape the dramaturgy and languages of performance. In *Tomorrow's Parties*, the fragmented, overlapping utopian and dystopian narratives of the future given through direct and clear language speak to our cognitive processes shaped by our media-saturated, information-bombarded lives and experiences in hypertextual structures and virtual environments. Both media-dominated stages and barer ones illustrate how theatre performance has increasingly become engaged with media not only as technological mediums but also as a sociocultural structure with a burgeoning impact.

The mediatization of theatre, whether manifest or not, engages with the contemporary moment differently, depending on a work's approach to theatrical representation. On the one hand, media can be used as an element of dramaturgical, scenographic and/or narrative design in a way that adheres to and repeats the representational structures of dramatic theatre tradition. Examples of this are abundant – ranging from the 1997 National Theatre production of Patrick Marber's *Closer* and Lyceum Theatre-Traverse's co-production of Enda Walsh's *Chatroom* (2005) to Robert Lepage's *887* (2015) and Headlong and Royal Court co-production of Jennifer Haley's *The Nether* (2013). I will return to some of these examples in the coming chapters. It suffices here to briefly illustrate this mode of mediatized theatre with an example focusing on the theatre production of Haley's play. In *The Nether*, the mirrored set design on the Royal Court stage with moving screens and projections of actor/character's faces, videos and wireframes creates layers of different realities, namely, the virtual and real worlds where the play takes place. In this production, technologies are used as scenographic and narrative tools to represent and comment on the multiple realities and ethics of the digital network age. Media is both the subject and the central scenographic instrument which figuratively stages the relationship between the virtual and the real onto the stage, translating the dramatic world into the here-and-now of performance.

However, dramatic theatre's traditional use of a linear and conceptually coherent narrative form which depicts the world as a closed-off, unchangeable fictive whole is incompatible with the mediatized coordinates of contemporary society, or as Hans-Thies Lehmann puts it, with the 'globalized and multiply mediatized [thus,] less "surveyable" and manageable than ever world' (Jürs-Munby 2006: 11). Using various technologies within the cohesive and unified frame of drama that generates a consistent totality with an identifiable social reality, *The Nether* speaks more to a world and consciousness based on continuity and unity than the contiguity, inconsistency and fragmentation that define the fast-paced, information-bombarded, globally networked coordinates of late capitalist society, where the boundaries between reality and its representation blur. Nevertheless, this is not to suggest that dramatic mediatized forms do not reflect on our media-saturated cultural ecology. Rather, it is to stress that these modes of theatrical expression, unlike the Wooster Group's or Forced Entertainment's critical takes on technology and media age, are limited in terms of their capacity to interrogate and expose the workings of social, cultural and political discourses under mediatization. Instead of challenging, dramatic mediatized forms tend to reproduce the dominant narratives, motives and structures of the late capitalist system. In other words, to use Jacques Rancière's theory, such works adhere to and repeat the *distribution of the sensible* – 'a system of coordinates defining modes of being, doing, making, and communicating that establishes the borders between the visible and the invisible, the audible and the inaudible, the sayable and the unsayable' (Rancière 2013: 89). By reproducing the *sensible*, namely, what is deemed natural and reasonable (with no rational alternative)[6] by the dominant social order, *dramatic* mediatized dramaturgies dissolve 'the bond between perception and action, receiving message and "answerability"' (Lehmann 2006: 184). In other words, the dramatic theatre model engages with the realities of the contemporary in a more *culinary*, to use Brecht's notion, and consumerist rather than critically engaged and dissident manner. In such theatre works, we 'find ourselves *in* a spectacle in which we can only *look on*' (Lehmann 2006: 184).

That said, there has been a tendency to use forms and aesthetics of media technologies as scenographic, compositional and/or narrative tools in a subversive manner that reverses and destabilizes representational mechanisms and languages of theatre. For example, the non-linear, multi-layered and multi-perspectival design of *L.S.D.*, generated through technologies and media aesthetics, denies a linear, singular and unified dramatic representation of reality and offers a theatrical language that accommodates and speaks to our mediatized ontology and consciousness. This kind of approach in performance, which aligns with aspects of postdramatic theatre, deploys media as a critical tool that forecloses the voiding of an alternative discourse and perspective on late capitalism and its metaprocesses. It presents a new way of looking at the realities of technologically disseminated, globalized capitalism, a possibility for a dissident thinking that might generate a crack in our established and accepted framework of thought, perception and action in the *sensible* order. In other words, such theatre works refuse to let us remain contentedly as we are by challenging the *sensible* and revealing its perceptual and epistemic underpinnings. Rancière calls this act of disruption and exposure 'dissensus' – a form of disagreement with the consensus, the given structures and narratives of the dominant social order that excludes differences and possibilities for opposition. The aesthetic resistance to the proliferation of familiar representational structures is, therefore, a political response to the ubiquitous, agreed-upon machineries and discourses of late capitalism.

Certain aspects of these mediatized postdramatic compositions, such as intertextuality, discontinuity, subversion, fragmented forms and multi-perspectival presentation, resonate with postmodern aesthetics. The postdramatic and postmodern are connected; as Karen Jürs-Munby highlights, postdramatic theatre theory focuses on the application of postmodern and poststructuralist discourses to contemporary theatre (Jürs-Munby 2006: 13–14). Nevertheless, although the concept of postdramatic theatre contains elements of postmodern theory and style, 'it is not based on the application of a general cultural concept to the specific domain of theatre, but derives and unfolds from within a long-established discourse on theatre aesthetics itself, as a deconstruction of one of its major premises' (Wessendorf in Jürs-Munby 2006: 14). The postdramatic framework offers a theatre-specific model and 'a new multiform kind of theatrical discourse' (Lehmann [1999] 2006: 22) that considers contemporary theatre and performance landscape particularly in relation to 'the spread and then omnipresence of the *media* in everyday life' (Lehmann [1999] 2006: 22). As indicated, this relation to mediatization can be presented overtly in themes and form or implicitly integrated or unconsciously manifested in a performance's aesthetics. Due to its focus on theatre and on theatre's relation to media culture, 'the postdramatic' is more apt a term than 'the postmodern'.

The increasingly salient relationship between media and theatre has galvanized a deal of scholarly and critical attention. More and more undergraduate and postgraduate courses across the UK have started offering modules that explore media–theatre interactions such as digital performance; interactive digital multimedia techniques; performance art, new media and bioart; digital theatre crafts; intermedial performance practice and so on. In addition, academic associations and federations like TaPRA (Theatre and Performance Research Association) and IFTR (International Federation for Theatre Research) have formed working groups such as Performance and New Technologies, Intermediality in Theatre and Performance and Digital Humanities in Theatre Research, all of which tackle the ways in which new media technologies influence theatre practices and research. Undoubtedly, these developments foreground the inevitable impact of new media technologies and mediatization on theatre and call for the recognition and interrogation of this phenomenon in relation to theatre praxis and studies. As Tim Etchells rightly argues, '[Y]ou have to think about technology, you have to use it, because in the end it is in your blood. Technology will move in and speak through you, like it or not. Best not to ignore' (Etchells 1999: 95). Furthermore, these changes highlight an evident tendency in current theatre research towards the performance aspect of theatre in relation to mediatization.

Scholarly examinations have generated a variety of discussions about the ontology, phenomenology and sustainability of theatre performance. It is beyond my scope to investigate these discussions in detail, yet it is important to provide a cursory view of some of the central debates in order to substantiate the predominant focus on performance. The prominent debate between Peggy Phelan and Philip Auslander about *liveness* is based on two different perspectives: while Phelan argues that the incorporation of media-generated images and technologies into theatre threatens the theatre's ontology as live performance (Phelan 1993: 146), Auslander criticizes the binary opposition between the live and the mediatized and questions whether there 'really are clear-cut ontological distinctions between live forms and mediatized ones' (1999: 7). For Auslander, the live is supplanted by the mediatized double, not only physically on stage but also in the individual's perception (1999: 3–5). This idea resonates with our everyday lives where we engage with virtual environments and, as a result, perceive and conceptualize live experience differently from the here-and-now kind of liveness. Hence, Auslander argues, in theatre 'the experience of liveness is not limited to specific performer-audience interactions but refers to a sense of always being connected to other people, of continuous, technologically mediated temporal co-presence with others known and unknown' (2012: 6). This sense of liveness also contains 'connections and interactions between human and non-human agents [which] can produce a feeling of "liveness" and a sense of the machine's agency and – because it exchanges symbols – even of a subjective encounter with a persona' (2012: 6). As a result, we could consider that liveness is neither an intrinsic quality of an object nor 'an effect caused by some aspect of the object such as its medium, ability to respond in real time, or anthropomorphism' (2012: 9). Rather, in order for liveness to occur there needs to be an inter-responsive, interactive process through which an audience consciously engages with an object and accepts and responds to its claim of liveness. The question of liveness, as briefly evidenced here, focuses majorly on theatre performance, on the composition of bodies in performance whether they are on stage, in the auditorium or across the ocean connected to performance via their screens. Although the performance aspect is understandably the primary topic in relation to theatre ontology, it would also be interesting to explore how changes in perceptions and conceptualizations of live experience, corporeality and real-virtual dimensions influence the textual aspect of theatre – *often* a part of its ontology.

Considering contemporary performance practice, Matthew Causey argues that Phelan's and Auslander's arguments about the ontology of performance are 'unsustainable and even inaccurate because they create binary distinctions among media delivery systems that are challenged in what [he defines as] postdigital condition' (2016: 428). Postdigital, according to Causey, is not about an endpoint or the obsolescence of digital technologies. On the contrary, it is about *recognizing* the ingrained presence of these technologies in our lives, defining power relations, systems of control and consciousness. Therefore, Causey argues, the question for artists who are completely entrenched in the aesthetics of the digital 'resides not in the type or aesthetic use of technology [on stage], but in learning to think like a machine, digitally' (2016: 440). A postdigital performance that *thinks digitally* is one that is formed with a consciousness of the digital and engagement with its language and conceptual frameworks in order to resist its ideological machinery and turn 'the system back against itself' from within (2016: 432). Causey's arguments are inventive and easily relate to an analysis of writing for the stage in mediatized culture.[7]

Along with liveness, intermediality and digital/postdigital performance have been widely researched topics in the field which comprises such categories as posthumanism and cyborg theatre, virtual theatre and social media theatre. For example, *Intermediality in Theatre and Performance* (2006) and *Mapping Intermediality in Performance* (2010) tackle the mounting influence of emerging media forms on theatre and how each media technology is remediated in performance, and, as a consequence, shapes aspects of performance ranging from embodiment, spectatorship to temporality and spatiality. Both works tend to explore such interesting constituents and structures of theatre often, if not always, with a focus on live performance. Special issues by *The Theater Journal* such as 'Digital Media and Performance' (2009), 'Digital "Issues": Rethinking Media in/and/as Performance' (2016) and 'Theatre, the Digital, and the Analysis and Documentation of Performance' (2016) explore the use of digital technology in performance practice and consider how the use of digital scholarship informs and shapes theatre research. Steve Dixon's *Digital Performance* (2007) gives an extensive account of contemporary trends in theatre and performance art in relation to digital technologies. Bree Hadley's *Theatre, Social Media, and Meaning Making* (2017) investigates how our social media-saturated lives have shaped theatre-making, spectatorship and theatre industry. Drawing on Patrick Lonergan's *Theatre & Social Media* (2016), Hadley furthers the interrogation of social media theatre by analysing performances by Paul Sermon, Blast Theory and Brian Lobel, among others. These accounts importantly map and theorize the current theatre landscape in which media culture and technologies play a significant role. However, at the same time, they epitomize the predominant tendency in theatre scholarship to consider the theatre–media relation in connection with the act and event of performance[8] and disclose a certain blind spot: playtexts.

Why have playtexts been overlooked? Or, why have texts been less popular than performance while growing number of plays, thematically and aesthetically considering the impacts of media on society and consciousness, have been written for the stage? I will explore these questions shortly. However, before that, it is important to highlight that the text–media relation in theatre has not been entirely ignored; there has been some, albeit limited, research. In what follows, I will briefly investigate some noteworthy aspects of this existing literature. Then, I will look into the central question concerning the overlooked position of playtexts set above.

Playtexts and mediatization: Initial explorations

While laying the groundwork for this book, I asked a number of my students, colleagues and theatregoing friends to give me an example of a play that speaks to our media-dominated lives. Answers varied from Patrick Marber's *Closer*, Enda Walsh's *Chatroom* to Caryl Churchill's *Love and Information* and

Jennifer Haley's *The Nether*. These are undoubtedly accurate and relevant, as well as telling of the tendency to consider the relationship between playtexts and media technologies mainly in terms of the direct representation of technology and media culture in the plays' narrative content. This way of thinking about the dramatic writing-media relation is also in evidence in certain critical texts exploring theatre in relation to media culture and technologies.

In her analysis of theatre in a media culture, Amy Petersen Jensen analyses two plays written in the late 1970s and 1980s – *A Movie Star Has to Star in Black and White* by Adrienne Kennedy and *Speed the Plow* by David Mamet – and considers the direct presence of media forms, television and film, as complementary to the plays' storyline. Similarly to recent examples such as *The Nether*, the use of media as thematic content also functions as a critique within the plays of the interconnection between capitalism and media technologies. As Jensen puts, 'film and television are identified as pervasive entities through which authentic communication is subverted and material capitalism reigns' (2007: 113). A similar theme-oriented approach is manifest in Kerstin Schmidt's study of Jean-Claude van Itallie's plays (2005) and Michael Kustow's analysis of Mark Ravenhill's *Shopping and Fucking* (1996) and *Faust Is Dead* (1997) in *Theatre@risk* (2000). In their analyses of the plays, both critics focus on what the plays are *talking about* and foreground the shared theme of media's influence on consumerism. As I identified earlier, the connection between capitalism and media technologies is an important aspect of mediatization as a social phenomenon. Here, one cannot help but wonder how these plays' forms portray the reality that they thematize and whether any dramaturgical component such as characterization is restructured to speak to the late capitalist, mediatized context. I will explore these questions in Chapter 2, but suffice for now to say that plays that depict our mediatized environment solely in their thematic content tend to adhere to the traditional model of dramatic representation in their composition. They portray the world in a way that reproduces the prevalent images and narratives, which are continually circulated by media in line with dominant power structures. Such *dramatic* mediatized dramaturgies, which picture our media-saturated lives as a closed-off fictional totality, are in evidence in contemporary Anglophone theatre and are important to consider while investigating the evolution of plays. Accordingly, it is necessary to question to what extent these plays engage with the intricacies of mediatized culture, a culture no longer understandable nor representable through the traditional structures of dramatic theatre.

In an age where media pervades our lives and circulates the *sensible*, the structures through which we artistically signify and engage with the world cannot be thought outside of mediatization. In other words, theatre's mode of representation and perception is directly connected to and influenced by the media-saturated, info-rich, fast-paced world 'outside'. Therefore, it is important to consider not only and simply what a playtext or theatre performance is *speaking about* in relation to our mediatized world but also, and more importantly, the ways in which it *speaks to* the social and perceptual conditions. Rather than mere thematization of our socio-cognitive situations in a mediatized culture, it is through reconsideration and restructuring of sign usage, through 'the implicit substance and critical value of its *mode of representation*' (Lehmann 2006: 178; emphasis in original) that theatre or dramatic writing can critically reflect on experienced reality, and interrupt the prescribed narratives of the dominant social order.

The question of form has caught the attention of such scholars as Arnold Aronson and Patrice Pavis who emphasize the importance of exploring the tissue of the text and its new formal languages in order to understand how dramatic writing responds to the media age (Aronson 1999; Pavis 2003). It is important, they argue, to look beyond the representation of new technologies in the content of the written text. Aronson highlights this in his analysis of the works by American playwrights Mac Wellman, Suzan-Lori Parks and Tony Kushner, and Pavis does in his study of French-language plays such as Bernard-Marie Koltès's *Dans la solitude des champs de cotton*, Joël Jouanneau's *Allegria* (1999) and Eugène Durif's *Via Negativa* (1996). In his discussion of Kushner's *Angels in America*, for instance, Aronson arrives at the conclusion that the multi-plot, non-linear and multi-character aesthetics speaks to the multi-layered, hypertextual world of cyberculture and to the contemporary mind that is familiar with and shaped by this culture (Aronson 1999: 196). Drawing on this idea, *Mediatized Dramaturgy* also scrutinizes plays that deploy media aesthetics and mediatized contexts, implicitly or explicitly, in their dramaturgical architecture as a critical tool, subverting the dramatic paradigm and representational structures, and interrupting the circulation and proliferation of the *sensible*. As shall be explored shortly, these plays challenge the logocentric, causal logic of dramatic representation, based on an idea of the world as a unified and consistent whole. These texts certainly do something beyond mere thematization and dramatic representation of mediatized existence and consciousness; they not only address and talk about it but also embody the cultural, social and cognitive ecology in interesting ways through their subversive mode of representation.

An important aspect that we tend to overlook while analysing the dramaturgical elements of playtexts, as this handful of critical texts show, is that even when there is no direct thematic reference to the media-saturated age or explicit use of media technologies in a play, it can still accommodate and critique our mediatized world and perception. There is, for example, a correlation between fragmented, non-linear narrative and our sense of the world, space and time, or between unidentified speakers and our changing sense of subjectivity and identity in an age where we generate identities in the virtual world. *Mediatized Dramaturgy* considers such implicit manifestations of mediatization and investigates how the fabric of the text speaks to the contemporary without always having to reproduce any technology or media-specific setting on their thematic layer.

In addition to the organization and thematics of plays, mediatization has also affected the overall genre of playtexts in that playwrights have started experimenting with new media forms and platforms such as Twitter, and presented inventive approaches to playwriting, textual aesthetics and spectatorship. John H. Muse's '140 Characters in Search of a Theater: *Twitter Plays*' provides an insightful account of some of the ways in which Twitter has engendered new forms of plays and reshaped both playwriting and the spectatorial experience. We will return to and explore such imaginative formations in Chapter 6 with a focus on mediaturgical plays at the core of whose formation, composition, presentation and reception lie media technologies.

Besides being the source and milieu of new kinds of playtexts, social/digital media has also provided a new environment for the adaptation of classic plays. A well-known example is the RSC's Twitter adaptation of Shakespeare's *Romeo and Juliet* as *Such Tweet Sorrow* (2010). The adaptation of old texts into new environments and the convergence of different media and realities – virtual, textual and physical – has generated new research into the use of media-based adaptations of classic works as teaching, learning and research tools. For example, focusing on the implications of social media for Shakespearean research and pedagogy, Stephen O'Neill considers the interactive quality of digital media platforms and highlights their potential as objects of critical analysis and teaching–learning tools through which users can shape the content of the plays and engage with them differently.[9] There is a continual and rising interest in this field of mediatized theatre: Robert Allen discusses the process of his adaptation of Strindberg's *A Dream Play* as hyperseries broadcast on the internet,[10] while Rebecca Wotzko investigates the appropriation of applied drama within the micro-blogging platform Twitter as a means to increase students' social media literacy and awareness about the reliability of mainstream news media.[11] These are important and timely topics that require detailed discussion. In this book, I focus only on original playtexts and not on adaptations because my research question aims to grasp the evolution of contemporary dramatic writing, how its form and content have changed in relation to mediatization, and what the new formations and transformations mean in today's theatre and culture.

All these critical discussions provide significant and well-founded perspectives on the evolution of plays in a mediatized culture and theatre stage and show that there is a rising interest in the subject matter. However, it is significantly limited in comparison to our theoretical enquiries about performance genres, performance aesthetics, performance ontology and phenomenology in relation to the media age. It is striking that, despite the rising interest of playwrights in mediatized culture and the increasing engagement of theatre practitioners with media, the question of the playtext as a part of the mediatized theatre landscape has attracted less scholarly attention. But why have playtexts been overlooked in a theatre scene populated by media technologies? Or, why, despite the increasing number of plays written in and about the mediatized times, are playtexts left in the shadow while the performance dimension of theatre has been widely researched?

The question of the text: Dramatic writing for the mediatized age and stage

One response to this question could be that media aesthetics and manifestations of mediatization are seemingly less pronounced and perceptible in writing than they are in performance. For example, the binaural head in *The Encounter*, the cameras and screens in *Fräulein Julie* and in the Wooster Group's *Hamlet* and *L.S.D. (. . . Just the High Points . . .)* or the earphones in Tim Crouch's *An Oak Tree* are easily discernible as on stage. However, media in written text, as Patrice Pavis argues, 'is not, as it is onstage, a foreign body; it actually places itself in an intertextuality in the widest sense of the word' (2003: 192). In a similar way, the impact of media can be an entrenched, taken-for-granted and even unconscious experience due to the widespread presence of media in society and individual lives. Playwrights writing in a media-saturated world might not be aware of its influence on their perceptual faculties and writing techniques. The impact of the media may be embedded in the flesh and blood of texts, as it were, and so become hardly recognizable. Simon Stephens's *Pornography*, for instance, does not necessarily place technology at the heart of the narrative. Apart from a few references to iPhone and computer, there is not a clear reference to media as there is in Haley's *The Nether*. Nevertheless, the play's fragmented composition relates to our cultural consciousness, which is accustomed to brief and fast-moving images and memories, the objectification of the other and social disintegration, all of which are products of mediatization. Hence, it would be a mistake to think that, compared to media influence on the performance aspect of theatre, plays are not affected by or unresponsive to changing sociocultural and cognitive conditions.

Another reason for the relatively minor interest in the impact of media on plays could be due to the changing status of text in comparison to performance in theatre with the move towards the materiality of performance in European and North American theatre since the 1960s. In *Postdramatic Theatre*, Hans-Thies Lehmann criticizes the subordination of the staging to the primacy of written drama in dramatic theatre where the playtext is the determining factor even when 'music and dance [. . .] predominated the "text"' (2006: 21). The notion of the postdramatic puts forward an idea of theatre that has emancipated itself from the dominance of the dramatic text and from the hierarchy between text and performance, and treats the written component of theatre as just another element in performance dramaturgy and scenography. In questioning the primary position of playtexts in the *dramatic theatre* tradition, an issue raised earlier by Antonin Artaud among other historical avant-gardists, Lehmann does not propose a *textless, antitext* or *non-text-based* theatre. Nonetheless, the idea of postdramatic theatre and its performance-oriented approach have been misunderstood as such. One of the reasons for this misconception is Lehmann's own deliberate avoidance of the study of postdramatic theatre's textual dimension or the creative possibilities new writing may offer to the performance process. This is not, however, because the author argues for the exclusion of text from theatre or fails to recognize the evolution of dramatic writing. Rather, Lehmann, albeit briefly, refers to playwrights and the new potential and role of dramatic writing in theatre. He considers Heiner Müller and claims that '[i]mportant texts are still being written' (2006: 17). He also touches on Elfriede Jelinek, Peter Handke, Sarah Kane and René Pollesch, among other playwrights, as illustrating the persistence of playtext and proposes a new role for it in the processes of postdramatic theatre. Considering such instances in *Postdramatic Theatre*, we can claim that Lehmann reserves the category of postdramatic theatre for the performance dimension of theatre, without denying yet at the same time without scrutinizing 'the continuing association and exchange between theatre and text' (2006: 17).

The text's less popular position in the discussions of the theatre–media relation is also based on the conflation between the idea of the dramatic text as primary centre of performance and the dramatic paradigm – the philosophical category of the 'dramatic' as a representational design for a unified world. This separation, present in *Postdramatic Theatre*, relates to the dissolution of the idea of text as the authoritarian element in theatre and to the crisis of representation, deepened by the advent of new audiovisual, digital and social media technologies. Within the parameters of mediatized culture, performance is considered a visual form, and the written text is treated 'as a banal subsidiary of the mise en scène' (Pavis 2003: 191). Moreover, this conflation positions *any* playtext within the logocentric predicament of the dramatic that is problematic in relation to the *unsurveyable* present of the media age. It also leads to a binary view: 'dramatic' as text-based and 'postdramatic' as non-text-based theatre (Tomlin 2009: 58). Such binary categorization suggests that if the written text has a central role in the performance process, it cannot be considered in relation to postdramatic aesthetics and its transgressive logic that resists and goes beyond drama as 'the logos of a totality' (Lehmann 2006: 40). This viewpoint is problematic because it defies the capacity of playtexts to accommodate and critically map our media-saturated lives that are no longer representable through the logic and aesthetics of dramatic theatre tradition.

That texts have been overlooked while considering the theatre–media relation does not indicate that plays are obsolete or incapable of capturing the realities of the media age. Without a doubt, as the crisis of representation and the change in the traditional aesthetics of theatre in view of the mediatized world have affected performance, they have also influenced playtexts and led to a re-evaluation of dramatic writing, generating new forms that defy 'the authority of the dramatic paradigm' (Lehmann 2006: 27) in response to mediatization. In her analysis of contemporary stage-plays and their dramaturgy, Gerda Poschmann looks into the position, treatment and workings of the text in contemporary theatre and puts forward the notion of the 'no longer dramatic theatre text' (in Jürs-Munby 2009: 46). This idea offers an apt category for identifying the transgressive plays that destabilize dramatic logic in a bid to talk about the contemporary world and its realities. In this respect, Poschmann's concept is central to the discussion of mediatized dramaturgy. Therefore, in what follows, I will delineate this notion and how it challenges and resists the dramatic paradigm.

Textual intervention: 'No-longer-dramatic' text

Gerda Poschmann coins the term 'no longer dramatic theatre text' (Jürs-Munby 2009: 46) to indicate the shift in the ways playtexts are written and the role of written texts in the theatre. Lehmann reads such plays as a new mode of theatrical sign usage (2006: 17) and a critique of what he considers the potentially untenable role of dramatic representation in the media-saturated, globalized world. The distinction between the 'no-longer-dramatic' text and *postdramatic theatre* is that the latter refers to performance rather than the written text per se. In 'no-longer-dramatic' plays the '"principle of narration and figuration" and the order of a "fable" (story) are disappearing' (Poschmann in Lehmann 2006: 18); rounded and psychologically motivated characters, dialogue form and linearly structured, recognizable dramatic plot dissolve. These formal features can be easily identified with postmodern aesthetics such as discontinuity, multiplicity and the dissolution of integrated, three-dimensional characters. However, the postmodern as a category remains too broad in its parameters to define theatre and dramatic writing, as Lehmann explained as the reasoning for the choice of postdramatic as a performance-specific term. Likewise, the 'no-longer-dramatic text' offers a text-oriented viewpoint in theatre studies without ignoring its links to a postmodern form and framework. Besides, these two theatre-centric categories consider the societal and cognitive shifts beyond the postmodern period which largely demarcates changes that took place before the digital age. In this sense, these aesthetic and theoretical categories work in continuity and congruence with postmodernism.

These plays still tell stories and relate to the world without reverting back to well-made plays and dramatic unity. They are beyond dramatic representation, which does not mean that they are without representation at all or they do not contain any dramatic elements. Rather, it means that these plays are not shaped according to or governed by the dramatic paradigm or the *representative regime* – 'an artistic system of Aristotelian heritage' (Rancière 2013: xiv) that operates through reproducing and establishing the *distribution of the sensible*, of what is defined as visible, audible and sayable by the ideological organizational system. Instead, their no-longer-dramatic form, which corresponds to Rancière's *aesthetic regime* of art, subverts mimetic representation and provokes a shift or an interruption in the *distribution of the sensible*. It is in this way that these plays bring about an intervention or possibility for *politics* and dissensus – a possibility to interrupt the representation of the *sensible* under dominant ideology and reveal the invisible and unsayable that we have become desensitized to under mediatization. Hence, these plays offer textual bases, sources or outlines for performance, which respond to an increasingly 'less "surveyable" and manageable than ever world' (Jürs-Munby 2006: 11), a world of screens and mirrors where simulation takes the place of narration.

These texts are fundamentally connected to mediatization. That is, the subversive dramaturgy of no-longer-dramatic texts, which destabilizes the dramatic paradigm and, relatedly, the conforming reproduction of the dominant ideology, speaks to a world and consciousness constructed by prevalent technologies and media culture. For example, in Caryl Churchill's *Love and Information*, media technologies and the phenomenon of mediatization are at the core of its thematic and formal architecture as it talks about our information-bombarded lives through numerous, bite-sized scenes. On the other hand, in Churchill's *Heart's Desire* there is hardly any mention or representation of media technologies, but the rewinding and replaying of scenes, which evokes VCR technology, challenges linear plot composition and dramatic unity, while the flow of fragmented utterances speaks to the fast flow of images and information. The plot structure, particularly the reset device, reflects the power that the media exerts on consciousness. In every reset, Churchill erases the preceding scene and replaces it with a new version, which seems to function as a form of censorship as it suggests the dominance of the current scene over the previous and seeks to erase a problematic past in favour of a perpetual present. This could be read as a reference to the media's shaping of 'reality' and individuals' perception of it, and to how it presents a partial perspective on events in line with the dominant ideology, persuading people to accept prescribed narratives as the truth.

The no-longer-dramatic plays problematize the written text's formerly privileged status over performance, and act as one of the elements in theatre – whether they are a source material, a base or a reference point for the stage action. Importantly, these texts are not written *for* the stage in the traditional sense; that is, they do not suggest or require a performative translation of the textual material on to stage. Instead, they are written, as Pavis suggests, 'against the stage [. . .] or, at best, *in spite of* it: the stage is not there to illustrate and clarify the text, it must provide an apparatus which opens up new perspectives for [and of] the texts' (2016: 190). Through the subversive aesthetics developed in response to the unsurveyable present, which postdramatic theatre tackles in relation to performance, these texts not only present a textual connection to and reflection on our mediatized world but also offer challenging possibilities for the stage to problematize and disrupt figurative representation. This mode of dramatic writing therefore presents the text as open material for the theatre and deconstructs the traditional harmony and unity between a text and its performance. Instead, it proposes a productive tension between text and performance enabled by the writing's open and porous form, which invites director, actors and 'spectators to become active co-writers of the (performance) text' (Lehmann 2006: 6). Moving beyond and against the erstwhile centrality of dramatic writing, the no-longer-dramatic playtext asks for new directorial, performative and spectatorial approaches, and it 'suggests itself as a relativized element for performance from the outset and points to its own indeterminacy and status as uninterpreted material' (Barnett 2008: 16).

'No-longer-dramatic' plays often result in postdramatic performances. However, it is important to note that postdramatic theatre does not completely reject dramatic plays to work exclusively with 'no longer dramatic texts'. There are postdramatic attempts to reinterpret traditional written drama in a way that strips the dramatic text of its teleological and logocentric narrative and treats it as an element of the performance text with no primacy. The Wooster Group's 2001 production *To You, the Birdie! (Phèdre)*, which is broadly based on Racine's *Phèdre*, and *Brace Up!* (1991, 2003), based on Chekov's *Three Sisters*, provide examples of postdramatic interpretations of dramatic texts. Here, similar to the Wooster Group's use of a classic text in *L.S.D.*, the plays are treated as found objects and source material for the compositional process through which they are deconstructed, disintegrated, redesigned, quoted and so on.

Drawing on the significant gestures in the contemporary theatre landscape which I have delineated in this chapter, *Mediatized Dramaturgy* explores the ways in which playtexts have evolved in an age of theatre marked by mediatization and its possibilities. Focusing on Anglophone theatre since the 1990s, which still has a strong and evolving culture of dramatic writing, this book considers how playtexts respond to the prevalent influence of media technologies on society, opening up critical spaces for interrupting the *sensible* and for dissident questioning of the workings of our late capitalist mediatized culture. This study combines theatre theory, sociology and media theory through the concept of mediatized dramaturgy and offers reflections on the ways in which certain modes of playtext negotiate the new reality of the mediatized society through their form, creating a crack in our familiarized frameworks of thought, perception and action that have been shaped by the late capitalist cultural technologies of the media. As mentioned earlier, the analysis of plays is not limited to the texts themselves. Importantly, it refuses the historical dualism of text and stage, of writing and performance. As a result, while investigating the changing structure of plays and their critical-performative potentials, I will also consider the relationship between text and performance by studying certain stage productions.

Chapter 2 explores playtexts that *overtly* thematize mediatized culture in their narrative context. These plays depict our media-saturated lives and environment in line with the representative regime as a self-contained reality that is organized by causality and linearity. The plays offer intriguing meditations on the different phases of our late capitalist mediatized society, ranging from the early days of the internet in Mark Ravenhill's *Faust Is Dead* to the recent context and concerns of our techno-dependent, multi-reality existence in Jennifer Haley's *The Nether*. What separates these plays from the others to follow in the chapters that focus on the formal components of dramaturgical structure – language, characterization and plot – is the fact that the fabric of these playtexts does not suggest an engagement with the technologies or mediatized contexts that they overtly thematize in their narrative content. In response, the chapter investigates to what extent such plays speak to a world and consciousness dominated by media, when mediatization remains merely on the thematic layer of their composition.

2

Plays of discord

Mediatized thematics and traditional dramatic form

'[T]heir kids spent twenty-four-seven on the Net [. . .] they never see their kids anymore,' foretells the Chorus in Mark Ravenhill's *Faust Is Dead* (1997: 121), referring to a community that raises money to prepare their children for the future. This scene foreshadows the world of Jennifer Haley's *The Nether* (2014), as the character Sims describes contemporary reality: 'Eighty per cent of the population work in office realms, children attend school in educational realms – there's a realm for anything you want to know or do or think you might want to try. [. . .] Real children are hard to come by these days. It's not like they play outside anymore' (2014: 17). Written almost two decades apart, both plays comment on our increasingly media-saturated world and how it has altered our lives, illustrating a trend in contemporary theatre. As discussed, since the 1990s the British stage has been populated with plays that address the ubiquitous impact of media technologies on contemporary society. Examples are abundant – ranging from Martin Crimp's *The Treatment* (1993), Patrick Marber's *Closer* (1997), Lucy Prebble's *The Sugar Syndrome* (2003), Enda Walsh's *Chatroom* (2005) to Chris Thorpe and Hannah Jane Walker's *I Wish I Was Lonely* (2013), Tim Price's *Teh Internet Is Serious Business* (2014) and Gary Owen's *Killology* (2017). These plays put the mediatized age at the heart of their thematic content and acknowledge the ways in which pervasive technologies shape the social and cognitive coordinates of our current existence. For instance, *Chatroom* and *The Sugar Syndrome* tackle internet impersonation and its impact on relationships, while *Faust Is Dead* and *The Nether* address hyperreality and the mediatization of perception. The ethics of virtual reality has also been a popular theme in British theatre in the last decade, explored in plays such as *Killology, The Nether* and *Teh Internet Is Serious Business* – each offering a different angle – often with an emphasis on the uncertainty of the boundaries between reality and virtual world that lead to harm, offence and the violation of privacy and rights.

These plays acknowledge the social, cultural and cognitive shifts occurring as a result of our media-saturated environment and bring the mediatized world to our attention, reinforcing theatre's immediate relation to society. While directly thematizing current technologies and the new realities these technologies have generated, some of these plays, such as *Faust Is Dead* (*Faust*) and *The Nether*, adhere to the aesthetic logic of dramatic theatre, depicting the image-soaked, multi-reality world through the traditional structures of realist dramatic form, and portraying it as a stable, unified totality. The underlying motive for this aesthetic choice is multifaceted. However, one fundamental reason for representing the world as it 'is', namely as we perceive it, as profoundly shaped by media, is to make sense of the complex realities and uncertainties of our time via a familiar, easily recognizable form. Hence, the plays follow the deep-seated tradition of dramatic theatre that is based on causal logic, linear structure and meaningful order – a design that depicts our globally networked, pervasively mediatized, fast-paced world as a surveyable whole. This dramatic design begs the question: How and to what extent do *dramatic mediatized plays* respond to our experienced reality in the contemporary world?

Before exploring this question in relation to the thematic and formal designs of *Faust* and *The Nether*, it is important to highlight that adherence to the logic and machinery of dramatic representation implicates the *reproduction* of the culture and structures of the dominant social order and its prevalent perceptual dispositions as communicated and imprinted on us by media. This is basically due to the fact that how we represent the world we live in is directly connected to how we perceive it, which is profoundly influenced by mediatized late capitalist culture, power relations and its technologies. As Hans-Thies Lehmann underlines, the 'mode of perception in theatre cannot be separated from the existence of theatre in a world of media which massively shapes all perception' (2006: 185). The technologies and processes of mediatization, and therefore of late capitalism, inscribe the dominant power structures and social order that define Rancière's concept of the *distribution of the sensible*. This regulatory system and its machineries support and communicate a particular social reality and standardize what is acceptable, shaping our collective consciousness accordingly in a way that impedes the possibility of dissensus. By dissensus he suggests an individual's or a group's subversive intervention into the prevailing organizational system – a system of meanings and values, identifying the perceptual coordinates and boundaries of a society (Rancière 2013). Extending his thoughts on politics to aesthetics, Rancière argues that the *representative regime of art* replicates the status quo and the hierarchical *distribution of the sensible* in accordance with which it shapes the society's perceptual horizons. Considered in line with this idea, the dramatic representation of the mediatized world reproduces the prevalent narratives and structures of late capitalism. In relation to this, this adherence to the structures of dramatic tradition, while thematizing the intricacies of the contemporary world, limits plays' capacity to critically challenge what is deemed *sensible* or common sense through the deep-rooted, widely consented and almost invisible processes of mediatization. In what follows, I explore this point in relation to *Faust* and *The Nether* with a focus on the playtexts' thematic content and dramaturgical design and discuss how they mimic the culture of mediatized late capitalism within their dramaturgy. Following the analysis of each playtext, I briefly investigate some aspects of their first productions and their engagement with the text's dramatic aesthetics.

Thematization of mediatization

Faust: Thematics

Ravenhill's *Faust* meditates on our media-saturated society and its effects on our existence. The play centres on three characters: Alain, Pete and Donny. Alain is an intellectual, a thinly veiled conflation of Michel Foucault and Jean Baudrillard, who promotes his new book on the 'death of man' and 'the end of history' on *Letterman* as the play opens. Through Alain's characterization, Ravenhill questions perception and reality in an age where people are inundated with reproduced images gradually transformed into a giant simulacrum without any reference or relation to experienced reality.

Pete, on the other hand, is the son of a Bill Gates-like software tycoon who steals his father's software program 'Chaos' with the aim of profiting from it. After being sacked from his teaching job, Alain decides to 'live a little' (Ravenhill 1997: 3). He meets Pete, who is running away from his father, and they set out on a road trip across America. There is a continuous Faustian power struggle between Alain and Pete: while Alain-Mephistopheles has experience and knowledge to offer Pete, Pete-Faust is searching for experiences and is willing to do anything to have them. From another perspective, as Caridad Svich argues, both characters function as aspects of Mephistopheles and Faust with 'the socio-political framework of the text serving as the ultimate comment on the Faustian bargain the world has made for itself in the name of progress' (Svich 2003: 85). Ravenhill's use of the Faust myth contributes to and highlights the critique of capitalism in *Faust* and its manipulative power apparatuses that function under the pretence of progress and civilization.

The Faustian subtext is reinforced with the introduction of a Gretchen-like character, Donny. Donny is a teenage boy who, due to a traumatic childhood and estrangement from his mother, has been self-harming and sharing his acts of self-punishment on the internet as a way to gain affirmation from others and to feel meaningful. Like Gretchen, Donny refuses to escape from the outcome of his deeds and cuts his throat while broadcasting his act online. Donny's death, as we shall see, is a planned act that later turns him into sensational TV show material. Ravenhill also incorporates a Chorus that presents a number of parables and commentaries underlining the mediatized context of the play and its critical concerns about human subjectivity and media-constructed reality and consciousness.

Ravenhill locates this media-driven fictional world specifically in America. This evidently evokes Baudrillard's road trip through America, particularly when Alain identifies it as a place 'within our century' (Ravenhill 1997: 101). In other words, America as the fictional setting is not simply a physical milieu in *Faust* but a conceptual framework. This particular context epitomizes the late capitalist age as the final form of social system with no alternative where, according to Alain, we experience the end of reality and progressive history while simultaneously living through the illusion of them in a hyperreal world of simulations. Throughout the play, Ravenhill illustrates the ontology of omnipresent mediatization, rendering the boundaries between reality and its simulation indistinguishable, and demonstrating its connection to neoliberal capitalism. The Chorus speaks to this socio-cognitive context. The first and final Chorus sections picture a dystopian view of the world that is 'not getting any better. It's just going on, on and on and on.' In the face of this reality, the speaker feels estranged: 'I don't feel a thing. [. . .] And I wonder what made me that way' (Ravenhill 1997: 137). This desensitized consciousness manifests in Pete and Donny's individual attempts to capture reality and feel it. As mentioned, another Chorus part tells a pre-internet story of a church community raising money for their children 'to be part of the future [. . .] so they can spread the word way into the future' (Ravenhill 1997: 121). However, the Chorus reveals that, with the arrival of the internet, the children have gradually become addicted to it and spend most of their time in the virtual space (Ravenhill 1997: 121). The picture the Chorus presents here, albeit a rather technophobic and partial one that dominates the entirety of Ravenhill's play, denotes the pervasive presence of media in our everyday lives and our growing dependency on them.

Alain and Pete's road trip in America sets the narrative backdrop for the representation of mediatized experience and consciousness. Pete and Donny are the epitomes of this state of being and consciousness. Pete, the son of a media mogul, is the embodiment of the kids in the Valley of the Geeks that spend 24/7 on the Net and experience the world through a screen. He depends on his camcorder and computer in order to make sense of the world. Mediatized reality, the 'spectacle', to use Guy Debord's term (2010), becomes the prerequisite for Pete to connect with reality and constitute social relations. This is in evidence in the desert scene where Pete treats the camcorder and mediated image as the surrogate of reality that renders this reality 'safe':

> (Looking at the desert at night)
> **Alain**   This is a very beautiful place.
> **Pete**   I guess it's okay.
> I kind of prefer it on the TV.
> I prefer it with a frame around it, you know? [...] when you actually see it, you know ... it's a little scary.
> *He takes out the camcorder, looks through it.*
> That's better.
> I kind of feel okay now.
> This always works for me. Some guys it's Prozac but with me ...
> (Ravenhill 1997: 113)

Pete's immediate reaction to a new, real-life experience is to record it – an action now familiar within contemporary reality. It is not unusual to see people recording the sunset or a political demonstration, posting it on social media, comment on it and so on, while the sunset or the demonstration takes place. Similarly, in another scene, Pete agrees to a sexual encounter with Alain as long as he records it all and they 'make it like on TV':

> **Pete**   (*TV commentary voice*) Lost under the stars surrounded by the splendour of nature and the mysterious awesomeness of Death Valley, the kid is initiated into the strange world of the homosexual.
> (Ravenhill 1997: 114)

It is through the mediated representation that Pete understands and relates to reality. He takes refuge in this alternative *framed* reality which distances him from the sheer experience as it replaces it. Given that the mediated image offers a sense of reality that is more familiar than the real thing itself, it is not surprising that Pete daydreams about *buying* and *consuming* 'totally real experiences' in this late capitalist hyperreality: 'I'm gonna keep the peace in Bosnia. I'm gonna take Saddam Hussein for a pizza. I'm gonna shoot pool with the Pope and have Boris Yeltsin show me his collection of baseball stickers' (Ravenhill 1997: 112). This is the condition Alain theorizes and tries to communicate on television, namely, a world in which there is an absorption of one state of the real into another, an extensive flow of facsimiles, dominating the world and creating a new model of reality, *hyperreality*, 'a real retouched in a "hallucinatory resemblance" with itself' (Barker 2008: 343). Ironically, it is this distanced and desensitized state, which the Chorus comments on, that Pete experiences and retreats into while, at the same time, he strives to leave by cutting himself:

> *He [Pete] removes his shirt. His chest is covered in cuts.*
> Everything's a fucking lie, you know? The food, the TV, the music . . . it's all pretend. And this is the one thing that's for real. I feel it, it means something. (Ravenhill 1997: 126)

Pete's act of self-mutilation as a means to feel connected to reality and as a reaction against his estranged relation to the world behind a screen also indicates a search for an autonomous connection to himself and to others. In the search for a *real* sense of the world and the self, the perception and positing of the body as the truth presents an interesting, yet naive, position. Ravenhill's idea – stimulation of sensations through the body as a means to feel connected to reality – suggests that the body is outside culture and unaffected by the mediatized, hyperreal sociocultural landscape. Nevertheless, the body evolves within and in relation to cultural and social experiences and ecologies and experiences the same mediated connection to the world.

Similarly to Pete, Donny often has a mediated connection with and experience of the outside world. He cuts himself and broadcasts his self-harming performances on the web. Unlike Pete, Donny is critical about his media-driven life and wants to break away from it and have real connections with 'real' people beyond the computer screen: 'Had enough of just communicating with all you guys in a virtual kind of way. Had enough of it all just being pictures' (Ravenhill 1997: 134). As a last act of his Faustian search for something *real*, Donny decides to make his actions '[t]otally real' (Ravenhill 1997: 134). He cuts his throat in front of Alain and Pete while broadcasting it publicly on the internet. Interestingly, Donny's act turns him into a sensationalist reality TV product as it attracts the attention of media conglomerates: 'every TV show, every talk show. Ricki and Oprah both got the same show: "Death on the Net". And Stevie already has a song about it. Which he has performed unplugged and is now showing three times an hour on MTV' (Ravenhill 1997: 134–5). Donny becomes a spectacle himself and then a reproducible version of his own experience and existence, a commodity. Although his suicide supposedly takes him out of the virtual world, his attempt to go 'live' on the web ironically draws him back into the vicious circle of simulation. As a result, Donny's pursuit of real experience ironically culminates in an entanglement in late capitalist hyperreality, which

Alain sees as a confirmation of his argument that '[r]eality finished and simulation began' (Ravenhill 1997: 132) as the former evaporates into the latter and becomes indistinguishable.

Ravenhill reinforces the narrative commentary on the dissolution of reality into media-generated experience and perception through the Chorus' piece on the 1992 Los Angeles riots. The Chorus here presents 'excerpts from the "rioting" following the Rodney King trial, which Pete supposedly witnessed and video-recorded' (Ravenhill 1997: 63). The riots broke out when four Los Angeles Police Department officers were acquitted of all assault charges despite the discovery of a video recording of their violence against Rodney King, an African American from Pasadena. The court's decision and the video footage increased public sensitivity to the endemic racial inequality and injustice and led to riots. As the video footage of the uprisings was broadcast on television, similar public reactions took place in other US cities. The reference to the riots has a critical position in the play since it comments on the dissolution and simulation of historical facts, namely, how our perceptions and memories of historical events are constructed, shaped and communicated by the media. The Chorus directly draws our attention to how the constant broadcasting of the riots has constructed viewers' perception of historical reality: 'It's happening just like they [the media] said. Whole city is blowing apart' (Ravenhill 1997: 107).

The fact of individuals' dependence on media images as a gateway to reality is made even more pronounced when the Chorus remarks that people stole VCRs during the chaos rather than food. This critique of our dependency on the image and the spectacle is accentuated when Pete asks Alain: 'What is the point of food in the house when you have nothing to watch while you're eating it' (Ravenhill 1997: 107). The scene shrewdly addresses our dependence on media-generated and framed experiences, historical events and truths as the source and guarantors of reality. This, however, does not deny the fact that King's bruises and the LA deaths were real events and traumas. Nevertheless, the televised version of historical events that is edited, reconstructed and often embellished becomes the reference point for reality. This, as Ravenhill hints, is the inevitable state of our mediatized existence and perception. However, it does not deterministically suggest that there is no reality outside or without the mediated image, but that the boundaries between reality and its representation have been greatly blurred, and this has irrevocably altered how we perceive and relate to the world.[1]

Faust: Form

Faust's dramaturgical design frames the complex realities of this world through the unified narrative form of drama which, I argue, remains restricted in terms of its capacity to critically engage with the socio-cognitive circumstances and prescribed narratives of mediatized culture. To begin with, it is important to stress that, written in the late 1990s, *Faust* refers to a world that is different from that of *The Nether* and ours in the 2010s and 2020s. Social media platforms such as Facebook, Twitter and Instagram, which profoundly shape how we communicate and receive information about the world, did not exist in the late 1990s. Nevertheless, the increasing influence and manipulative power of mass media and information-communication technologies defined the period. Ravenhill depicts some of these conditions such as the changing sense of reality from a singular sense of a physical 'now' to a multi-reality platform where reality and its representation are no longer distinguishable.

Faust has nineteen chronologically and thematically connected scenes. The Chorus scenes seem to diverge from the linear storyline; however, they provide relevant commentaries that complete the narrative arc. For example, in scene 7 the Chorus refers to the Rodney King riots through a snapshot of a mother and son's underprivileged living conditions ('we ain't got no food in the kitchen' (Ravenhill 1997: 107)). This sub-narrative clearly resonates with Donny's story in scene 15 where he reveals more about his poor background: 'she [his mom] worked nights in the store and so I'd go there after school, hang out with my mom "til like six in the morning"' (Ravenhill 1997: 129). In addition, the narrative homogeneity is also maintained through scene 8 which starts with Pete repeating the closing line of the Chorus – the son's words: '[w]hat is the point of having food in the house when you have nothing to watch while you're eating it?' (Ravenhill 1997: 107). Complementing the unified, causal plot, the time and space are structured, coherent and realistic: the story takes place in present-day America with direct or implied references to real-life people and events such as Madonna, Letterman and the Rodney King riots, and it unfolds through a clear, chronological linearity. Through this dramatic design, rooted in a unity of action along with structured time and space, *Faust* pictures the world as a cohesive, surveyable whole with clear distinctions, if not binary oppositions, between reality and its mediatized representation.

To illustrate, on the thematic level the play remarks on our changing sense of reality through a particular emphasis on the merging of reality and its simulation through, for instance, Pete's constantly mediated contact with the outside world. This is also evident in the Chorus's reference to the media's construction of the Rodney King riots as the basis for historical truth as opposed to the real event itself. However, on the formal level, these instances of mediatized reality, where reality and its representation are no longer distinguishable, are depicted as distinct states of a meaningful, recognizable whole. For example, the scene where Pete meets Donny in an online chat room is introduced in the stage directions as a different setting that functions in line with narrative coherence, structured time and unified sense of reality both in the dramatic universe and the outside world: '*Pete is on the Net, tapping at the keys*' (Ravenhill 1997: 122). The play demarcates the dialogue in the chat room and outside of it by using capital letters without risking the homogeneity of the plot or altering the portrayal of the world as a closed-off totality:

> **Pete**   [. . .] Just some fucking actress, Donny, huh? Just some fucking fake. Fuck you. I hate that. That really gets to me. I have to tell him. I'm gonna tell him.
> Pete *types and* Donny *types his responses.*
> **Pete**   <DONNY, YOU ARE A FUCKING ACTRESS, YOU THERE, DONNY?>
> **Donny**   <SURE, I'M HERE.> (Ravenhill 1997: 125)

Here and throughout *Faust*, what we see is the representation of *mediation* or mediated communication. To put it simply, the portrayal of online presence and communication is not necessarily different from the use of media such as newspapers, telephones and television in earlier drama as a part of mimetic representation. The virtual experience in *Faust* adds to the sense of dramatic unity and one single reality. In addition, the scenes that thematize mediatized reality – Pete's desire for and dependence on a mediated perception of the outside world and the manipulated reality of the Rodney King events – are pictured from within the fictional universe. The mentioned layers of reality – virtual, framed, copied or represented by media – do not leak into the horizons of the fictional cosmos or risk its homogeneity with multidimensionality and multi-reality. Instead, *Faust*'s plot structure situates the real and its representation as binaries, as two distinct states and experiences, reinforcing the dramatic vision of the world as a stable whole with a sense of reality distinct from its image, while thematically suggesting that the non-referential hyperreality or multidimensional, mediated perception of reality has radically shifted the perception of physical reality.

Ravenhill's approach to character complements the mode of the plot structure. The main characters – Alain, Pete and Donny – are three-dimensional characters whose background, motivations, actions and thoughts are clearly presented. In the play, we learn about the background to Alain's decision to experience life a little more, Pete's relationship with his father and the reason for his escape, and Donny's problematic childhood. Each of these characters is a recognizable representation of an individual 'who appear[s] and behave[s] in a certain way and who carries within him [*sic*] a certain ethos' (States 1985: 91). Characterization here is perhaps not as detailed as in the naturalistic dramas of Henrik Ibsen or Anton Chekhov. Nevertheless, the play portrays the human subject as a deep, psychologically motivated, unified individual, as a recognizable person with coherent subjectivity, whose being and consciousness are not altered or multiplied due to her mediated connection to the world and changing sense of reality. For example, Donny's online and offline identities, and the multiple subjectivities his character contains after being simulated, objectified and circulated by the commercial mass media, are portrayed in line with cohesive dramatic characterization, depicting him as an identifiable character with individuality and autonomy. Additionally, Alain and Donny, who are objectified through Pete's camera and computer, are consistently pictured as individual characters with depth and unique subjectivity as opposed to being portrayed as hybrid, multi-layered characters with overtly constructed identities. This and other instances in *Faust* show that Ravenhill's characters represent the human in a media-saturated world of changing realities, subjective states and perceptions as a stable, cohesive individual whose subjectivity is yet not radically transformed by the symbolic and informational structures, or at least not yet identified in this drama as such.

This representation, through the traditional structures of dramatic theatre, of changing socio-cognitive coordinates and relationships in an increasingly media-saturated culture at the turn of the century offers some significant remarks on the culture and evolution of playtexts in the Anglophone theatre. Thinking in line with the deep-seated realist tendency in British theatre, Ravenhill identifies the representational logic underlying the play with his desire to 'capture the truth of this new world we live in' (Ravenhill 2003). In addition, the tradition of dramatic theatre provides a familiar aesthetic language and intelligible frame which offer a meaningful, recognizable order – something we seek in the face of the conditions and experiences of the multiply mediatized world. By making the contemporary comprehensible through a familiar form, Ravenhill aims to make his audience engage easily and directly with the drama and 'think more critically about The Way We Live Now than they might have done before' (Ravenhill 2006: 132). *Faust* achieves this to a certain extent as it acknowledges significant aspects of our mediatized lives, such as the implosion of reality in an increasingly media-driven environment, and our alternate identities or multiple existences on different media platforms. However, representing the 'less easily surveyable' (Lehmann 2006: 11) world as a closed-off, intelligible and, therefore, easily consumable whole limits the critical meanings that the play's thematics put forward for questioning. The dramatic logic and style, based on representing the outside world as we see it, tend to reproduce how we perceive reality, which is shaped by the dominant social order and increasingly more by media's representations of it. This suggests that *Faust*'s traditional dramatic design repeats the given perceptual and social codes through a sense of order, unity and consensus that closes the fictional world off to potential challenges to or ruptures in these prescribed structures of the *spectacle*. This mode of engagement formed through the comfort of accustomed structures suggests what I call *awareness with acceptance* – a sense of attention to the issues the play foregrounds that authorizes us to become conscious of them without offering the space for challenging and alternative narratives outside the dramatic parameters.

Faust: Performance

Premiering at the Lyric Hammersmith Theatre in 1997 by the Actors' Touring Company (ATC) under the direction of Nick Philippou, *Faust* on stage closely followed Ravenhill's text in terms of its media-saturated landscape, thematic context and dramatic aesthetics. In order to create the world of *Faust* and accentuate its narrative plot, ATC fashioned a multimedia environment: Pippa Nissen designed the stage with moveable screens with a monitor at the back wall of the stage and two large screens showing the walls of the play's hospital and motel settings.[2] On to these screens real-time images of the stage action were projected, shot by video-artist Alain Pelletier, who also played Alain, and pre-recorded images from the David Letterman show, the LA riots and Death Valley. The TV screens continuously showed images in relation to the onstage action. For instance, in the scene where the Chorus – presented as a young citizen of Los Angeles at the time of the 1992 riots – recounted his mother telling him off for stealing a VCR instead of food, the TV set at the back of the stage mediated the live action. The onstage Chorus was complemented by the mediated one on TV, a video-chorus of 'American teenagers [that] keep reminding us of the confusion of the coming generation' (Hemming 1997: 235). Furthermore, Pete's dependence on his camcorder and his inability to grasp reality without the mediated image were materialized on the stage, for instance, through pre-recorded footage of the Death Valley desert.

The use of technology complemented the play's realist design and narrative context, portraying a world becoming increasingly dependent on and controlled by media images. The ATC's intention to *translate* the playtext into the here-and-now of the stage was evident in each instance of its set design. For example, the juxtaposition of the physical reality of the staged action and its mediated version via live footage made visual the growing presence of technologies in our everyday lives and our tendency to experience the world behind screens. Ravenhill's comment on ATC's use of technology illustrates the representational and thematic drive of the multimedia design:

> What I engage with is narrative. But when we all worked together I became excited about the way it [video] could be used more thematically. To what extent are we living in a bubble of images and news? So then the use of video seemed to be integral to the whole theme of the piece. (Ravenhill in Callens 2003: 63)

Without doubt, the multimedia design on stage brought to its audience's attention media's increasing presence in our lives and its influence on society, human relationships and perception towards the end of the twentieth century, signalling what is to become a pervasively media-driven culture in the following century. It represented a strong commentary on the sociocultural and cognitive shifts and an invitation to consider our existence and experiences through the context of the dramatic universe – a closed-off, unified whole. However, while the structure of dramatic theatre facilitated an easily identifiable representation of these shifts, it simultaneously reproduced the sociocultural and perceptual motifs that we are repeatedly exposed to and consequently consented to. As a result, the stage production sealed *Faust*'s world and critical meanings from probing readings in line with the world we live in and how we perceive and represent it in and outside the theatre. As technologies have evolved rapidly in the twenty-first century, new realities and environments have emerged, accompanied by new plays, addressing the continually changing conditions and contexts of our existence and consciousness. Almost two decades after *Faust*, Haley's 2013 play *The Nether* responds to a world in which virtual reality offers a new 'contextual framework for being' (Haley 2014: 17) in a similarly direct and representational manner by using the form and conceptual framework of dramatic theatre.

The Nether: Thematics

Haley's play presents a hybrid world where virtual reality has become a state one can choose to migrate to and, relatedly, where ethical questions about our actions have become more confusing than ever due to our multi-reality existence. *The Nether* focuses on the investigation of the Hideaway – one of the domains in the Nether (that used to be the internet) – by Morris, a Nether detective. Morris seeks to find out about the crimes against children committed in this domain founded and owned by Sims (in-world name)/ Papa (name in the Hideaway). Morris enters the Hideaway undercover as a guest called Woodnut in order to find out about Papa/Sim's and other visitors' criminal actions against children. As the play progresses, one understands that, in the Hideaway, no one is a child; in this virtual realm, everyone involved has an adult *behinder* in the real world. Therefore, the children in the virtual world are masked personas of adults: Iris, the girl at the heart of the story, is actually a middle-aged science teacher called Doyle. The play takes place in two worlds as the story moves between the in-world interrogation room and the Hideaway, and the characters take on and perform alternative identities in the virtual realm. This generates an intricate narrative as we find out that Woodnut (female detective Morris) has fallen in love with Iris (a middle-aged man), and Iris/Doyle with Papa/Sims who sees the Hideaway as a useful safety valve that allows people to release their secret desires without infecting their in-world life.

The Nether questions the ethical boundaries that attend the rising influence and presence of media technologies. Is an unethical or illegal action committed in a representational world a crime? How does engagement in virtual environments affect people's actions in real life – are they immoral, criminal acts or preventative opportunities? Is it possible to separate virtual existence, actions and thoughts from those of the real world in an age where virtual reality technologies, social media platforms and info-communication networks shape our relation to and perception of reality? Who are we and how can we take responsibility for our actions when we exist as someone else?

Throughout the play, often in the interrogation scenes, Sims and Doyle imply that the real world is a repressive place and there is an urge to escape from the restraints of reality into the emancipating environment of the Nether:

> **Sims** [speaking to Morris:] [T]his world, has been so perverted by other people's ideas of what it should be. You and your speeches on images creating reality and why don't we make a better reality – look around! Look at this room. Look at what you've created. A place to twist people. A place to terrorise them. (Haley 2014: 62)

Visitors to the Hideaway find a refuge from who they are in the physical world and an opportunity to be who they want to be and do what they want to do, as Papa suggests, 'to live outside of consequence' (Haley 2014: 21). In the Hideaway, one chooses his/her identity – age, ethnicity, gender – from a set of looks provided. Doyle, a middle-aged teacher, chooses to *be* the little girl Iris, while Sims, a successful businessman, is Papa, and the female detective Morris is the behinder of the Papa's new customer-guest, Woodnut.

The real and the virtual at first seem to be separate. The characters maintain their in-world lives and relationships. However, as the play progresses, the boundaries between in-world presence and virtual existence blur, and this affects their relationships, how they think and act in the physical world. Morris, whose father became a shade in the Nether, implies that his absence affected her as a child. Now, as a detective, she reveals that the people who shift from the real world into the virtual realm and then are taken back again to the physical reality struggle 'to accept themselves again' (Haley 2014: 26). The boundaries between reality and representation blur most strikingly in the scene where Woodnut (Morris) repeatedly kills Iris with an axe in the Hideaway:

> **Morris** (*reading from a report*) And in those moments, standing in the carnage of her small body, the hot smell of everything we have inside rising around me, [. . .] I look down to find her body gone. What have I done, have I done something, have I done nothing, is this all nothing, is everything nothing? A giggle at the door, and she reappears, [. . .] she keeps coming, and now it's not just my hands covered in blood, it's my face, it's my body, I can taste it in my mouth, [. . .] I have never felt so much with every nerve, felt so much, felt so much . . . feeling. (Haley 2014: 53)

While the act of killing is virtual and not actual, what Morris as the undercover agent *feels* is real and actual due to the advanced technology that facilitates the experience of real sensations (Haley 2014: 24). Although the character seems to distinguish the real and the virtual, the boundaries become hard to differentiate:

> **Morris** But if there has been no consequence, there has been no meaning – no meaning between her and myself, between myself and myself – and if there has been meaning, then I am a monster. (Haley 2014: 53)

Haley's play does not offer answers to the questions about the ethics of virtual reality that it poses, but leaves them open for critical enquiry. Besides this specific thematic focus, the play also addresses the performance and presentation of the self on social media, and the impact of media-saturated lives on human consciousness and relationships. This is a shared thematic preoccupation in both *Faust* and *The Nether*. Let's briefly return to *Faust* as an earlier example that foreshadows aspects of changing social behaviours and perceptions in the globally networked, digital world of *The Nether*. As mentioned earlier, in Ravenhill's play Pete often prefers to relate to others behind the screen of his camcorder and computer, and he is comfortable 'only when [real life] experience can be mediated and consumed' through technological commodities (Wallace 2005: 272). In Pete, we see a consumer of not only experiences but also relationships. His reluctance to have an emotional connection with Alain, his hasty and distant attitude towards him during an intimate moment, and his desire to experience a direct connection with another human when this relationship is mediated all suggest a change in our interpersonal relationships. Such moments in *Faust* resonate with the fact that as a result of 'virtual proximity' being a defining aspect of human connection incrementally since the beginnings of the internet, the majority of our relationships are based on what Zygmunt Bauman calls 'liquid love': '[c]onnections [that] are too shallow and brief to condense into bonds' (2003: 62) and 'easy to enter and to exit' (2003: xii). Similarly, Doyle's addiction to the Hideaway illustrates how technology shapes our relationships, and how ironically, as Baudrillard claimed before Bauman, it 'devours communication and the social' when we search for connection and intimacy through virtual proximity (1994: 80). Doyle prefers the relationships in the Nether, the 'beautiful family [and] sympathetic community' to his in-world ones and is ready to leave his in-world bonds behind in order to cross over (Haley 2014: 21).

In relation and addition to this, *The Nether* comments on the illusion of intimacy when Papa repeatedly reminds Iris that the Hideaway is a business, hinting at the capitalist motives and discourses underlying various social media platforms that offer a sense of proximity and connection. It is also in evidence when it is revealed that once visitors 'start expressing real emotion, it's off to boarding school', namely, that they are expelled from the virtual realm (Haley 2014: 44). This, perhaps in a far-fetched manner, resonates with the fact that today our 'cyberintimacies slide into cybersolitudes' (Turkle 2011: xlvii), as we falsely identify our online connections as intimate relationships. This explains Donny's desire to stop communicating with people online and meet people 'for real' in *Faust*, as well as Morris's yearning for direct communication and relationship with her father in *The Nether*. Both plays, however, suggest that in an age where '[t]echnology has become the architect of our intimacies' (Turkle 2011: 590), even our search for intimacy may be interrupted by and culminate in 'the illusion of companionship' (Turkle 2011: 590) and the confusion of posts or chats on social media with 'true' communication.

The Nether: Form

Considering the story and themes of *The Nether* analysed here, we see that the play directly addresses some of the significant and morally troubling issues in mediatized culture. Its up-to-date and overt thematics, with which anyone living in the digital age is familiar, presents us with important questions not only about the ominous potential of the internet but also about the ethics of our decisions, actions, lifestyles and perception in a media-driven culture. However, I contend that the use of traditional dramatic form with its closed structure to portray this multi-reality world puts forward a vision of reality that is no longer in tune with the socio-cognitive circumstances that the play thematizes and therefore limits its critical scope and reception.

To elaborate, *The Nether* is formed of short, linearly structured scenes that follow a coherent, causal storyline, and structured space and time. The two settings in the play – the physical world (the interrogation room) and the virtual world (the Nether/the Hideaway) – are presented with great clarity: there is no confusion as to where the scenes take place and when they unfold within the play's time schema. Haley introduces the time of the play as 'soon' at the opening of the play and makes sure that this vague concept of temporal space is structured within the boundaries of a linear timeline. As the play opens and the plot advances, it becomes clear that this unspecified future is indeed presented through the familiar dramatic order of beginning, middle and end. The final scene, distinguished from the previous numbered scenes and labelled as 'Epilogue', is not structured within the linear storyline as it reiterates an earlier scene where Papa brings Iris a birthday cake. In the Epilogue, the major difference is that, this time, the intimate interaction takes place between Iris and Papa's behinders, namely, between Doyle and Sims. The Epilogue closes as Doyle and Sims express their love for one another without their virtual personas. Although the concluding scene is not given within the chronological framework, it still sits within the narrative frame because it seems to be an imagined dialogue possibly playing in Sims's mind after learning about Doyle's suicide. Hence, rather than undermining the linear construction, the final scene complements and reinforces it.

The mode of characterization follows the same dramatic framework. Throughout the play, there is a clear distinction between the in-world characters – the behinders – and the virtual ones in the Hideaway. One does not know who is the behinder of whom at the beginning of the play, yet due to the mode of character presentation this becomes clear as the story unfolds. Nevertheless, in this state of initial ignorance, there is no uncertainty about the difference between the real and the virtual or an overlap between these states because the boundaries are evident, stressing the clear binary opposition between reality and its representation. Each character in physical reality and in the Nether is formed and presented as a three-dimensional psychological individual: Sims, for example, is a successful businessman and founder of the Hideaway who firmly believes that he is protecting the in-world children by diverting his paedophilic desires to the virtual world. His alternative self or avatar in the Nether is Papa – a fatherly persona who enjoys prepubescent girls and runs a brothel-like business where guests are free to experience child rape and murder. The multi-realities and subjectivities, which in the contemporary world of Facebook, Twitter or Instagram are not clearly separable, are represented as connected, yet distinct through apposite use of character names. That is, on the thematic level, the narrative gestures towards the blurring of boundaries between reality and representation; for example, we know that Doyle spends a lot of time in the Hideaway as Iris – to the extent that he wants to migrate to the alternative reality and become a shade. Whereas, on the formal level, the play's structure delimits the characterization to a unified representation of subjectivity (i.e. we know when the character is Doyle and in the physical world, and when he is Iris and in the Nether), leaving the layered, multiple and hybrid subjectivities outside the realities that the play attempts to thematically address.

Ultimately, the insightful thematic engagement with contemporary mediatized culture – something postdramatic theatre tackles in text and performance (e.g. Martin Crimp, Heiner Müller, Elfriede Jelinek, the Wooster Group, Builders' Association) – is stymied by a dramaturgical structure that portrays the world as a recognizable, unitary whole. Considering the world today, which is identified with economic and political uncertainty, info-rich, fast-paced and always-on culture, globally networked yet socially disintegrated individuals and all-pervasive simulations encouraging the spectacle of consumption, the attempt to represent the contemporary in a teleological, orderly manner is not surprising. However, the desire for logical order and causative structure is no longer adequate to fully articulate and *critically* grasp the complex social and cognitive conditions of a ubiquitously mediatized culture. This does not mean that plays that talk about mediatized society through traditional dramatic structure do not display interesting and relevant aspects of it. Rather, it suggests that old conventions of representation have become limited and limiting in their ability to speak of and to a world where perception, and therefore representation, is majorly shaped by media technologies and the sociocultural environment they have engendered.

This also suggests that as a consequence of its realist, dramatic form, which reiterates the prevailing power structures and what they imprint on our perception as acceptable majorly through media technologies today, the play affirms these social codes and relations. Reproducing the commonly agreed-upon ways of being and thinking through a recognizable frame confines the possibilities for questioning these from within and obtaining subversive perspectives on the world we live in as an alternative to the *consensus*. Therefore, the direct thematization in *The Nether*, which invites its audience to critically engage with its questions about the world we live in, actually reiterates the familiar perceptual frames and social codes, namely, the *sensible* of our media-driven everyday reality. Plays that thematically engage with aspects of mediatized culture through the structures and conventions of dramatic theatre doubtlessly bring the themes to our attention. However, this form of engagement is likely to engender consensual awareness as opposed to subversive attention – *awareness with acceptance* – and keeps us within the perceptual parameters of the prescribed narratives of the dominant social system. The interpretation of *The Nether* on the Royal Court stage followed the play's dramatic form and reinforced its meanings and effect.

The Nether: Performance

In 2014, Haley's *The Nether* received its European premiere in a co-production between the Royal Court Theatre and Headlong, directed by Jeremy Herrin. In a similar way to ATC's *Faust*, the stage production of *The Nether* presented a dramatic interpretation of Haley's text that depicted the virtual and the real settings as well as the clear shifts from one to another. Following the explicit and implicit cues in the text, Es Devlin designed the in-world interrogation room as a featureless, colourless, high-tech space. There was minimal use of props in this clinical setting – two chairs, a table and projected images on the walls. On the other hand, the Hideaway, as the playtext suggested, was designed to present an environment that was the opposite of the cold, dark in-world space: a dream-like, colourful, Victorian-themed house surrounded by trees and filled with lavish furniture. The set was raised on a suspended platform enclosed by mirrored walls, creating a magical feeling.

Although the performance constantly shifted back and forth from the in-world setting to the Nether, the clearly partitioned set presented the two worlds as two distinctly separate spaces and realities within the boundaries of theatrical representation. This was not only because of the manifestly separated sets but also due to the carefully devised actor–character combination that separated the real character from her virtual counterpart. That is, as the performance progressed, the audience figured out that the detective (Amanda Hale) was Woodnut's behinder in the Hideaway (Ivanno Jeremiah). Likewise, Doyle from the in-world domain (David Beames) transformed into Iris (performed by child actor Zoe Brough). Here, we see the clear separation between real-life self and virtual identity, which preserved a uniform, realistic characterization since each character on page was embodied by a separate actor on stage, despite the fact that the virtual and the real were the same person. This characterization does not correspond

Figure 1 *The Nether*. Photo credit: Es Devlin.

to the ways in which we experience subjectivity in mediatized culture where our real-life and virtual experiences and beings are intertwined, producing a multiple, heterogonous, divergent ontology.

The only actor–character combination that did not change in the real and virtual domains was Sims/Papa who was played by Stanley Townsend. However, the same actor for both in-world and virtual subjects was not necessarily confusing for the audience or a reference to the mediatization of the self because Townsend used different costumes in different realms to distinguish the subjectivities and states. Despite this, some might argue that the use of live actors in the virtual realm created a sense of uncertainty as to the reality of the Hideaway: 'the live actors of Herrin's production ensure that the distinction between real and virtual remains blurred [and] that the audience is never quite free of a nagging doubt that the Hideaway is entirely virtual, entirely unreal' (Stowell-Kaplan 2015: 161). However, questioning its reality is yet another way of thinking about the real and the virtual as binary oppositions, rather than considering the virtual as a new dimension interrelated with the physical reality. Relatedly, the presence of a live actor in the representation of a virtual realm, when the real and the virtual are clearly defined through the set design and characterization, does not necessarily lead to the blurring of the two dimensions. The mode of staging kept these two realities strictly and deliberately within the closed-off universe of *The Nether* without causing a leak into the here-and-now of the auditorium.

In addition, it is apt to mention here that, before the performance began, the audience encountered several terminals placed at different parts of the Royal Court through which the audience members could interact with the Nether – an online platform created by Michael Takeo Magruder along with Drew Baker and Erik Fleming. This supplementary design did not only offer an engagement with the world of *The Nether* beforehand but also rendered the *fictional virtual* world accessible to and present within the audience's physical reality. This was an intriguing aspect of the production and one that initially suggested the intermingling and co-presence of different realms – physical reality, fictional/dramatic world and the virtual realm (onstage and in real life). However, later one found out that our input into the virtual world was separated from the world of the play and the outcomes of our interactions were to be displayed in an artwork throughout the building. They were not an interaction with *The Nether* and the fictional realm within it. In other words, though promising as a design idea, the use of stations only allowed our interactions to be supplementary to the theatre event rather than a aesthetico-critical design letting our reality blur and leak into the worlds of *The Nether* and its real-life digital extension at the Court.

Additionally, casting a *trained* child actor to perform the virtual character Iris, whose in-world *behinder* is an adult man, fortified the dramatic framework as she dexterously personified the character and stayed within the boundaries of the dramatic illusion. This was a deliberate choice given the discomforting theme of child abuse. Other theatre pieces such as Milo Rau's *Five Easy Pieces* (2016) and Markus Öhrn's *Conte d'amour* (2010) deal with the same theme with reference to real events (the cases of paedophile serial killer Marc Dutroux and Josef Fritzl, respectively) yet in ways that radically undermine dramatic representation. While, in Öhrn's piece, all the adult and children parts are performed by adult actors, in Rau's production every part is enacted by child actors (apart from Peter Seynaeve, the only adult actor on stage in the interchanging roles of Dutroux and director-facilitator, possibly Rau's proxy) in a metatheatrical way on stage and by both child and adult actors in the pre-recorded film images. Rau's piece is especially interesting in relation to Herrin's *The Nether* as it casts child actors to talk about a disturbing real-life event yet continually breaks the theatrical illusion by emphasizing the theatreness of the stage action and actorly-ness of the children. On the other hand, *The Nether* uses a child actor in an entirely fictional setup to enact a virtual false-identity character (a doubly fictional character) who is actually an adult in the play to show the online domain as it appears on the screen to the characters in *The Nether*. The child actor might offer the possibility of subverting the dramatic illusion momentarily by causing something unquestionably real to break the dramatic illusion and confront the audience.

Nevertheless, using a *trained* child actor who would try to stay within the dramatic representation, to represent an online world based on constructed identities, does not aim for and accommodate such subversion. There is a difference between a professionally trained child actor, who is asked to enact a character realistically and who fleetingly breaks the dramatic illusion by accident (where we agree to suspend disbelief and become aware of the nature of *live* performance), and a professionally trained actor who, as in Tim Crouch's *An Oak Tree* (2005), is asked to perform the tasks given to her rather than fully embodying them in a realistic style. In the first scenario, the accidental act can surely take the audience out of the play's world momentarily, yet this is not the critical-aesthetic motive of the overall design that would keep the audience aware of theatre's 'theatreness' all the way through.

The realistically conceived characters and their dramatic embodiment by the actors on stage could be challenged in interesting ways. For example, it would be interesting to see Iris being performed by an actor who does not look like the character at all – something Tim Crouch explores in his work, especially in *An Oak Tree* – in order to destabilize the boundaries of dramatic representation and open the possibility of questioning mediatized being and consciousness in a world of multiple realities. It would also be intriguing to see Iris and Woodnut performed by their behinder-characters/actors, that is, by Doyle (D. Beames) and detective Morris (A. Hale) in order to explore how this approach to staging *The Nether* would subvert unified and teleological representation, breaking away from traditional aesthetics to relate to our multi-reality, multi-consciousness world.

The production of *The Nether* undoubtedly portrayed our media-saturated lives through a dexterously choreographed setting and vividly represented story and characters. However, the easily identifiable dramatic frame, presenting the world as a surveyable whole, homogenized the intricacies of the ontology and phenomenology of mediatized society. Furthermore, rather than creating ruptures in the agreed-upon and often media-induced structures of the *distribution of the sensible*, which divorces those who can take part and be visible, audible and representable from those who are excepted, the dramatic aesthetics reproduced these structures and social codes. As a result, the *dramatic* dramaturgy (the dramaturgy of dramatic theatre) comforted rather than encouraging the audience to grasp and critically question the socio-cognitive experiences of the contemporary. It represents theatre for consumption (*culinary theatre*) – a form of theatre that reiterates the dominant power structures the media circulates, and relatedly, keeps its audience within the familiar social codes and narratives, leaving the dissident questioning of the world we live in outside the dramatic cosmos.

Conclusion: The problematics of dramatic mediatized dramaturgy

Faust and *The Nether* illustrate a common occurrence in contemporary Anglophone theatre practice, particularly in Britain: plays that *talk about* mediatized culture through the traditional structures of dramatic theatre – recognizable, linear plotline, structured time, unified space and psychologically motivated characterization. One may argue, as Sarah Bay-Cheng does, that 'dramatic structures and models of theatricality that are more akin to late-nineteenth-century realism [. . .] offer new possibilities for dramatic theatre in an era of new media' (2015: 689), and 'theatrical realism suggests an aesthetic distance that allows us to consider violent actions with a critical distance' (2015: 693). The majority of performances that tackle technology and digital culture in the twentieth and twenty-first centuries use a non-narrative, non-realistic, postdramatic aesthetics. This may suggest that a return to realist theatre aesthetics nostalgically brings back the old forms, and that the use of the old forms, while addressing the new socio-cognitive contexts, generates an aesthetic and critical distance (2015: 698). However, as I underlined earlier, realist aesthetics are not passé in the majority of Anglophone theatre. Moreover, although in theatre performance the aesthetics of the modernist avant-garde has been popular while addressing the techno-culture and its media forms, in dramatic writing, particularly in the British theatre, the dominant mode has still been the realist, dramatic tradition. Hence, rather than offering a distancing effect, dramatic realism actually limits the critical capacity to engage with mediatized culture in which the lived experience and perception of social reality and thus its presentation fundamentally differ from the understanding of the world in the nineteenth century, based on logical order of cause and effect, and the models that Henrik Ibsen, Chekov or Stanislavski used. In addition, filtering the contemporary through the sieve of dramatic logic and aesthetics suggests the representation of mediatized human existence, consciousness and relations in the way that media shapes them in line with the dominant social order. Dramatic mediatized dramaturgy therefore tends to reiterate what we conventionally accept as the social reality, without necessarily allowing a space for alternative ways of thinking about our times and existence. Therefore, a politics of content placed within the dramatic mediatized textual architecture does not necessarily bring about critical efficacy or engage us intellectually and emotionally.

This calls for attention to new trends in the dramaturgy of texts that resist and rupture familiarized representational aesthetics in order to offer possibilities for dissident thinking about the mediatized now. Resistance to representation is a political act *especially* in an age where our lives are inundated with media images. Such resistance, in other words, proposes a challenge to the reproduction of the *sensible*, and aims at a nonconformist and transformative perception of our existence through a transgressive approach to conventionally mimetic representation, to 'the perfection of reproduction' as a projection of an absolute perception of reality (Lehmann 2006: 116). Therefore, plays with such innovative form and critical value engage with the mediatized state of mind from within, and open spaces for alternative perspectives on and narratives about the world we live in. Drawing on these reflections, the following chapters explore the ways in which some contemporary playtexts reconfigure their dramaturgical structure to map, relate and respond to mediatized society and its sociocognitive repercussions. To this end, in these chapters I expand the critical scope from the thematization of mediatization to developments in textual dramaturgy by considering language, characterization, plot structure and media-based plays.

3

Dramaturgy of language
Tracing mediatized culture in words

If the bard were alive today, he'd probably write, '2B or not 2B'.
(Thurlow 2007: 221)

When Patrick Marber's *Closer* opened at the National Theatre in 1997, British theatre encountered one of the first representations of online communication on stage, with a scene set in a chat room. This scene also marked one of the first uses of netspeak through abbreviations ('Nice 2 Meet U') (Marber 1999: 23), expressive styles (capital letters to indicate shouting) and emoticons (❦) (Marber 1999: 27). In the same year, another innovative play addressing mediatized culture made an appearance: Martin Crimp's *Attempts on Her Life*. Unlike Marber's play, Crimp's *Attempts* does not use the media-generated language style. Instead, *Attempts* uses language in ways that suggest links to our changing social and cognitive conditions in a media-saturated ecology. For example, the unattributed speech raises the question of how much agency we have over our language and perception, bearing in mind our mediatized ontology and media-driven consciousness. Fast-forward to 2014 – almost two decades after these initial dramaturgical reflections on mediatized life and language – Christopher Brett Bailey's *THWD* engages with the contemporary through a striking and critical emphasis on language. The play makes hardly any reference to technology's impact on our lives through the *direct* use of media language – such as Twitter-style short text speak with hashtags – something that we see an early version of in *Closer*. Instead, similar to *Attempts*, *THWD* uses language to subtly evoke aspects of our mediatized lives and perception. The script, formed as a galloping torrent of words, loads the audience with bite-size information and snapshots, continually constructing and deconstructing meaning until language is finally pronounced dead. The overall affect is an existential and perceptual state that resonates with anyone living in this fast-paced, information age.

Since the late 1990s, playtexts have had this specific preoccupation with the language of mediatized culture – from Marber's open use of netspeak to Crimp's fragmented and depersonalized and Bailey's torrential, fast-paced language. These plays suggest a significant shift in the dramaturgy of language. While some of the plays engage with mediatized language in line with the vision and aesthetics of the realist dramatic tradition, others reconsider language in a way that subverts this deep-seated tradition in order to speak to the realities of mediatized culture and consciousness. Both dramatic and no-longer-dramatic dramaturgies of language in these plays offer intriguing reflections on our existence in a media-driven age. However, whether and how differing aesthetico-critical engagements with language in a mediatized culture cultivate a critical distance from our engrained socio-cognitive environment is a question yet to be explored. This chapter wonders: What does the shift in the dramaturgy of language, produced whether deliberately or unconsciously in playtexts, contain? How does it work in relation to dramatic representation and its crisis, particularly in the mediatized age, where the globalized, fast-paced, information-intensive, politically and economically uncertain state of the world is rendering language less reliable and less capable of identifying the realities we live in? How, if at all, do new modes of language use open up critical spaces to engage with mediatized society and consciousness? Before we delve into these questions, it is useful to briefly consider how language has evolved in a mediatized culture and identify some general aspects of mediatized language.

Language in a mediatized culture

Language is a layered construct with various aspects. It is important to identify some of these in order to understand its position and meanings within our media-saturated social, political and cognitive ecology. To begin with, language is a primary means of human communication, not simply and only a medium for social interaction and expression of ideas, but also the central medium through which we construct our ideas of the world and understand, interpret and communicate reality. Language, therefore, serves as an ideational mechanism generating representations of the world (Fairclough 1995: 17), reflecting and fashioning reality. Language, therefore, as Hans-Georg Gadamer argues, 'is not just one of man's [sic] possessions in the world; rather, on it depends the fact that man [sic] has a *world* at all' (2004: 440).

As a human-made construct, language is unquestionably in conversation with and a product of the social world; it evolves through convention and social interaction, through repetition from speaker to speaker, and from one generation to another. There is no such thing as a non-historical, non-cultural or non-social use of language. Besides, language is always already shaped by and often a product and instrument of the dominant power structures. It serves to construct and sustain these structures, as well as being an influential force that shapes power relations and the sociocultural realities these relations may engender. Language carries with it 'the power of those concrete contexts into which it has entered [and which is] permeated with the intentions of other speakers' (Bakhtin 1973 cited in Holborow 2015: 124). Hence, language is an ideological technology, if not the 'most powerful ideological instrument' (Postman 1992: 123), given that ideology influences the ways in which and the tools through which we give meaning to the world. It defines how we identify, perceive and understand reality, it forms our ideas of the world and our position in it and it reflects and produces power structures and evolves in line with dominant intellectual interests. Often the ideological role and workings of language are veiled, first because ideological structures and narratives are deeply ingrained in our everyday lives, and second because language is perceived as an innate human trait that evades immediate critical attention.[1] While the invisibility of language as an ideological instrument helps power structures continue, this does not mean that the buried agenda cannot be unveiled and subverted. Language can be used as a mechanism by the ruling power to impose and maintain their power; yet, it can also be used as a subversive instrument for resistance against the dominant social, ideological and cultural structures.

In the context of language and its connection with prevailing power structures, it is important to mention discourse. Like language, discourse represents reality, but while doing this, discourse involves language as well as other symbolic means. While language is more about the set of rules and patterns, discourse goes beyond the rules and level of semantics and grammar to grasp and identify how language makes meaning in different social, political and cultural situations. Discourse, in this respect, can be considered as a system and set of representations that form the ways in which we perceive reality. Discourse, Foucault argues, refers not only to 'individualizable groups of statements' (1972 cited in Mills 2003: 53) (e.g. feminist discourse) but also to a mode of language use based on a 'complex set of practices which try to keep them in circulation and other practices which try to fence them off from others and keep those other statements out of circulation' (Mills 2003: 54). In relation to the idea of language as an ideological technology, discourse 'can be both an instrument and an effect of power, but also a hindrance, a stumbling block, a point of resistance and a starting point for an opposing strategy. Discourse transmits and produces power; it reinforces it, but also undermines it and exposes it, renders it fragile and makes it possible to thwart it' (Foucault 1978: 100–1).

Language today is deeply connected to the new media technologies and cannot be considered outside the phenomenon of mediatization, pervading our contemporary society, culture and consciousness. Nevertheless, this is not to say that the impact of technology on language is a new phenomenon. Technology as social, cultural and ideological machinery has always influenced language. With the invention of the printing press in the fifteenth century, an increasing number of books were in circulation and newspapers appeared which not only revolutionized society but also generated and spread new varieties of language. The advent of the telephone in the nineteenth century and the arrival of broadcasting media in the early twentieth century, among other technological advancements, engendered new linguistic styles and discourses (Crystal 2001: 26). However, the impact of new technologies on almost all aspects of our personal, social and political lives as well as on language has never been as radical, rapid and widespread as it has been since the late twentieth century. In our contemporary media-saturated society, in which media technologies, language, society and power structures are more deeply interlinked than before, language has become mediatized.[2] Language, in other words, has evolved in line with new technologies and the socio-cognitive and ideological realities these technologies have generated and/or sustained.

Since the 1990s, the internet – with its numerous extensions and platforms such as emailing technology since the mid-1990s, text messaging and social media since the early 2000s, and Twitter since the mid-2000s – has drastically influenced language use. The internet, as David Crystal argues, has triggered a linguistic revolution (Crystal 2001: 5). For example, the concise form of text messaging and Twitter posts requires that we communicate in increasingly succinct language. In 2001, *The Guardian* newspaper launched a text poetry competition inviting people who 'had 160 characters inside them waiting to come out in the form of a poem' (Keegan 2002). The winning poet reflexively wrote: 'txtin iz messin, / mi headn'me englis, / try2rite essays, / they all come out txtis' (Hughes 2001). The language styles the new media technologies have introduced, which have been quickly and globally adopted, offer a language beyond dialect (Hjarvard 2004: 94). Stig Hjarvard attributes this linguistic invention to the concept of *medialect* – 'linguistic variants that arise out of specific media' (Hjarvard 2004: 75) and 'spread to other medialects as well as to traditional written and spoken communication' (Hjarvard 2004: 95). For instance, text message abbreviations (2day, CU, B4), phonetic spellings (bcoz, luv), emotional noises (hehehe for 'laugh') and the creative iconicity (<3 for 'heart', itself a visual representation of 'love') are also used in emails and chat rooms.

To consider language in the mediatized culture or language as mediatized, however, is not simply to consider it in terms of the *direct* and noticeable impact of media technologies on syntax, grammar or linguistic styles. Mediatization of language also refers to the linguistic and discursive representations of and engagements with larger social, cognitive and cultural changes. Such shifts in language are often hard to discern because they are deeply rooted in the social and perceptual processes we experience in a mediatized age which have been so absorbed into our everyday lives that they have become almost imperceptible. Mediatization of language is therefore about both the direct and implicit manifestations of our mediatized culture in the way we use language, and the language we are exposed to through which we identify the world and ourselves in it. For instance, fragmented, fast-paced, shortened modes of language use suggest our contemporary cognitive conditions and lifestyles, shortened attention spans and sped-up sense of time, shaped through our immersion in social media and inundation with bite-size information. In addition, mediatized language cannot be considered outside the capitalist system and its power relations, which new technologies and media platforms, more often than not, are a product of and tend to sustain. The language of news media and advertisements, for example, is filled with direct manifestations of consumer capitalism that bring about and shape a collective consciousness and behavioural pattern that sustains consumption and a neoliberal political economy.

Mediatized dramaturgy of language

'Mediatized dramaturgy of language' simply refers to the form of language that has altered, deliberately or unintentionally, in relation to the media technologies we use every day and the realities of the mediatized culture we live in. As I briefly discussed at the opening of this chapter, with the penetration of new technologies into every stratum of our lives, the theatre scene has encountered, since the late 1990s, an increasing number of plays that evidence aspects of mediatized language.

As mentioned, some plays have used mediatized language overtly to generate a realistic representation of the technology that the characters are using. For example, following the path Marber's *Closer* lay down, Lucy Prebble's *Sugar Syndrome* (2003) and Enda Walsh's *Chatroom* (2005) incorporate netspeak into the heart of their dramatic representation, set scenes in online chat rooms and portray youth culture and identity politics in the internet age. Besides the explicit and immediately familiar uses of mediatized language, there have been changes implicit in the form of language in plays that suggest links to our media-driven, info-saturated, accelerated lives without having to use any technological lingo or direct references to technology in texts. Various plays show evidence of a subtle mediatization of language that addresses contemporary subjects' fast-paced lives and fragmentary, multi-directional consciousness. John Jesurun's *Everything Rises Must Converge* (1997) and *Firefall* (2006) illustrate this form of language use. In these plays, the non-linear, quick bombardment of words with no obvious connective logic evokes how, in a media-saturated socio-cognitive context, we communicate and think in the mode of dissociated circuitry. These plays reflect on social disintegration, the difficulty of communication and the desire to make sense of the world through reliable, homogenous language. More examples of subtle mediatization of language could be found in plays such as Suzan-Lori Parks's *365 Days / 365 Plays* (2006) and Caryl Churchill's *Love and Information* (2012), in which bite-sized language echoes aspects of our existence in the information age. This dramaturgical pattern calls for further discussion, which I shall return to shortly in relation to Crimp's *Attempts* and Bailey's *THWD*, exploring how the aesthetic and critical considerations of language in these plays speak to the contemporary.

It is important to note here that, whether overtly or implicitly mediated, the mode of language use in playtexts relates to the contemporary socio-cognitive environment with varying degrees of critical depth. The definitive factor here is the aesthetic and critical stance on traditional dramatic representation. In certain plays, as I shall explore in relation to *Closer*, the use of language reiterates the realist dramatic form and reinforces the representation of the world as a closed-off totality, often reproducing the social, cultural and ideological structures of the dominant order. Whereas, in others such as *Attempts* and *THWD*, language use acts as a part of the overall no-longer-dramatic architecture and challenges the dramatic model while addressing the less easily surveyable and representable contemporary realities. Hence, I argue, the use of language in line with traditional dramatic form corresponds to the intricacies of mediatized culture in a limited way, restricting the level of critical understanding of the times we live in. The no-longer-dramatic language mode evokes aspects of this culture and opens possibilities for a critical questioning of our otherwise unnoticed mediatized ontology and consciousness. This, however, does not suggest that the former does not relate to the contemporary social ecology at all. Instead, it indicates that dramatic mediatized plays retain and reproduce the embedded socio-cognitive context we live in without necessarily opening cracks for critical rethinking, while the no-longer-dramatic model does.

Mediatized dramaturgy of language: From dramatic to no-longer-dramatic design

Medialect in drama: *Closer*

Marber's *Closer* tells the story of the romantic turmoil between four characters: a photographer (Anna), a stripper (Alice), a dermatologist (Larry) and an obituary writer (Dan). Alice falls in love with Dan; Dan falls in love with Anna, who takes Dan's picture for the cover of the book he has written about Alice. The dynamic of this love triangle changes when Larry meets Anna, initially through an internet chat room, a scene I will elaborate on shortly. The relationship between the four characters then leads to a cycle of betrayal – ending with all of them estranged (despite what the title implies). Underneath the representation of these intertwined and often ostensibly self-interested relationships lie subtle references to a certain socio-historical and geographical context – London (and the Western world in general) in the 1990s – a post-Thatcher society characterized by the rise of self-interest and individualism. All of the characters in Marber's play emerge from and signify these individualistic and self-interested modes.

In scene 3, Marber reinforces this contemporary and 'darkly savage' social context through the use of a cyberspace setting and the new global dialect: medialect (Saunders 2008: 1). In this scene, Dan and Larry talk to each other via a cybersex chat room when Dan pretends to be Anna, 'a sex-obsessed woman, a "cum-hungry bitch" with "epic tits" who titillates the man at the other terminal, finally faking an ecstatic textual orgasm of jumbled letters and "oh-oh-oh"s' (Dixon 2007: 469). Marber, like Ravenhill in *Faust Is Dead*, identifies this world as a place where real human connection and intimacy have become problematic and hard to achieve, and where, as Larry emphatically indicates, everything has become a version of something else.

Closer is based on the 'dramatic' idea of the world and is relatedly structured as a well-made drama with a chronologically organized and consistent plot, structured time and space, plausible situations and clearly identifiable characters. The way Marber deploys language corresponds to this construct in which language serves as a tool to reflect the world as a unified whole. Language constitutes a definitive point of origin based on a linear signification process that structures meaning through a coherent and recognizable relationship between the representation and the represented. In this, Marber's approach to language evokes the naturalist dramas of Henrik Ibsen, Anton Chekhov and George Bernard Shaw, where language is part of the realistic composition, representing the world as a complete and surveyable whole and corresponding to the dialects and sociolects of the period. The incorporation of netspeak into *Closer*'s acts as a part of this overall dramatic structure, and situates the drama within the historico-social realities of the late 1990s – the beginnings of the contemporary globally connected, information-rich digital age.

Closer is certainly one of the first plays to remediate the aesthetics of chat language, yet not the only one to use chat rooms for its setting and thematic content. Later plays such as Enda Walsh's *Chatroom* (2005) and Lucy Prebble's *The Sugar Syndrome* (2003) both situate their narrative in a virtual environment and focus on themes such as human relationships, identity and self-representation in a digitally connected world. Nevertheless, innovatively for the late 1990s, *Closer*'s scene 3 uses netspeak features such as abbreviations ('Nice 2 Meet U'; 'RU4 real?' (Marber 1999: 23–6)), the loosening of grammatical rules ('Youre v.forward'; 'Life without riskisdeath' (Marber 1999: 23–7)) and emoticons. Moreover, this scene mainly consists of short and quick exchanges, resonating with the characters' physically detached and emotionally disengaged states. For example, when Larry's office phone rings as he is about to masturbate, turned on by Anna's (Dan) messages, he picks it up and responds to a medical case. Similarly, in the same scene, Dan *'lights a cigarette'* and *'clicks the balls on his Newton's Cradle'* (Marber 1999: 25). This blank and impassive attitude towards the other, which is also evident in the rest of the play as characters easily stop and start relationships and cheat on each other, speaks to a representation of the outside world as made up of self-interested individuals and social fragmentation. This resonates with Zygmunt Bauman's 'liquid love' – a mode of relationship, arising out of late capitalism with new technologies as one of its tools, and characterized by relations that are 'easy to enter and to exit' (2003: xii). The swift and impersonal language use along with the cybersex chat-room setting reflects the consumerist tendencies of human relationships. In doing so, the scene reiterates the underlying theme of self-centred individualism, objectification of the other and the deteriorating state of human relationships in an increasingly mediatized, capitalist society.

In addition, Marber occasionally uses capital letters – ('**Larry**: WHAT D'YOU HAVE TO DO TO GET A BIT OF INTIMACY AROUND HERE?' (1999: 73)) – and underlined phrases – ('<u>Don't say it</u>, don't fucking say, "You're too good for me." I *am* – <u>but don't say it</u>' (1999: 58)). These language patterns, used throughout the playtext, though originating from written language, imply a connection with the linguistic style used in chat rooms, SMS messaging and online text documents, particularly when considered in relation to the medialect and online context used in scene 3. Such signs and styles in written language, including emoticons and abbreviations discussed earlier, have become familiar forms to our consciousness as we have started using text messaging, emailing and other media communication platforms since the late 1990s. In this respect, the way Marber scatters these patterns throughout the play does not introduce a new, unfamiliar form, but reproduces a commonly shared mode of linguistic communication and interpretation (e.g. a character is yelling or emphasizing his/her point). They also function as implied stage directions within the text, making the presentation of the dialogue conform to the tone of the dramatic narrative. The use of medialect, therefore, adheres to the aesthetics of mimetic representation and, by extension, reproduces the dominant ways in which we identify and relate to the world around us. Marber himself underlines the use of language as an element within the parameters of dramatic illusion to accommodate and represent the way people speak as they do in real life: 'I felt the people in the play would speak as they do' (cited in Sierz 2001: 190). This realist dramatic drive underlying the dramaturgy of language in the play is neither unusual, nor unfamiliar or bygone. On the contrary, as discussed in Chapter 2, it is still a central aesthetic mode in Anglophone theatre practice. Hence, the dramatic frame and the medialect as a part and instrument of it provide an easily recognizable and accessible picture and language. Within its dramatic universe, the play acknowledges the changing mode of human communication and relations both with regard to emerging technologies and to rising individualism and social disintegration in the late capitalist, mediatized culture. It addresses our desire for and failure to connect in this society and relates this to the growing impact of media technologies on our relationships and perception. This thematic focus, reinforced with the realist dramaturgy of language, is prescient of the social disintegration, 'liquid love', monetized romance and instant gratification culture of the twenty-first century.

Despite acknowledging aspects of our mediatized lives in interesting ways, the play's unified, easily identifiable fictional cosmos can speak to the world we live in only to a limited extent. This is mainly because of a dissonance between how realist, dramatic form defines the world and the realities of our mediatized, globalized lives that are hard to accommodate within the sealed-off, fixed cosmos of drama. For instance, our socially disintegrating, individualistic existence in a mediatized, capitalist world is no longer straightforwardly manageable or representable through the idea of the world as a closed-off totality or through a reliable, coherent language for that matter. Language in the dramatic tradition is a stable and consistent meaning-making system through which we come to a clear understanding of the world we live in, who we are, our sociocultural environments and so on. However, this mode of language is limited in grasping at our fast-paced, info-bombarded, multi-perspectival minds or our politically and economically unstable living conditions in a media-driven post-truth culture. Language used in line with the realist, dramatic paradigm can certainly refer to such realities. However, it would struggle to create critical distance from within a fixed, impenetrable cosmos, which replicates the predominant social order and its set viewpoints and value systems – 'the distribution of the sensible' – (Rancière 2013: 89) as a meaningful, homogenous whole. By reproducing these prevailing structures, the play reiterates, reaffirms and retains rather than destabilizes and questions the normative outlook that we are immersed in and consciously or unconsciously consent to in our everyday lives. Hence, the *dramatic* mediatized dramaturgy of language addresses and acknowledges aspects of our mediatized culture to an extent, yet it does not engage with them in a subversive, critical manner to open up spaces for questioning the engrained politics of this culture.

Mediatized language 'Beyond' drama: *Attempts on Her Life* and *This Is How We Die*

Unlike *Closer*, Crimp's *Attempts* and Bailey's *THWD* do not directly represent or use mediatized language. Instead, these plays speak to our mediatized selves by subtly embodying and critically engaging with aspects of mediatized culture through their individual approaches to language. The dramaturgy of language here is in line with the overall subversive aesthetico-critical position of the plays. That is, while reflecting on the contemporary, both plays destabilize dramatic representation and propose a dramaturgical model *beyond* drama – still containing some characteristics of drama without being governed by its logic (Lehmann 2006: 44). As shall be discussed shortly, the subversive aesthetics at the heart of these plays correspond to the form and idea of no-longer-dramatic texts, which challenge the teleological dramatic form and the representation of the world as a unified, fixed reality through reliable, consistent language. By destabilizing the realist dramatic design, *Attempts* and *THWD* also refuse to reiterate the ways in which media images and language shape the perception of the world in line with the dominant power structures of the late capitalist order. Instead, through their dramaturgy of language, these plays open spaces for resistant, critical reflection regarding how mediatization has affected our subjectivity and perception; and the intricate relationship between language, ideology and mediatization.

To elaborate, Martin Crimp presents the model for *Attempts* as a series of 'scenarios' in his introductory note: 'Let each scenario in words – the dialogue – unfold against a distinct world – a design – which best exposes its irony'

(2005: 202). *Attempts* is a series of seventeen distinct scenarios – outlines of fragments of events, dialogues or narrative passages that are juxtaposed 'just like a montage in the pictorial arts' without having to generate a chronological order or a meaningful and complete story (Zimmerman 2002: 115). Each scenario displays a different perspective on 'Anne' (Anny, Anya, Annushka), the much talked-about, yet absent and unknowable, figure in the play. Anne can be anybody and anything – a daughter, a terrorist, a porn star or a car – and Anne can be anywhere, from European capitals to North African countries. The use of scenarios that are based more on contiguity than causality clearly contrasts with the coherently connected scenes of a dramatic play such as *Closer*. In this respect, Crimp's play epitomizes what Gerda Poschmann defines as the 'no longer dramatic theatre text' (cited in Jürs-Munby 2009: 46). Crimp does not entirely remove the dramatic form. He still uses naturalistic elements such as logical conversational progression and recognizable discourses and styles – adverts, art criticism and pop-songs – through dialogues, monologues or lyrical forms in English as well as Eastern European and African languages. Nevertheless, what is striking about these easily identifiable aspects of the script is that, despite their recognizability, it is unclear where the words emanate from since Crimp replaces character names with dashes, undermining the traditional unified relationship between speaker and character, and between speaker and language. Language, as I shall explore shortly, does not seem to have a definitive source, an individual speaker, but is communicated by what Gerda Poschmann names *Textträger* (cited in Barnett 2005: 140–1) – namely, text bearers that are responsible for delivering the text rather than representing it. When considered in line with the overall no-longer-dramatic aesthetics of the play, the mode of language in *Attempts* resists representation, as we know it. In doing so, I shall argue, Crimp's language speaks to certain aspects of mediatized culture such as the dissolution of the perception of reality as a unified and stable whole, the question of agency and subjectivity, and globalization.

Likewise, Bailey's *THWD* challenges dramatic logic and aesthetics without completely breaking away from certain aspects of dramatic form such as the dramatic arc. However, overall the play resists a realistic and easily identifiable narrative context, structured time and space, recognizable dialogue and language, psychologically motivated characterization and so on. Bailey's play is structured in a surrealistic, dream-like style that continually subverts the idea and representation of reality as a unified and coherent fictive cosmos even when the storytelling becomes more relatable. The playtext is formed of a stream-of-consciousness style torrent of language, bombarding us with information, images, sounds, and meaningful and meaningless words. As we encounter the flood of words and try to make sense of the collage of absurd images such as a cigarette-smoking mouse and a swastika-shaped man, we gather the underlying tale about young love between two misfits who are 'tucked up by static and watched over by satellites' (Bailey 2014: 37). Then, as we dig deeper into the fragmented flow of words and images touching on masculinity, violence, technology and climate change, we see the reflections of the contemporary world – one in which language is abused and is no longer reliable. Bailey's play deliberately makes meaning in order to deconstruct it over and over, leaving us with no single, unified narrative or a trusted language through which to make sense of the world. In this, the play asks: How do we perceive and relate to reality and each other in an age where the relationship between language and meaning has broken down?

While thinking about the dramaturgy of language in these plays in relation to mediatization, I have drawn on Arjun Appadurai's 'mediascape' and Gertrude Stein's 'landscape plays'. With 'mediascape', Appadurai refers to the world as presented by and received through media. Stein's 'landscape plays' are plays imagined as landscape paintings made of language, in which language does not tell a linearly ordered story, create an identifiable fictive universe or present chronological narrative with believable characters as it would in dramatic composition. Combining aspects of these notions, I consider *Attempts* and *THWD* as 'media-langscape' plays: while the no-longer-dramatic mode of language evokes aspects of landscape plays, the thematic and formal references to mediatized culture overlap with the mediascape. In what follows, I will argue that this form of language use destabilizes not only the representational role of language to portray the world as a recognizable, coherent whole but also, and relatedly, the idea of a reliable language through which we make sense of the world around us and on which our perceptions of reality are based. Challenging language, as we know it, the plays shake our familiar perceptual constructions of reality, the self and the other. In doing so, the no-longer-dramatic, mediatized mode of language also resists the replication of the language and discourse of dominant power structures – the orderly, *sensible* language (largely constructed and communicated through media today) – shaping the sayable and unsayable, and thus how we perceive and define the world we live in. Instead, they offer a different perspective on our contemporary mediascape, a possibility for rethinking our ontology, consciousness and relationships embedded deeply in a media-driven, late capitalist era from within, by turning its language against itself. The following sections discuss how language use in these plays addresses and offers critical engagements with mediatized world and consciousness, subjectivity and late capitalist ideology.

Dramaturgical engagements: Mediatized world and Consciousness

The form of language in both *Attempts* and *THWD* is closely connected to the overall composition of the plays. In his opening note, Crimp asks the play to be composed in a way that reflects 'the composition of the world beyond the theatre', which in the late 1990s referred to a world that was rapidly becoming more globally connected, pervasively mediatized and increasingly consumerist (2005: 2). *Attempts* opens with the scenario 'All Messages Deleted' in which individual phone messages from different people are left for Anne. The fragmented nature of this initial bite-sized scene that loads us with bits of information resonates with the entirety of the play – throughout which Anne is linguistically constructed and deconstructed. In the second scenario, 'Tragedy of Love and Ideology', we are informed that Anne is a political character in a script that the speakers of this scene are writing, whose values are destroyed by her lover's political masters in the name of business, rationalization and so-called individualism and choice (2005: 14). Then, Anne is introduced as a daughter to a 'Mum and Dad' in the sixth scenario through the use of an intimate narrative language:

- Some of the strange things she says to her Mum and Dad as a child: 'I feel like a screen.'
- 'I feel like a screen.'
- She's lying there, isn't she, with the tube in her poor thin arm, looking terribly pale, whiter in fact than / the *pillow*.
- 'Like a TV screen', she says, 'where everything from the front looks real and alive, but round the back there's just dust and a few wires.' (2005: 30–1)

More fragments of information follow: Anne is presented and talked about as a particle physicist in 'Particle Physics', as an artist in 'Untitled (100 Words)' and, most interestingly, as a car in 'The New Anny'. Throughout, we shift from one context, landscape and discourse to another. We are bombarded with bits of information about Anne and snapshots into her life that never lead to a clear portrayal of who Anne actually is or accommodate her as a three-dimensional character with a voice, a presence in the play.

The use of short, fragmented and non-linear language, in line with the overall plot design, evokes our mediatized lives in which we are constantly inundated with bite-sized information and, relatedly, our attention spans get shorter. Crimp's use of language resonates with various aspects of the mediatized age in the late twentieth century, preceding the current digital culture, and of the contemporary. It speaks to some of the ways in which our perception of the world alters in accordance with the changes in our sociocultural ecology. For example, it evokes the ways in which our perception is shaped and how it operates when we surf the internet and continually encounter new information, rapidly processing multiple bits of information, different texts, contexts and images.

We can see a similar connection in the layered structure of the second half of 'Pornó'. In the first part of this scenario, Anne is referred to as an underage porno actress; here the speaking characters identify her porn activity as a feminist act and her earnings as a part of her progressive lifestyle. The satirically delivered information about Anne gets more intriguing and her identity becomes harder to pin down as the scenario evolves. In the second half, the text is divided into two strands. In one strand, language is broken into small pieces defining an aspect of Anne, and finally portraying her as our saviour, who 'will save us from the anxiety of our century' (2005: 79). The simultaneously running second thread uses the particular discourse of airplane instructions and depicts Anne as a hostess who will save us from the metaphorical plane crash, namely, from our century. The short, multi-layered and disjointed language, which presents bite-sized information about Anne and the world, echoes aspects of how we perceive and experience the world around us today as we zap from one television channel to another or as we engage with and disengage from various content when browsing the internet. This is also in evidence in our everyday habit of media multitasking, that is, using two or more media at the same time (e.g. watching TV while responding to an email, and checking the weather or posting on our mobile phones). It is important to note here that besides speaking to our media-driven everyday lives and cognitive experience, the use of language in the above-mentioned scenes critically acknowledges other aspects of our mediatized being and sociopolitical landscape. I will discuss these topics in the following sections.

The overall plot composition in *THWD* is rather different from that of *Attempts*. Bailey's play, written in what resembles a stream-of-consciousness style, presents an unending spring of words and images, often obstructing a coherent meaning or truth and an easily recognizable context. The playtext is formed and performed as a *diegetic* monologue in which the first-person narrator Chris tells his story. It also resembles a dramatic monologue poem with references to the interior and exterior worlds of the speaker/character. In relation to this, there are no speech prefixes or character names, but a dream-like, free flow of language jumping from one image, context, space and time to another while presenting the surrealistic road trip story of a young boy and his equally eccentric girlfriend. The torrential language inundates us with abrupt fragments of information and imagery, and, as a result, creates a continual sense of uncertainty and dissociation from what the language aims to communicate, what the meaning is. The opening image of the world as a place where 'a generation of forever babies [are] bathing in radio waves and rocket fuel', and of the contemporary as 'a time of one gender, one race, one homogenous, milk, all-tolerant whole' under 'satellite and sedation' (Bailey 2014: 7) brusquely jumps to an advertisement-like context and language critiquing the consumerist and materialist culture: 'cut this coupon out and get off your next visit to our digital marketplace. You can buy fishguts and stolen radios without even getting off the victoria line. Isn't progress a wonderful thing?' (Bailey 2014: 8). Then, we meet the speaking character, who we link with Chris, as a school-aged boy that sets off on a road trip with his peculiar girlfriend. The jump cuts evoke the aesthetics of film, television and our hypertextual practices such as surfing the internet as well as our consciousness, shaped through media multitasking and info-heavy culture. Furthermore, the roller coaster-style narrative flooding us with a plethora of information, fragments of imagery and snippets of scenes is presented often in a free verse style with a musical rhythm, and always in lowercase:

> we cannot picture the future because we cannot imagine living through, surviving, the present. the past; we know what that looks like. it looks like sepia photographs and telephones you had to do this with (*mime rotary phone*). [. . .] we are still processing the past. still dealing with it. but the future? the future is a car crash or an orgasm. we live everyday with a sense of acceleration. everyday more and more technology, more and more communication, more and more information as the world shrinks to the size of an iphone . . . . (Bailey 2014: 56)

The style engenders a sense of urgency, a rapid flow of information, and asks its reader to read the text in a fast-paced manner while implicitly assuming they would be able to understand the speedy fragments of thoughts and images. Without doubt, Bailey's language evokes the experimental, political and personal style of the Beat poets. Nevertheless, the short, fragmented and rapid mode of language also speaks to *our* fast-paced lives, accelerated consumerism, info-loaded consciousness and shortened attention spans; to a world where websites would lose a third of their traffic if they took two seconds to load,[3] and major mobile phone companies promote the culture of acceleration that we unthinkingly accept: 'Anything worth doing is worth doing faster.'[4] Also, it resonates with our evolved ability to rapidly shift from one set of information to another, from one reality to another, and our desire to break reality into easily intelligible and consumable bits.

While speaking to the mediatized world and consciousness through the above-mentioned aspects of language use, both plays do something conspicuous – something different from how *Closer* addresses the mediascape. As mentioned earlier, they structure language and the overall dramaturgical design in a way that refuses the representation of outside reality as an easily identifiable, unified whole with a definitive, logical order. The use of fragmented, short and often fast-paced modes of language in *Attempts* and *THWD* reinforces the no-longer-dramatic architecture and subverts our search for a set, clear-cut understanding of the unpredictable times we live through. Such dramaturgical resistance to the representation of our increasingly more complex and less surveyable reality through a reliable language and in an easily recognizable frame at the same time suggests a critical resistance to the reproduction of prevalent beliefs and values. In so doing, the plays offer a space that is neither closed-off to the realities of our mediatized culture nor uncritical of its influence on modes of perception and representation, but one that exposes its machineries and socio-cognitive parameters. In a world where information and news are given in soundbites, books are condensed into fifteen-minute app-based stories,[5] and romance can be accessed through a swipe; everything is packaged and made more easily consumable than ever before. Disrupting the representational reproduction of this sociocultural landscape in an affirmative manner, the dramaturgy of language in *Attempts* and *THWD* represents a critical infringement from within and demonstrates the intricacies of mediascape and culture of acceleration we inhabit today while refusing to offer an effortlessly consumable experience.

Dramaturgical engagements: Mediatized subjectivity

While critically reflecting on the mediatized world through language, the plays also consider the position of the human subject in this environment and engage with the question of how our sense of subjectivity has evolved. I shall elaborate on this question and the notion of *mediatized subjectivity* in relation to the dramaturgy of character in Chapter 4. However, there is a close connection between the words spoken and who is speaking them. Moreover, language, shaped profoundly by technologies and mediatized culture, is at the heart of the changes in how we perceive and identify the world and, relatedly, how we define and grasp our position in it. Therefore, it is important to explore subjectivity in this chapter and briefly explain the concept of mediatized subjectivity here. For the scope of this section, suffice it to say that the notion refers to the ways in which our understanding and experience of selfhood and agency have been shaped by our use of and exposure to media technologies and the sociocultural and cognitive consequences they have created. Examples of this are in abundance – ranging from our changing sense of self in relation to the self-made images we communicate to the world through social media, to our so-called self-governing performance of prescribed discourses, images, identities that constantly inundate our everyday lives. Crimp's *Attempts* offers various instances exploring mediatized subjectivity through its intriguing approach to language, while the aesthetico-critical exploration of the same subject is less at the centre of *THWD*. Hence, my analysis will concentrate more on the former than the latter without bypassing the relevant aspects of Bailey's text.

As explained earlier, each scenario in *Attempts* displays a different facet of 'Anne'. The scenarios involve a variety of recognizable discourses and styles through short or long dialogues, monologues or lyrical forms. What is striking about the identifiable language is that, despite its recognizability, it is unclear where the words emanate from, or who speaks them, since Crimp replaces character names with dashes, undermining the traditional unified relationship between speaker and character. The anonymity of language, based on the disjunction of language from speaker, is not a new form in drama and theatre, but features in earlier works. In the early twentieth century during the rise of modernism, several playwrights wrote plays in which individual character names – a fundamental tenet of dramatic plays – were replaced by categorizations or allegorical names. For example, in August Strindberg's *A Dream Play* (1902) and Luigi Pirandello's *Six Characters in Search of an Author* (1921) the characters are mainly defined by their social or occupational roles rather than names – the Director, the Father, the Lawyer, the Poet. In the second half of the twentieth century, Beckett took this feature further in *Act Without Words II* (1950s), *Breath* (1969) and *Not I* (1972) by attributing letters instead of names to the speakers and by completely removing individual and symbolic names. Instead, he used anonymous language and voices. These experiments sowed the seeds of anonymity in late twentieth- and early twenty-first-century plays – exemplified in the works of Peter Handke, Heiner Müller, Elfriede Jelinek and Sarah Kane. The way Crimp divorces the language from the speaker puts a noticeable emphasis on language as an autonomous mechanism, separated from the *individual* as its source, through creating a tension between the recognizability of the language and the non-identity of its speaker. The particular mode of language use here invites one to ask: If language is not the creation of an individual, then who is the originator and regulator of language?; what is the position of the speaking subject in relation to language and the structures operating it, and what does this form say about contemporary subject's agency today?

Crimp's unattributed text deploys a mélange of recognizable discourses and styles taken from a great many sources, some of which clearly reference to media forms and their capitalist logic. In 'The New Anny', introduced earlier, Anny the brand-new, sleek, fast car (Crimp 2005: 234) is presented through the familiar advertising discourse that we are accustomed to seeing on television or the internet. The commercial style of the scenario implies the clichés, the ideological agenda behind adverts, promoting consumerism and a world conforming to capitalism. It also turns the feminine into a product. What is interesting here is the unexpected and direct revelation of the ideological underpinnings that adverts normally cover up by presenting capitalist aspirations of luxury, success and security: 'In the ideal world of Anny there are no places for the degenerate races [. . .] the mentally deficient [. . .] the physically imperfect' and no room for 'gypsies, Arabs, Jews, Turks, Kurds, Blacks or any of that human scum' (Crimp 2005: 237). This exposes the messages hidden behind advertising industry and media discourse, and the racist and separatist undertones of some media products that reflect and sustain the dominant ideology. However, Crimp's overtly identifiable text clashes with the lack of unified characters or attributed speakers of the text. The speakers, without names, age or psychological depth, are separated from the text. Here, language appears as an autonomous medium with multiple origins and discourses rather than with a fixed individual source. Instead of fully developed characters with agency over language, the anonymous speakers seem to act as *Textträger* – text bearers that are responsible for delivering the text rather than representing it or claiming ownership and control over the words they convey.

Some other scenarios in *Attempts* offer multiple clichés from different sources in various configurations, yet the recognizable language in each continually poses the same question concerning the origin of the words given the absence of psychologically developed, knowable characters. In the scenario 'Pornó', Crimp presents the audience with a selection of familiar discourses and styles different from the focus on a single, media-specific discourse and pattern in 'The New Anny'. Unlike the unidentified, multiple speakers of 'The New Anny', in 'Pornó' Crimp identifies the principal speaker as '*a very young woman*' (Crimp 2005: 269). However, despite this, the speaker still functions as a text-bearer rather than an individual character as demanded by the text – she has no name, and the familiar patriarchal discourse of the porn industry that she delivers contradicts what would seem to be her interests. This incongruity between the speaker and the text raises the question of how female identity, voice and language are constituted increasingly in accordance with the desires of the dominantly patriarchal discourses of the media, represented here by the porn industry. This is not to suggest that all media forms, platforms and products adopt a patriarchal view, or that female identity is the only constructed one. Rather, the scene highlights the role of media in disseminating role models and constituting identities.

The scenario, however, does not continue as one would expect and seems to shift location and speaker, unlike, for example, 'The New Anny'. Later, the language divides into two strands, spoken simultaneously: the language of a heroic and almost poetic narrative, and the recorded discourse of aircraft passenger information:

- Anne will save us from the anxiety of our century . . .	- During the flight . . .
- [translation]*	- [translation]
- . . . and usher in an age in which the spiritual and the material . . .	- . . . we will be coming round with a list of duty-free goods.
- [translation]	- [translation] (Crimp 2005: 277)

These linguistic styles are familiar, yet their anonymity and irrelevant juxtaposition create an epistemologically unstable context. Additionally, in the scenarios 'The Camera Loves You' and 'The Girl Next Door', Crimp uses a lyrical verse form similar to chorus pieces. Here, the text is completely unidentified with no speaker or speech prefix. The song in 'The Camera Loves You', for instance, is about media-constructed identities, celebrity culture and the aspiration to become 'a megastar' (Crimp 2005: 223–4). The discourse echoes the language of a pop-song or of television (The camera *loves* you (Crimp 2005: 223–4)), particularly in relation to reality TV programmes such as *Big Brother*, which promotes celebrity culture and encourages housemates to market themselves as commodities.

Crimp presents a noticeable text, but again withholds the identity of the speaker. Divorcing the text from the speaker here, and in the previous examples, *Attempts* suggests that the well-known language that we all speak does not authentically or entirely originate from individual speakers. Instead, language appears to be given to the text bearers through which they understand the world. This form places language at the centre as an independent component of the playtext or the protagonist,[6] without an individual speaker or a particular point of reference and definitive interpretation, putting the individuality of the speaking subject and her autonomous agency into question. Even in scenes such as 'Untitled (100 Words)' and 'STRANGELY!' where they are presented as individual art critics and border guards, the text bearers are not directly identifiable, three-dimensional, psychologically motivated characters with clear motives or developed personal history and characteristics. Crimp intentionally restricts the speakers' individuality by withholding information about them and undermining their autonomy of language and thought. The dissolution of the idea of self-knowing, self-governing individual at the heart of the play points at our changing sense of agency and subjectivity in the face of mediatized culture. Crimp's incorporation of media discourses and aesthetics into the language of the play along with the purposeful tension between recognizability and non-identity of language speaks to how media shapes our perception and our subjectivity, namely, how our sense of the self and position in society are subjected to social structures and discourses larger than us. It highlights the increasing influence of media as ideological tools of global capitalism on human consciousness, identity and language.

As the analysis of the scenarios indicates, instead of a single recognizable discourse and style, Crimp blends different modes from a range of sources, offering a linguistic landscape, a networking of different voices and discourses. Hans-Thies Lehmann identifies this as a 'textscape' (Lehmann 2006: 148) – a theatre of voices that discards 'an originary source/agency of discourse' (Crimp 2005: 32) and multiplies 'sending agencies/sources on stage that lead to new modes of perception' (Crimp 2005: 32). Elfriede Jelinek takes a similar view through her notion of 'language surfaces' (*Sprachflächen*) which are, as Karen Jürs-Munby explains, 'montages of playfully and deconstructively manipulated quotes from a wide variety of different spheres and genres [. . .] intermixed with what reads like the author's own "voice"' (Jürs-Munby 2009: 46). Crimp's language surfaces or textscapes, like those of Jelinek, are striking not only because they accommodate multiple voices and discourses but also because they are radically deindividuated. The de-personalized and pluralistic mode of language – a form that goes against and beyond the traditional aesthetics in dramatic theatre – evokes the anonymity and multiplicity that we experience in mediatized culture. Crimp's media-langscape play critically addresses the increasing dissolution of a sovereign voice and identity. It speaks to the contemporary subject's experience of becoming, not entirely but increasingly, the products of the consumption-driven, mediatized culture.

A similar connection between textscape and mediascape is hinted by Bailey's *THWD*. The gush of words within the first-person narrative style seems to derive from, and is written and spoken by the playwright Chris himself or a fictional representation of 'Chris'. Despite the clear presentation of the first-person narrator as the words' source, the language seems to stand on its own, independently from its speaker. Language is in fact the central character in *THWD*. To begin with, the text does not provide a character name or a speech prefix to identify the sole speaker or, perhaps, multiple originators of the words. This is easily unnoticed as, in monologue form as opposed to dialogue, the speaker can easily be implied within the text and not presented overtly through a prefix. The torrential load and rapid frequency of words generate the feeling that no matter how hard speaker Chris is trying to maintain agency over the words, the language takes over the speaker and it speaks itself. The Sisyphean struggle against the loss of control over language and meaning is emphasized at the end of the playtext: 'we pronounce this language dead' (Bailey 2014: 62). The death of language and meaning implies our limited agency over meaning, over how we see, identify, relate to and construct the world and reality around us. This inevitably poses the question: Who has agency and control over language, meaning, construction of reality and subjectivity if not us? Bailey's play does not answer this question clearly. Instead, it implies a connection between our crumbling experience of autonomy and the media-saturated, fast-paced culture we live in through the use of found and recognizable discourses, for instance, about political correctness, and through direct references to the self as socio-linguistic, ideological constructs rather than results of our own free choice. Moreover, the words carry traces of various cultural figures and works, ranging from Samuel Beckett's *Not I*, Allan Ginsberg's poetry and David Lynch's films, to *Pulp Fiction* and GodSpeed You! Black Emperor,[7] emphasizing the speaker's eclectic voice and language as opposed to its individuality or authenticity. While these carefully chosen texts make critically engaging references to the unstable, precarious world we live in, they also pose questions about our deep-seated belief in our autonomy, challenging the pillars of capitalist individualism and pointing towards the constructedness of subjectivity particularly in a media-saturated, image-soaked, late capitalist culture.

The disconnection between language and the individual as the source of words and meaning in *Attempts* and *THWD* adds to the plays' overall no-longer-dramatic form. It refuses to represent the contemporary human, whose sense of selfhood, agency and perception is profoundly shaped by prevalent technologies and media culture, as an autonomous, stable, and easily knowable character. Without doubt, this form destabilizes not only the traditional notion of character as we know it but also our understanding of our subjectivity that is extensively fashioned by the capitalist discourse on individual autonomy and free choice – an illusionary vision of the self often reinforced and circulated via numerous media. The plays offer an aesthetic and therefore critical resistance to this view and open a vista for dissident reflection on our mediatized being and subjectivity.

Dramaturgical engagements: Mediatization and late capitalism

In Chapter 1, I explained the direct connection between mediatization and late capitalism, how media is an ideological technology as well as how the culture media technologies have generated operates in line with the dominant ideology, namely, neoliberal capitalism. Bearing this in mind, it is important to stress the close link between language and ideology. This relationship between language and ideology is critically explored through the dramaturgy of language in *Attempts* and *THWD*.

The language surfaces in *Attempts* contain ideologically loaded advertising and news media discourses that we are familiar with from our everyday exposure to news and commercials on television, radio, online media platforms and so on. The use of these familiar, ready-made styles and texts stresses how our language and therefore perception is shaped in line with capitalism. The commercial language of 'The New Anny', along with the use of the trademark symbol in 'The Threat of International Terrorism™', resonates with the consumerist undercurrents of almost all media today, the seeds of which were planted long before the initial days of the digital age in the late 1990s. Notions such as terrorism and God are presented as commodities similar to products such as Barbie™, Minnie Mouse™ and *Vogue*™, suggesting the shaping power of consumer capitalism over our social, political phenomena and our value systems. The objectification of the human (Anne being a car, a porn star, etc.) and commodification of everyday social reality acknowledge and draw attention to the consumerist culture we live in. It is easy to see the correlations between the aesthetic choices in *Attempts*' scenarios and adverts such as Protein World's 'Are you beach body ready?' which objectify women's bodies and promote a sleek, one-dimensional body image for profit. The presentation of races and ethnicities such as Jews, Arabs and gypsies as 'degenerate races' (Crimp 2005: 39) or 'human scums' (Crimp 2005: 39) in the advertising language of 'The New Anny' patently stresses the bigotry underlying capitalism, which is not a new phenomenon but is more widely circulated due to pervasive technologies. Fast-forward to the late 2010s, Crimp's critical use of language resonates with numerous instances, ranging from David Cameron's description of refugees as a 'swarm of people' (2015: BBC News Online) and French far right politician Jean-Marie Le Pen's comparison of asylum seekers to the barbarian invaders (2015: rt.com), to the British tabloid *The Sun*'s publication of Katie Hopkins's piece calling migrants 'cockroaches' (Hopkins 2015: *The Sun*) and, surely, to Donald Trump's numerous racist Twitter posts. Although written before the Twitter age, *Attempts* evidently picked up on what was to come in a media-saturated society that had been a product of capitalist power structures for a long time. In so doing, *Attempts* exposes the relationship between language and late capitalism, and relatedly, mediatized culture.

Globalization is another aspect that *Attempts* reflects on through its use of language. In 'The New Anny' and 'Pornó', Crimp incorporates foreign languages. These languages are presented through the marker –

'[translation]' – after every line where the foreign language should be placed in performance. Crimp's dramaturgical technique, particularly when the direction of the translation (in relation to English) and the choice of language are considered, reflects critically on globally mediatized capitalism. Before analysing this aspect, it is necessary to grasp the connections between globalization and mediatization as metaprocesses and by-products of late capitalism, and the position of English as the lingua franca of the globally networked village that we live in. Globalization is variously defined but fundamentally relates to the concept of (inter-)connectedness and thus mediatization. One definition identifies globalization as a process through which the world has become a smaller and more closely connected place due to rapid advancements in transportation, information and communication technologies.[8] In this shrinking world, our understanding of geography, time and physical distance has changed. Also, different cultures interact with each other and have become accessible to larger numbers of people.[9]

Besides environmental and cultural interconnectedness, globalization refers to an economic, political and ideological phenomenon, the extension of capitalism, under neoliberal policies, on a global scale, fostering consumerism and cultural standardization.[10] As ideological apparatuses, media performs many functions for global capitalism, monopolized for the most part, by Anglo-American, European and Japanese corporations. Despite the multinational status of corporations, they take their lead from Anglo-American management systems hence foster English as the dominant, common language across borders for international business. English has become the language of the globalized world – 'the first global lingua franca' (Crystal 2001: 1). The dominance of English, as Stig Hjarvard points out, is a centuries-long trend following British imperial colonization (2004: 77). However, in today's world, this dominance is mainly due to American economic power. The use of English in media, communication and information technologies has rapidly disseminated the consumerist discourse of capitalism to the world – borders and cultures notwithstanding. English is the language of computer games, the internet, blockbuster films, and international political, legal and commercial documents. Media technologies and platforms do not merely render English the global lingua franca, but also contribute to the Anglicization of global culture and dissemination of the consumerist lifestyle and capitalist vision. English, spoken with various dialects and by numerous non-native speakers, produces a monoglossic environment. This does not mean the end of cultural and linguistic diversity; monoglossia does not exclude other languages, but implies a hierarchical tendency over polyglossia. The globally connected world is not an English-speaking world, but a polyglossic world where different cultures and local languages interact and are not bound to disappear in the shadow of English, but to be dominated by it.

In 'The New Anny', lines are initially uttered in an African or Eastern European language, and then translated into English. The direction of translation, intentionally requiring every phrase to be uttered finally in English, indicates its dominant position in relation to the 'other', initial language. That is, the line is only 'complete' once it has been successfully rendered in English. The use of English as the dominant language alongside the capitalist commercial discourse can be read as a reference to English as global lingua franca and the language of global capitalism. The translation underlines how media conglomerates, operating globally, render English as the common language while also subtly instilling capitalist and consumerist ideas. The scenario critically highlights English not only in a common linguistic context, enabling information transmission across the world or intercultural communication; it is also an ideological, linguistic mechanism homogenizing socio-economic and cultural differences and shaping human perception in line with consumerism.

The thematic content and the commercial context of the scenario reinforces the reference to the globally mediatized, capitalist world that the act of translation presents. The advert implies that Anny is a mass-produced global product: 'The *Anny* crosses the Brooklyn Bridge [. . .] the Sahara [. . .] the vineyards of Bordeaux [. . .] dawn through North African villages' (Crimp 2005: 237). This indicates an imperialist undertone – the advert is not just selling the Anny locally but to the world, underlining the global mobility of the Anny as a commodity. This does not mean that the Anny is available to everyone. The advert hints that the car is only for the elite, offering an uncontaminated world and 'affirm[ing] what is repressed by the slick dreams of beauty, luxury and security designed to make the car attractive to buyers' (Zimmermann 2002: 121). This scenario also draws attention to mediatization as a part of globalized neoliberal agenda that systematically penetrates into and dominates social and individual lives through mass communication, information and other media forms. Crimp's specific choice of languages from developing areas such as Africa and Eastern Europe rather than France, Germany and Japan underlines the hierarchical workings of global capitalism: the economically powerful countries operate the system increasingly effectively thanks to universally prevalent technologies, and the rest adapt to the structures and languages of the ruling mechanism.

In 'Pornó', the translation changes direction and the choice of languages is slightly different: the words of the principal speaker, a very young woman, '*are translated dispassionately into an African, South American or Eastern European language*' (Crimp 2005: 269; emphasis in original). Considering the direction of translation in this scenario compared to 'The New Anny', it could seem that the positioning of a third-world language as the ultimate language implies a subordinate status for English. However, the intentional change in the direction of translation seems to be a strategy to underpin English's authority. The order of translation locates English as the leading common language that the media use to connect different cultures and to transmit information. English is the media's mother tongue through which people experience the world. Other languages appear as the impartial or *dispassionate* providers of information transferred from English. The suggestion that information is disseminated objectively – from the language of global capitalism to that of local cultures – works as a critical tool. The dispassionate tone creates the image of impartial information flow; however, language is the language of the culture industry, shaping worldviews, rather than a transparent tool for communication and information transmission. This emphasizes the fundamental relationship between power and language. Additionally, it underlines that the global lingua franca does not generate an exclusively monoglossic world; on the contrary, it acknowledges the existence of other languages – a polyglossic world where English acts as the common language. The use of foreign languages in *Attempts* hints at the role of media technologies and on the unaccomplished promise of the global village, suggested by Marshall McLuhan in the 1960s, with the hope of a democratic and egalitarian globalization of media. 'The dream of a global village, in which equals share information and culture does not describe the reality of today's global media' (Croteau and Hoynes 2003: 343). Instead, as the critical dramaturgy of language in *Attempts* implies, Western nations and corporations, more often than not, control media and its global use.

Multi-lingual dramaturgy here exposes two significant aspects of globalization: multiculturalism and global capitalism or cultural hegemony. On the one hand, the use of foreign languages refers to the polyglossic sociocultural landscape of the globally connected world. On the other, the directions of the translations, which differ in both scenarios, ironically highlight English as the 'master language'. With this formal strategy, in addition to the use of media-related discourses, Crimp emphasizes the consumerist ideology underlying the use of English as the language of commerce, politics, information, media technologies and platforms. The critical reference to the globalized world is neither merely formal nor linguistic. The thematic concerns of the scenarios with their capitalist and discriminatory advertising discourse, and the patriarchal and consumerist discourse of the pornography industry, suggest a critique of global capitalism.

Language and its ideological basis and function are at the heart of *THWD*, highlighted through overt references to language as a weapon, constructing and regulating the reality of our lives under satellites and media-induced sedation. In the surrealistic world of the play, which eerily speaks to the contemporary world, language is a tool in the hands of the powerful, a controlling force, shaping and policing entire populations and collective consciousness. The play openly depicts and criticizes this with reference to the notion of political correctness:

> political correctness has gone mad. gone mad. and i ask for a definition of mad and i am lead to understand that this cliché itself, with its casual use of the word mad, proves there is yet more linguistic whitewashing to be done if the perceived goal is to be the achieved goal. and i ask you, who is the straightjacket built for? have you heard our fresh cliche uttered by anyone of colour or minority persuasion? or is it the kneejerk chant of the great white alone? i have never met a black man who did not call himself a nigger, a rentboy who was not proud to be a whore. these are letters, words, sounds made with the mouth, they are meaningless, they are weapons of our own construction of a mutual agreement based on idiocy. (Bailey 2014: 8)

Political correctness is clearly not a coincidental notion as Chris starkly unpacks it here. He uses it to address language and meaning as a construct, camouflaging the obscenity of reality through pretty expressions and labels, and allowing the great white to rule. As the play moves on, Chris intensifies the critical focus on language and how we use it to police society, regulate thought and identity. After being accused of being misogynist by his girlfriend, he asks: 'why put boundaries around what we think?' (Bailey 2014: 23). Then, upon her suggestion, he ventures into deconstructing and destabilizing the overarching concepts – the 'isms' – creating another linguistic concept:

> jissum.
> jissum.
> jissum.
> jissum.
> ya know when?
> jissum.
> ya say a word so many times that it loses
> jissum.
> its meaning – becomes just sound – (Bailey 2014: 27)

Ironically, the more he tries to make meaning through language, the more unreliable the words become. The broken, flawed, inconsistent and often hasty form of language here and throughout the play fail to mean, to make logical and complete sense of the world, and to present an identifiable representation of reality as a unified, familiar whole. He responds to his girlfriend's frustrated comment – 'chris. go fuck yourself' (Bailey 2014: 31) – by *literally* fucking himself, a response that emphasizes the disintegration of language in the face of a rapidly and radically changing world. As Chris stresses earlier, words have been emptied of meaning, and no longer relate to reality as we expect. Instead, language digresses from meaning and conceals reality behind labels, concepts or manufactured and misleading 'truths'.

The divorce between language and meaning, between language and reality, which positions language as a mechanism that cannot be trusted anymore, speaks to the *post-truth* age we now live in – a by-product of the digital age where raw emotion, opinion and ideology are prioritized over scientific knowledge and evidence. In the post-truth age, politicians, media conglomerates and international corporations use social media and news platforms such as Facebook and Twitter to propagate fake news and dishonest fabrications as alternative facts. Relatedly, the death of language, dramatically pronounced in *THWD*, does not necessarily refer to a literal end of language as a communication tool. Instead, it critiques the misuse of language to hide or distort reality and truth, the fact that language as a meaning-making mechanism, through which we make sense of the world, has evaporated:

under satellite and sedation
[...]
these words, they leave my lips and explore like bricks like bricks like
   bricks,
mean nothing, mean air, mean i had an impulse,
i had nature, i had the evolutionary toolkit to be
able to form this sentence and the humility to
know that it means nothing.
[...]
and with our savage tongues we reclaim the
future
and pronounce this language dead. (Bailey 2014: 53–5)

Nevertheless, despite using language to deconstruct itself and pronouncing the end of language, the play does not do anything that manifests its death. If anything, it is the opposite. While critiquing the dysfunctionality and thus the end of language as we know it, *THWD* seeks ways to make sense of the contemporary world through an alternative language. In response, the play actually revives and foregrounds language by subverting the ingrained and familiar connection between language and meaning. It brings language under critical attention, allowing us to view our ontology in a mediatized, capitalist system. In this way, *THWD* produces a deeply eloquent mode of language that digresses, undermines and dissents from the deep-seated, normative language shaped and circulated globally by media platforms in line with late capitalist ideological structures. Language is not dead. It is dismantled and transformed to grasp and relate to the uncertain, less representable and surveyable times we live in.

Considering the inventive and distinct forms of mediatized language in *Closer*, *Attempts* and *THWD*, some of which are deliberate and obvious while others are implicit, one cannot but wonder how these texts are construed in performance. While considering the transformation from playtext to performance, one question stands out: Do the productions in question reiterate or challenge the mode of mediatized dramaturgy and what meanings do the related performance choices generate?

Mediatized dramaturgy of language: From text to stage

Closer: Computers and online culture as representational décor

The chat-room scene in *Closer*, where we see one of the first examples of internet context (i.e. chat-room cybersex) and medialect use in theatre, provides directors with clear instructions. In the text, Marber asks two actors to sit in front of two different computers and communicate with each other online by typing their messages, which simultaneously appear on a large screen (1999: 23). *Closer* premiered at the Royal National Theatre in London in 1997 and was directed by Marber himself; hence, doubtlessly, the production closely followed the textual setup. The two actors sitting behind their computers in the same physical space remained silent throughout their entire online exchange followed by the audience on the screen.

Nevertheless, what seemed to be a live, online interaction was a pre-recorded construct that Marber and assistant stage manager Emma B. Lloyd engineered through the use of a particular computer containing the whole script: 'though it looks real, the actors are only pretending to type. [. . .] I watch them carefully and when they touch the first key for a sentence I activate a quick key which makes the whole thing appear on the big screen' (cited in Gardner 1998). Throughout, including the carefully calculated chat-room scene, Marber adhered to the well-made dramatic structure of the play.

Figure 2 *Closer*. Photo credit: NT Archive/Hugo Glendinning.

He constructed the theatrical representation through coherent, linear plot composition, structured time and space, and identifiable characterization and language. Such design evidently aimed to avoid the irruption of the real into the fictional universe of the drama. The use of computers with pre-set text as opposed to the use of instant, live chat, which carried with it the risk of the real breaking in, generated a controlled, fixed representation – a closed-off world. The chat-room scene, which indexes the growing internet use and online behaviours such as 'catfishing' (impersonating someone else online) and medialect, was a part of the dramatic vision: portraying human relationships in the late 1990s through a unified and manageable fictive cosmos.

Given the fact that *Closer* was produced in the early days of pervasive digital culture and communication, the production introduced a novel experience and language onto the stage, acknowledging the complexities of human connection and bonds changing in an increasingly media-driven, capitalist order. However, the use of a realist dramatic frame, which depicts this complex reality as a unified, sealed-off and easily surveyable experience, poses a problem. As discussed in Chapter 2, the mediatized world is no longer easily representable through the frame of traditional dramatic theatre. The dramatic theatre not only portrays a reality that no longer completely and plausibly corresponds to the ways in which we perceive the world and form relationships but also frames it through the recognizable filter of dramatic representation – flattening complexities and positioning us in a comfortable state from which we easily consume the theatre work as we consume relationships, images and information in a late capitalist, mediatized culture. Hence, despite the explicit use of mediatized language as a thematic and its critique of the changes in human relationships, *Closer* offers a vision of a world that is closed to critical understanding and interrogation of the intricacies of our existence beyond the prescribed social, ideological framework. Nevertheless, this does not suggest the exclusion of dramatic theatre from the cultural scene, but an invitation to critically engage with its workings and the concurrent shifts and their aesthetico-critical value in contemporary theatre culture. Relatedly, dramatic theatre and the emergence and abundance of playtexts and productions continue to attempt to portray mediatized culture through representational aesthetics, namely, through dramatic mediatized dramaturgy. These plays, such as Enda Walsh's *Chatroom* (2007), Lucy Prebble's *The Sugar Syndrome* (2003), Sarah Ruhl's *Dead Man's Cell Phone* (2007) and *The Nether* (2013), and often their productions, still offer a view on the contemporary and present a slice of our media-saturated lives. However, dramatic theatre as a form keeps this view within the boundaries of the conditions, discourses and actions of the mediatized age rather than reconsidering form to generate critical distance from the everyday socio-cognitive environment in order to rethink it.

Attempts: Critical aesthetics of a media-saturated stage

A few months before *Closer* brought the internet as a setting and social reality on to the National Theatre stage, Crimp's *Attempts* opened at the Royal Court Theatre Upstairs (March 1997, dir. Tim Albery) and offered a technologically and aesthetically more intricate performance. Drawing on Crimp's formal and thematic references to mediatized society, Albery's production deployed 'video screens, stage screens and photographic montage sequences [that] flicker and change with the efficiency of robots' (de Jongh 2007: 311). In addition to media technologies populating the stage, eight performers from different ethnic and gender backgrounds delivered the lines with clarity and great adherence to the words on the page (Sierz 2006: 195).

At the heart of the performance, among technologies and performers' bodies, lay language which, through Albery's use of musical form, underpinned the various tonalities, perspectives and discourses offered in Crimp's text, as Albery explains: 'if, for example, you had one scene which was an aria, it

Figure 3 *Attempts on Her Life*. Tim Albery production; photo credit: Donald Cooper.

would be followed by an ensemble, then a duet, and then a quartet' (cited in Sierz 2006: 196). In other words, the audience encountered an orchestration of text fragments, ranging from 'jingling lists, overlapping dialogues, [to] quasi-Eastern European translations and answer-machine soundbites' (Foss 1997: 313). By treating the scenarios as musical pieces, Albery underlined the multiplicity and non-linearity of the voices. He also presented the audience with 'repetitiousness and verbal recyclings of most scenes' (Macaulay 1997: 312) as well as 'multiple perspectives in sliced-up prose' (Billington 1997: 312) onto the constantly shifting figure of Anne. Similar to Crimp's text, Albery's production refused a cohesive fable with structured time and space, representational action and figurative characterization. The production was overall an 'artfully cryptic, deliberately inconclusive and depersonalized' experience linked to the implied backdrop of global media hegemony and media-saturated individual lives (Foss 1997: 313).

This form of staging eschewed a naturalistic and easily identifiable theatrical experience. It refused to create a direct representational relationship between the stage and outside reality, and presented a mosaic, an unsolvable puzzle, of recognizable voices and images via depersonalized performers. Through the dramaturgical scepticism towards dramatic representation, the production engendered epistemological uncertainty on the part of audience, encouraging them to question the taken-for-granted connection between individual autonomy and particularity of language, and the ways in which our subjectivity, consciousness and perception of reality are constructed. Albery's *Attempts* offered an experience beyond representation as we know it by creating a puzzle through which it presented images, objects and instances for critical reflection. Hence, by focusing on the playtext's diverse and fragmented styles and discourses and presenting it through a hi-tech design, this production communicated some of the questions that Crimp, explicitly or implicitly, raises. The production, as Crimp requested at the opening of *Attempts*, 'reflect[ed] the composition of the world beyond the theatre' (2005: 202) – that is, inundated with technologies, images, and information, and saturated with simulacra. It is a world, as Crimp defines through Jean Baudrillard's words prior to the stage directions, in which '[n]o one will have directly experienced the actual cause of such happenings, but everyone will have received an image of them' (Baudrillard 1993: 80). Hence, a theatre performance that goes beyond the theatrical representation of the outside reality, which is immersed with and shaped by simulations of the real, is a performance that relates to the composition of the world, namely, to our mediatized lives and consciousness.

A decade later, in 2007, Katie Mitchell directed *Attempts* at the National Theatre. The production's narrative frame and setting were designed as a live TV broadcast – a decision made during the devising process as a strategic response to the complex form of Crimp's play. The live TV show setting provided the makers and performers with a detailed, tangible context through which to locate and realize the action, order and characterization of the play. In relation to this, the stage was covered in microphones and cameras, more in number than the actors, and the action was simultaneously projected live on the screens above the stage using close-ups, and grainy recordings as well as shiny television commercial aesthetics (Jones 2007: 309). Mitchell's production also accommodated a collage of TV spoofs, newsreader announcements, songs and dialogue, drawn on Crimp's text and the social, historical, cultural material that the performers introduced to the play as a part of its 1997 setting. Instead of updating the play to a 2007 context, Mitchell kept the production loyal to the period it was written in chiefly because, according to Mitchell, the references to terrorism meant differently after 9/11, and 1997 marked the New Labour period and the change in the political landscape (Kerbel 5). These rendered the past setting a better fit for the production than the contemporary moment. Accordingly, most of the technologies used on stage were historically specific and accurate rather than contemporary.

Along with the live TV show setup, Mitchell and the actors allocated characters to Crimp's unidentified lines so that 'they could have a secure understanding of the situation their character found themselves in and could respond accordingly' (Kerbel 4). Neither the setting nor the characterization was made explicit to the audience. These were mainly strategies for devising the piece, yet surely affected the outcome. Unlike Albery's version, Mitchell's

Figure 4 *Attempts on Her Life*. Katie Mitchell production; photo credit: Donald Cooper.

production had vaguely personalized characters rather than non-specified speakers. This still did not provide the audience with psychologically motivated, fully developed characters. Nevertheless, it generated a clearer implication of who these speakers might be and, relatedly, individualized the language. As a result, the tension in Crimp's text between familiar language and non-specified speakers was flattened and presented in a more coherently defined frame. Leaning towards naturalistic interpretation, Mitchell also omitted the first scenario 'All Messaged Deleted' that sets an uncertain tone, leading one to wonder who Anne might be. Mitchell wanted to avoid the audience considering Anne as an existing character and searching for her throughout the performance. In addition, she removed the spaces between the scenarios so that the play became a unified and continuous scene rather than separate individual pieces.

Such alterations adapted *Attempts* to the aesthetics and logic of dramatic theatre and shaped it into a recognizable representation of the world as a unified, coherent totality. While providing the audience with a more easily intelligible and consumable frame, the stage interpretation of the text, which originally resisted dramatic representation, bypassed the meanings the unidentified, non-linear, fragmented, language and overall structure offered. This is not to suggest that the production did not address the social landscape of the late 1990s; it certainly reflected aspects of mediatized culture and lives through technologically rich staging and explicit references to 'a society in which life is lived through a lens and every action is filtered by the media' (Jones 2007: 309). However, the engagement with the outside reality beyond theatre was more in tune with the mediatized framework we are embedded within. The dramatic model reiterated the discourses, social and cognitive circumstances that Crimp's text thematically and formally critiqued and exposed. Hence, despite its technologically sophisticated design, the production's suggestive language, characterization and setting located uncertainties in an identifiable frame, leading the audience to more easily intelligible meanings than the text originally pointed at.

Both productions responded to Crimp's suggestion for the use of foreign language in interesting ways. In the first production, Albery registered Crimp's suggested use of foreign languages. Crimp's text suggested that the English text and its translation be delivered by several speakers, free from the limitations of ethnic, linguistic or sexual background. Such textual flexibility opened the way for numerous interpretations that would shape the critical impact of the work. In his interpretation of *Attempts*, Tim Albery used Portuguese and Serbian[11] and integrated different English accents into the performance (Sierz 2001: 196). The use of Portuguese instead of an African or Eastern European language might have softened the critical potential and impact of the text. This is mainly because both African and Eastern European languages would underline the concern with globalization as a system of cultural and political hegemony, something that is not so readily evident in the use of Portuguese, the language of a Western country that used to be a colonial power, largely in Africa. On the other hand, Katie Mitchell's production staged the seventh scenario in Russian, before translating it into English. The scene was set in a location suggestive of a news studio: the Russian speaker delivered the lines live on stage while being simultaneously projected onto a screen. Her words were simultaneously translated into English. The choice of Russian could be for practical reasons, but it also evokes the global impact of capitalism contrasting with the communist history of Russia. It accommodates the experience of globalized capitalism and emphasizes its worldwide influence. By creating the television context on stage and employing a language other than English, Mitchell underpinned the play's concern with the connection between media and the global village.

This Is How We Die: Invisible mediatization on stage

Premiered at Norfolk and Norwich Festival (2014), Christopher Brett Bailey's *THWD* represents a provocative aspect of mediatized theatre. As opposed to Albery's and Mitchell's media-saturated productions, *THWD* opted for a technologically bare setting. On stage was a desk with a chair, where Bailey sat, and a lamp and a glass of water on the desk along with the text he read from throughout the performance.

The minimalist design and absence of hi-tech multimedia on stage, however, did not render the performance less connected to mediatized culture or less pertinent to it than the productions whose stages were intensively media-dominated. Technologically minimalist stages, as I highlighted in earlier chapters, might relate to the socio-cognitive aspects of mediatized culture through aesthetics and discourses that resonate with this environment and that can be grasped by a consciousness shaped by media and this very same environment. There is a fundamental, yet often unnoticed relationship between invisible mediatization on stage and our mediatized everyday lives in which media is so embedded that we do not easily recognize or critically engage with its influences or consequences. However, while the mediatization of society and individual lives often occurs due to the prevalence of media, invisible mediatization in theatre questions the wider social picture in the absence of technologies. In performances such as *THWD*, the performance, which often covertly accommodates aspects of mediatized culture and consciousness without having to use technologies,

Figure 5 *This Is How We Die*. Photo credit: Claire Haigh.

opens up critical thinking about the ways in which our society, ontology and perception are shifting in a media-driven cultural and political climate.

On an empty stage, Bailey sat at a small desk and inundated the audience with a torrential rain of words and images. Throughout, he galloped through the script; he decelerated and accelerated, then jump-cut to a different image, and carried on speedily without moving or gesturing, bombarding the stage and the auditorium with words. The speediness of Bailey's language drew us into the same mental space and pace like a vortex, contradicting with the stasis of bodies – his *and* ours – almost numbed and trapped by the incessant delivery. This affect, generated through the delivery of the text without the use of multimedia on stage, created a context that profoundly speaks to our info-saturated, fast-paced, commercially driven and highly technologized climate which we strive to grasp, adapt to and evolve with. The exposure to fast, non-linear language, loading us with snapshots of images and thoughts, without a unified and easily recognizable narrative, defamiliarizes us from our mediatized consciousness and ontology – desensitizes us to the technologies shaping them.

After Bailey declared language dead, he left the stage, and the audience waited in the dark looking for the traditional theatrical cues such as lights coming up and doors opening. None of these happened. Instead, darkness and silence took over the space, leaving us in a liminal, uncertain state, which was then dramatically broken by heart-pounding, elating instrumental music played by Bailey and a group of musicians. The music lasted for long enough to captivate the audience and pulled us into the heart of a felt experience. This pummelling disruption of our often-desensitized state in an info-heavy, fast-paced culture was a hopeful act. It invited one to engage with the contemporary realities outside and beyond the parameters set by the socio-cognitive environment we inhabit and the language we speak to identify it. Hence, the arresting shift in performance from racing words to equally rapid and deep musical expression did not lead to the end of language as Bailey suggested, but a critical re-focusing on it and on how we make meaning through words in an environment where language is no longer a reliable source of truth. Bailey used language as his central instrument to question how we make sense of the realities we live in, how our consciousness, subjectivity and relationships are shaped by the language we are exposed to and repeatedly use in line with the dominant ideological formations. Without the use of media technologies as scenographic or compositional elements in the performance, *THWD* engendered an experience that relates to and calls into question our mediatized social and cognitive lives. This mode of invisible mediatization evokes Tim Ethcells's definition of Forced Entertainment's works as being 'understandable by anybody brought up in a house with the television on' (Etchells 1999: 95). *THWD* is a piece that is comprehensible by anybody who uses the internet, instantly accesses information, communicates via text messaging, watches TV while checking Twitter and so on.

Conclusion: Dissenting words, language for a mediatized age

While commenting on *Attempts*' structure, Crimp hints at the limitations of traditional dramatic form in addressing the realities of a media-driven capitalist age such as 'the overload of information' and multiplicity of perspectives and choices – 'the nature of a globalised world' – generating 'many stories to tell' (cited in Kerbel 12):

> The normal way of writing a play, of representing the world, is to give the illusion that you have people on stage who are real people, who are experiencing real problems or whatever. The thing about that is that you can't necessarily get very far or you can't necessarily reflect a world that's full of multiple stories. (Kerbel 12)

Both *Attempts* and *THWD* as media-langscape plays respond to this need for a different form and aesthetic logic through the use of language and the critical value it contains. The no-longer-dramatic form of language in these texts, whether explicitly or implicitly mediatized, destabilizes our expectations and antagonizes our consciousness by presenting language in unfamiliar ways. It divorces language from meaning and from its speaker and decouples the familiar, intelligible language and its accustomed, expected signification. Such language use, along with the overall dramaturgical scepticism towards dramatic illusion, negates the traditional, predictable structures and meanings in theatre. Consequently, to go back to Rancière's terminology, this mode of language undermines the *sensible* through an unintelligible or unordinary form, which as a result exposes the processes underlying the agreed-upon, rationalized social ontology and consciousness regulated by the logic of capitalism and circulated and maintained by media. The no-longer-dramatic mode of mediatized language, therefore, offers an experience of the playtext based less on easy consumption of knowable meanings than on critically stimulating engagement with the formal innovations, addressing and questioning the mediatized, capitalist climate we are perceptually and experientially immersed in. In other words, resisting the logic and form of realist dramatic representation without completely breaking away from drama, this form of mediatized language offers fresh ways of thinking about the world we live in from within by using its language and mode of perception in order to disrupt it. Differently from traditional dramatic plays such as *Closer*, these plays present a form that not only speaks the language of the mediatized age but also critically speaks to and speaks out about its normalized, invisible blind spots. No-longer-dramatic mediatized language is dissenting and critical, resisting the reproduction of the dominant, normative logic through mimetic representation 'in an age of omitted images of conflict' (Lehmann 2006: 183), and, instead, offering alternative ways of seeing the social and individual ontology in a mediatized, capitalist world.

This chapter gestures towards another set of questions, particularly in relation to the recurring theme of subjectivity: How has the experience of subjectivity evolved now in everyday life and human consciousness is extensively shaped by new technologies and mediatized culture? How do playtexts address our changing understanding of the self and the other in an age where we have online and offline identities, we perceive and relate to the world through personal technologies, we are globally connected and we 'feel' autonomous? Who is the *mediatized subject*, and how does the dramaturgy of character respond to this?

4

'Characterizing' the mediatized subject

Let me start this chapter with a visualization: You wake up in the morning and your first move is to reach out to your mobile phone. You check social media and see a post *again* about a boat of refugees sunk somewhere in the Mediterranean; a second later, you receive a notification from your dating app and you message the person whom you think is a good match, at least *virtually*. Then, you quickly respond to messages, like some posts, participate in an online discussion and a poll about a political protest, send a group message to family to save time and so on. In this media-saturated setting, with which many of us can identify, our physical and social being, our sense of self – how we perceive, define and present ourselves – and how we relate to others are profoundly shaped by the technologies we use and the images, information and culture they produce.

Our existence in this media-driven age has undeniably evolved more radically than ever before through the technologies we have created. Our technogenesis – our co-evolution with tools and technologies – has reached potentially its most intense and extensive form during the twenty-first century; our sense of self and other, our subjectivity and intersubjective relations have all altered. In this media ecology, we have become more fluid, many-sided and deindividuated, and our social ties have potentially become weaker than before, albeit in a more widely connected world. We have inevitably become posthuman – a hybrid of the organic and the machine with a flexible, protean and decentred subjectivity. I define this change in our understanding and experience of our being as *mediatized subjectivity*.

It is self-evident that, as our subjectivity is changing, so is how we artistically interpret it. Considering characterization in drama and theatre, one wonders: how has the mode of character presentation in contemporary plays evolved and engaged with mediatized subjectivity? What does the unattributed characterization, as we have seen in Martin Crimp's *Attempts*, suggest about our ontology? What do the other shifts in character presentation such as the fragmented, multiple and fluid mode of characterization and the real–fictional hybrid character suggest about our understanding and experience of the self in a media-saturated age? And can such figurations help us rethink our ontology and generate a dissident understanding of our being, destabilizing our idea and experience of a subjectivity profoundly shaped by the media culture we live in?

This chapter explores these questions with reference to Simon Stephens's *Pornography* (2007) and John Jesurun's *Firefall* (2009). Through their inventive aesthetics of characterization, both plays challenge the liberal-humanist view of the human subject as an autonomous, unified and stable individual. Stephens's and Jesurun's plays approach this in different ways. For example, while there are no character names in *Pornography*, Jesurun uses letters and names in *Firefall* and attributes directives to each character that defy the creation of traditional three-dimensional, psychologically motivated characters. Nevertheless, despite the differences in characterization as well as in thematic content, both plays present epistemologies of the subject that destabilize the traditional dramatic configuration of subjectivity and expose and critically engage with the structures and workings of our mediatized ontology.

As in the previous chapters, the analysis of playtexts is followed by an analysis of their embodiment in performance. I explore the first productions of Stephens's and Jesurun's plays: *Pornography*'s world premiere in Germany (2007) and its British production in Edinburgh (2008), and *Firefall* in New York (2009). Additionally, it is worth noting here that while the productions of *Pornography* draw profoundly on the finished playtext, Jesurun's playtext acts more as a point of origin that evolves throughout the performance in relation to pre-recorded and live online material. Based on this, I will explore how different as well as similar approaches to text and technology speak to our contemporary ontology. Before analysing the plays and productions, let us unpack the notion of mediatized subjectivity and the changing aesthetics of characterization in relation to it.

Mediatized subject: A deindividuated posthuman being

Mediatized subjectivity is an ontological state with complex and interrelated aspects that fundamentally encompass how technologies and mediatization have affected our sense of being and relationships. Without a doubt, this state cannot be considered outside the late capitalist processes of subjectivation, as well as the media-saturated social ecology that shapes our body and mind, rendering the contemporary subject *posthuman*. Consider the ways in which we develop virtual identities on social media and relate to the outside world through this hybrid subjectivity; how our personal data is monitored and monetized, objectifying us as bits of information; or how our societies have become increasingly disintegrated and apathetic, albeit globally connected. These instances present a snapshot of our mediatized being. In what follows, I will explore the two major and interconnected aspects of mediatized subjectivity: deindividuation and posthumanism.

In order to understand the notion of mediatized subjectivity, it is useful to briefly recount the rise of liberal humanism in the Enlightenment. That said, the concept of a unified and stable inner self is rooted in Western cultural tradition that predates the Renaissance and Enlightenment. For instance, Plato's concept of the reality of pure ideas and knowledge derived from a belief in the transcendence of an inner self. Aristotle's philosophy, similarly, referred to a sophisticated formulation of the workings of the individual's mind.[1] Medieval thinkers expanded the idea of pure self beyond the realms of the mind through concepts of the soul and the emotions while, in the pre-Enlightenment era, René Descartes's *cogito* proposed the separation of the thinking mind from the material body. The Cartesian subject existed prior to and independent of society, divine authority and other external forces. Descartes saw the human subject as self-determining with an ultimate disembodied autonomy that was the autonomous centre of knowledge and will. Following Descartes's model, Immanuel Kant and Edmund Husserl's transcendental ego foregrounded the superiority of reason over emotion and considered the subject as fundamentally unchanging and sovereign. Enlightenment and post-Enlightenment liberal-humanist positions predominantly saw the human (generally and thus normatively male) as a self-governing agent and originator of *his* own actions and thoughts. This subject had a unique existence and a particular character, separate from and superior to other non-human animate and inanimate beings.

In the nineteenth century, the liberal-humanist idea of the subject started to dissolve following sociocultural and economic events – particularly the Industrial Revolution. Emerging philosophies challenged the notion of the sovereign subject from different perspectives. Following Karl Marx, Marxist thinkers focused on the construction of subjectivity through cultural conventions, socio-economic practices and political relations. The subject, according to Marx, was 'the ensemble (aggregate) of social relations' (Gergen 1996: 127) and the mainsprings of her actions were 'rooted in the whole social organization of man [sic] which directs his [sic] consciousness in certain directions and blocks him [sic] from being aware of certain facts and experiences' (Fromm 2013: 18). Drawing on Marxist critique, in the twentieth century, Theodor W. Adorno and Max Horkheimer argued that the capitalist economy called for the death of the transcendental self because 'reason itself has become merely an aid to the all-encompassing economic apparatus' (Horkheimer and Adorno 2002: 23). The culture industry circulated commodities and consumerist ideologies through 'the manipulation of taste and the official culture's pretense of individualism', so seducing humans into believing in individual agency and identity while shaping these very identities (Adorno 2005: 280). Similarly, for Louis Althusser, society and social consciousness were structured by the ruling ideology through its ideological state apparatuses such as the judiciary, schooling, the media and so on. These instruments of the governing regime interpellated individuals into pre-constituted forms of subjectivity while, simultaneously, understanding the individual as subject to these apparatuses (Eagleton 1996: xx). The Althusserian subject, therefore, was not an autonomous individual but an ideologically constituted one, a function of the state.

Arguing against the liberal-humanist subject, Michel Foucault introduced the notion of *subjectivation*, namely, the construction of the individual subject. He put forward a form of subjectivity that was not innate but contingent and continually evolving in line with specific historical, social, cultural contexts. Thus, he contended, people's actions, thoughts and decisions were always constructed through social practices and 'within structures that embody certain patterns of power and difference, calling [them] into being within their discursive framework' (Graham 2002: 193). As a result, Foucault focused on the genealogy of the self across history and argued that subjectivity was enmeshed in power relations and socially constructed in discursive practices. Human beings were subjected to power structures and relations that enabled and maintained their definition of themselves as individuals with identity and autonomy.

Considering the subject's position within the late modernist society, Zygmunt Bauman and Ulrich Beck identified the subject as an *individualized* one. 'Individualization', Zygmunt Bauman argued, 'now means something very different from what it meant 100 years ago and what it conveyed in the early times of the modern era – the times of extolled human "emancipation" from the tightly knit web of communal dependency, surveillance and enforcement' (Beck and Beck-Gernsheim 2001: xiv). The concept today refers to the inescapable condition of humans in late capitalist culture: it is 'a fate, not a choice; in the land of individual freedom of choice, the option to escape individualization and to refuse participation in the individualizing game is emphatically *not* on the agenda' (Beck and Beck-Gernsheim 2001: xiv). Individualization is about creating the idea of the human as an autarkic self with an interest in her own gains and success, while tying subjects 'into a network of regulations, conditions, provisos' and standardizing them to be pawns of mass culture (Beck and Beck-Gernsheim 2001: 7). As mentioned earlier, Adorno identified this as 'pseudo-individualism', the 'endowing [of] cultural mass production with the halo of free choice or open market on the basis of standardization itself' (2002: 445). Likewise, individualization is a subtle compulsion that adapts people to capitalist values. It is useful to note here that individualization differs from individuation. Individuation, Ulrich Beck noted, refers to a self-sufficient, autonomous individual, whereas individualization is about believing that one has agency while in fact one's individuality is significantly shaped by institutional, ideological, discursive systems. Hence, the individualized subject is an 'institutionalized' and *deindividuated* being whose subjectivity is regulated by the dominant power structures under the guise of sovereignty and profit (Beck and Beck-Gernsheim 2001: xx). This does not mean that the subject has no authority over her life. Rather, it is to highlight the increased control of ideological and symbolic systems over our subjectivities in high modern societies.

Taking these viewpoints forward, Judith Butler contends that a human's sense of autonomous subjectivity is a retroactive construction, namely, an 'act' which 'has been going on before one arrived on the scene', and occurs merely through the performance of social conventions and roles (Butler 1990: 272). Butler argues that social reality and the subject's sense of her position in this reality are not self-evident, fixed givens, but constantly constituted as an illusion by hegemonic social conventions and ideologies 'through language, gesture, and all manner of symbolic social sign' (Butler 1990: 270). According to Butler, we enact these ideologies through the performative act of speaking and embody them in actions. Thus, gender, race and identity in general are 'an act which has been rehearsed, much as a script survives the particular actors who make use of it, but which all the same, requires individual actors in order to be actualized and reproduced as reality once again' (Butler 1990: 272). It is through our subjection to and consensual practice of these structures that we attain cultural recognition in society, assume an identity and position ourselves in relation to others. Differently from Althusser's interpellation, where norms are imposed upon the subject without her participation, in Butler's view, human beings, at least to an extent, participate in the workings of these frames since they provide structures that we use to apprehend identity.

Importantly, Butler argues that human subjectivity is not simply restrained by the mechanisms and processes of subjectivation. Rather than an entirely ideological restriction, our subjectivation is an essential part of our social existence. It contains the possibility of us emancipating ourselves from these constructions that facilitate and sustain our subjectivation – our interpellation or subjection to ideological, institutional, discursive systems. Hence, subjectivation, for Butler, holds both subjection and its negation. The subject, according to this non-liberal-humanist viewpoint, is not fully denied access to their own subjectivity or agency. For Jacques Rancière, who defines the subject as a contingent, collective and relational being, as opposed to an agentless container of roles and identities, subjectivation is in itself an emancipatory act that allows for the subject's resistance to assigned roles. The subject resists her participation in or exclusion of the *distribution of the sensible* (Rancière 2013: 89) – the system that defines what is made (in)visible, (in)audible and (un)representable – by seeking agency and forming dissident responses to the consensus maintained and disseminated through neoliberal, mediatized structures.

Considering these theories of subjectivation in relation to the contemporary world, in which technologies as parts and instruments of global neoliberal capitalism spread into every aspect of our lives, we can infer that there is a close connection between the construction of the self and media technologies. We can take social media platforms as an example; they inundate us with ideas and images of the *desirable self* – one with an ideal physical appearance and socio-economic status, attainable through marketed products and services. Media as an instrument of subjectivation provides the platform where we perform identities and seek recognition in accordance with this desirable self and, relatedly, with the prescribed norms of the dominant social order. For example, Facebook and Instagram are forums where we present our private and public lives within these norms that generate social recognition or cultural intelligibility. This, however, does not come without a price as these platforms not only mine individuals' personal data and monetize it for marketing and political purposes but also reinforce the neoliberal act of individualization, giving us the false idea that, as autonomous beings, we control our virtual existence.

In addition to our sense of self, the processes of subjectivation in our media-driven culture have affected our perception of the other and our intersubjective relations. Individualization has promoted self-interest and rendered the subject less able or eager, Anthony Giddens argues, 'to take a serious interest in anything other than shoring up the self' (1991: 172–3). Likewise, Kenneth J. Gergen contends that the self-interest of the individualized subject makes her less sensitive to minority voices and the other, and more likely to suppress the other and cause social division (1999: 33). The contemporary subject has become increasingly uninterested in other humans, and society as a whole is left with 'a sense of profound isolation' (1999: 33) leading to social apathy and weaker social ties. In our media-saturated social context, despite our ability to instantly communicate with others, we experience a more intensified degree of social disintegration. 'Virtual proximity', Bauman argues, defines the predominant mode of human connection today, 'too shallow and brief to condense into bonds' (2003: 62) since they are 'easy to enter and to exit' (2003: xii). The subject, Bauman argues, has 'no bonds that are unbreakable and attached once and for all' (2003: vii). Prior to Bauman, Baudrillard argued that rather than creating communication, the media 'devours communication and the social' (1994: 80). The media, Baudrillard claims, overload people with information and dissolve the social 'in a sort of nebulous state dedicated not to a surplus of innovation, but, on the contrary, to total entropy' (1994: 81). Baudrillard's bold omens are certainly justifiable, to an extent. However, while new technologies doubtlessly generate communication and innovation, they also partly lead to a sense of social apathy and an anti-social culture in which we might overlook our coexistence with others. As Sherry Turkle argues, we have become *alone together* and our mediated intersubjective relationships and encounters tend to degrade our experience of other people and generate a collective loneliness, a 'failed solitude' (2011: 462) rather than strong social bonds and intimacy.

This aspect of mediatized society is directly connected to neoliberal global politics. Mediatization in late capitalist, highly modernized societies has galvanized, Stig Hjarvard argues, 'a *soft individualism* that depends on *weak social ties*' (2009: 160; emphasis in original) rather than a truly self-driven, self-dependent individualism or a strong social solidarity. Weak social ties are fundamentally about the composition and execution of power dynamics and structures in a society where less binding relationships can be more easily contained as a social unit, monitored and regulated. They reinforce social dissolution that creates the groundwork for media to disseminate norms influencing the masses, and to mine individuals' data, target them as consumers based on this data, as well as monetize them by selling their private data to corporations. Media, in this respect, 'both encourage and make possible a continuous monitoring of the wider social environment through weak social ties' (Hjarvard 2009: 169).

Social disintegration in mediatized, highly technologized societies is also connected to the process of objectification of the human by various media. The news and social media often treat subjects as material or sources of human-interest stories, a means to attract or divert the consumer's attention. It flattens the specificity of individual's stories and presents them as catchy and easily consumable objects, and thus trivializes the complexity of human lives. This objectification happens, for example, in news programmes and reality TV shows. From the dehumanizing political and media narratives about the refugees, the victims of the Grenfell Tower and of the war in Syria, to the commodification of individuals through celebrity culture and reality television, media has had a powerful role in shaping how we perceive each other, leading us 'to treat other humans as objects of consumption', as images on the screen, pieces of information to be quickly consumed (Bauman 2003: 75).

This suggests that we are becoming less attached, responsive and more indifferent to each other as a consequence of the pervasive culture of individualization, fuelled by the late capitalist system and sustained by media as its predominant instrument.

Nevertheless, these processes of subjectivation do not mean that we are doomed to remain within this social, cultural and political context with limited agency and weakening social ties. Rather, to return to Butler and Rancière, I contend that we are able to resist the means and workings of individualization and mediatized subjectivation *from within* by using the same technologies used to sustain our subjectivation to the dominant social order. In other words, by using social news media and other communication and information technologies with an awareness of their ideological underpinnings, we could better understand our subjective position and identity. It is through the tools, discourses, viewpoints and narratives of the prevailing power structure that we turn it against itself, and resist the *sensible* order and its processes of subjectivation, deindividuation and objectification. Can we not, for example, consider some internet memes as examples of this? After the company Protein World's advertisement campaign 'Are You Beach Body Ready?', showing a slim, white woman in her bikini, numerous internet memes went viral criticizing the indoctrination particularly of women with an ideal body image and racial and ethnic identity (Hackman 2015: *The Guardian* Online). The emergence of memes, sarcastically ridiculing the campaign and claiming our agency over our bodies and identities, is an example of self-directed subversion of and resistance to the normative neoliberal commodification and control of subjectivity.

It is important to highlight here that, despite being the key instrument of the late capitalist order, fostering individualization and social disintegration, media has also had positive impact on individuals and societies in numerous areas. These benefits range from instant global dissemination of information to the collective interaction and reaction to important sociopolitical events such as the #MeToo Movement and the Black Lives Matter movement. Thanks to digital communication and information technologies, we can instantly communicate with anyone across the globe and develop connections with new people anywhere. In this way, we expand our social circles into an entirely mediated state and ecology of global coexistence. Our interpersonal relations and experience of others become mediated which may cultivate a sense of social collectivity and engagement regardless of a shared physical space, as experienced in the Arab Spring. These are historical and significant steps that we should not overlook while questioning the influence of technologies and media culture on our subjectivity.

When we talk about our ontology in the highly technologized contemporary moment, it is crucial to identify the posthuman subject – an integral part of our mediatized subjectivity. To begin with, let me highlight that by posthumanism I do not simply mean technological prosthetics or bodily augmentations. Instead, posthumanism identifies our hybrid state, encompassing nature/organism and artifice/information. The posthuman subjective position is a flexible one as it alters through and adapts to our interactions with and evolution through media technologies. When we send an email to a friend, post information and images on Facebook, share viewpoints on Twitter, or when we track our sleep and movement on personal technologies, we become posthuman. The posthuman aspect of our ontology and our individualized state within the capitalist system are deeply connected. One example to illustrate this connection is the surveillance and mining of our personal data without our *informed* consent by international corporations and media conglomerates for commercial and political purposes. Even though we believe that we have full agency over our online actions and the privacy of our shared information (e.g. when we sign a consent form), we are often barely informed about how our personal data is used by the wider neoliberal machinery.

Let's take a closer look at the notion of the posthuman in order to grasp it better and relate it to mediatized subjectivity. Ihab Hassan introduced the term in the late 1970s to refer to the radical change in 'the human form – including human desire and all its external representations' (1977: 843) in view of the ever-increasing predominance of techno-science, media technologies and industrial production. As opposed to a liberal-humanist position, Hassan's posthuman subject is a dynamic and malleable entity, an amalgam partly determined by informational and symbolic structures. In the mid-1980s, when personal computers entered the market (among other technological advancements), Hassan's theory was adopted and furthered by such theorists as Donna Haraway and N. Katherine Hayles. In 'A Cyborg Manifesto' (1985), Haraway argued that human beings in the late twentieth century have become 'cyborgs', 'theorized and fabricated hybrids of machine and organism' (1991: 150), or 'of social reality as well as [. . .] of fiction' (1991: 149). For Haraway, the human subject as cyborg no longer has a unique, unified and autonomous individuality detached from the external systems and realities of the world. The cyborg is related to and composed partly of non-human symbolic structures, such as media and information technologies. Thus, the metaphor of the 'cyborg', rooted in poststructuralism and cybernetics, considers the subject as a symbolic construct conceived through the interaction of the organic with the symbolic and technological. Subjectivity, conventionally rooted in the mind, disconnected from the body or external forces, is relocated both within and beyond the material body.

In *How We Became Posthuman* (1999), Hayles extends Haraway's ideas with a critique of cybernetics' misreading of the posthuman as an omen for the replacement of humans by intelligent machines. Drawing on Haraway, Hayles argues that the posthuman is a hybrid with diverse components and borders that concurrently accommodate the organic and the symbolic, problematizing the entrenched liberal-humanist division between the body and mind, or in a more recent context, between the organic and its engulfing technological environment. Posthumanism does not propose an *anti-human* argument, but is a critical attack on the liberal-humanist subject. Posthumanism problematizes the idea that the individual is the sole originator of her capacities, exclusive of society or external realities. It rejects the idea of a subject that is consistently stable and intrinsically autonomous. By contrast, the posthuman subject is a fluid and flexible entity whose diverse components and borders are constantly being constructed, deconstructed and reconstructed (Hayles 1999: 3). Therefore, posthumanism is not simply about prosthesis, literal cyborgs, humanoid robots or science fiction. Rather, and particularly in the context of this chapter, it refers to the (re)construction of subjectivity through the subject's interaction with the highly technologized environment. Becoming posthuman means going beyond the boundaries of the so-called human and furthering the sense of subjectivity, not only through the extension of the material body beyond the borders of the organic skin but also through the expansion of consciousness and cognition. That is why, as I mentioned earlier, one becomes posthuman once one surfs the internet, socializes through Facebook or feeds information into online systems such as Wikipedia. As Hayles argues, 'as you gaze at the flickering signifiers scrolling down the computer screens, no matter what identifications you assign to the embodied entities that you cannot see, you have already become posthuman' (Hayles 1999: xiv).

To sum up, the *mediatized subject* undermines the liberal-humanist division between a changing body and a stable mind by proposing a heterogeneous and fluid subject position that is a hybrid of the corporeal and the symbolic, the physically real and its representation through semiotic systems such as media technologies. This mode of subjectivity refers to a decentred 'self of many possibilities' (Lifton 1993: 1) and identities exposed to multiple realities and, which 'loses its consistency, and becomes brittle, broken or shattered' (Elliott 2007: 145). The mediatized subject constantly shifts through her interaction with and exposure to technologies and the media-saturated sociocultural, political and economic conditions – without being anchored in a definite position. Robert Jay Lifton identifies this as a 'protean self', which he separates from other (contemporary or postmodern) theories of the self that associate 'multiplicity and fluidity with disappearance of the self, with a complete absence of coherence among its various elements' (Lifton 1993: 8). The protean self, by contrast, is 'the blending of radical fluidity, functional wisdom, and a quest for at least minimal form' (Lifton 1993: 5). It continually adapts itself to the changing sociocultural circumstances, with no clear end point or unified self. Proteanism is a 'balancing act between responsive shapeshifting, on the one hand, and efforts to consolidate and cohere, on the other' (Lifton 1993: 9). This view of the subject corresponds to an important aspect of the mediatized subject since it does not entail the complete abandonment of individual agency, but it emphasizes the fluid, continually shifting state of the subject. The protean, like the mediatized subject, is malleable; its subjectivity is constantly constructed and reconstructed through contact with media images and discourses. While challenging the anthropocentric idea of human essence as the absolute and original source of meaning and centre of the universe, the mediatized subject still holds the potential for an increased critical awareness and unorthodox subjective position. Although media technologies may 'have a very draining debilitating effect upon a subject's sense of self' (Elliott 2007: 152), the subject is not merely symbolic or completely agentless nor is it obsolete. Hence, unlike Jean Baudrillard's definition of the subject as a primarily passive spectator who 'cannot master – let alone control – the cultural logic of governing information diffusion' (Elliott 2007: 150) or Arthur Kroker's identification of it as 'possessed by the seduction of virtual reality' (2001: 145), the mediatized subject can hold a degree of agency over her actions and thoughts by questioning and resisting the very same structures that have deindividuated, objectified and socially disengaged her from what used to be a strongly tied social environment.

Theatre as a historical, social and cultural construct has never been independent of contemporary social changes and constructions of subjectivity. Considering the above-mentioned changes in our subjective position and intersubjective being, as well as our potential for destabilizing the processes of subjectivation to gain agency, I will consider below how these affect how we engage with the mediatized human subject in theatre, particularly through the dramaturgy of character, and how inventive modes of characterization could open spaces for critical and dissident reflection on our ontology in a media-driven environment.

Who is speaking? Mediatized subjectivity and characterization

The evolution of our sense of the self and the other in relation to new technologies and our mediatized culture has galvanized new aesthetic engagements with and formations of characterization in theatre text and performance. What and who we consider to be a character has altered, discarding some of the historical aspects of characterization as we have known it, while introducing new facets that address the complexities of mediatized subjectivity, once more leading to the question: 'Who is speaking?' It is useful to consider some of the important moments in the development of characterization in Western thinking and theatre, particularly since the rise of liberal humanism, in order to grasp characterization in the theatre of the media age. Before this, however, let me pause here and briefly identify the notion of *character*. By character, I refer to any configuration and portrayal of subject and subjectivity in a theatre text and performance. It is an ever-changing, flexible category that adapts to our ever-evolving ontology and epistemology – our being in the world and our ways of knowing it. Hence, a character can be defined as a three-dimensional, psychologically motivated person with an identifiable name and expression as we see in G. Bernard Shaw's or Anton Chekov's plays, as well as a depersonalized executer of the text – the role and the actions – with no easily recognizable presence or identity as illustrated, for example, in Crimp's *Attempts* or Sarah Kane's *Crave* and *4.48 Psychosis*. Character, therefore, can be considered, as Cristina Delgado-Garcia suggests, as an *onto-aesthetic category* since 'it is the aesthetic *form* that theatre gives to a particular *form of being* or notion of subjectivity: it is the form through which theatre thinks, produces and encounters subjectivity' (2015: 19–20).

Following the Enlightenment, several thinkers, dramatists and theatre scholars adopted the liberal-humanist approach to characterization. Historically speaking, Georg W. F. Hegel has been among the most influential philosophers. Criticizing Aristotle's identification of plot as the 'soul' of tragedy that situates the character as an agent of dramatic action, Hegel argues for a transformation from the self-enclosed objectivity of ancient tragedy to the absolute subjectivity that places character as the representation of the 'absolute inner' (Fuchs 1996: 26) and at the centre of drama. Characterization, for Hegel, should be a fully developed representation of psychologically and ontologically unique subjects with historical and personal backgrounds, lifelike manners and complexity of mind. Compared to the Greek notion of fate, the Hegelian character in Romantic or modern tragedies has more freedom of choice when she encounters unintentional circumstances and events. This mode of character suggests the representation of the human as a self-determined, strong-willed person with freedom to undertake actions (Nyusztay 2002: 64). This idealistic, Romantic view of subjectivity does not annihilate the other aspects of dramatic narrative: 'the narrative frameworks and symbolic networks remain potent, but only after they have been internalized and taken up into the post-Cartesian drama of human inwardness' (Lundin 2005: 155). Likewise, Gotthold Ephraim Lessing's and Denis Diderot's works depend strongly on liberal-humanist characterization, namely on the idea that every character 'is defined by its own unique moral character' (Martinson 2005: 54), inward thoughts and feelings, and self-determined actions. Lessing and Diderot's viewpoint cultivates the realistic approach to character presentation, the connection between characters and real-life individuals. Relatedly, they extend their view of characterization to the aesthetics of acting, arguing that acting should be 'natural' and 'follow a logical sequence [. . .] a logical motivation of action' (Höyng 2005: 226) to generate a complete picture of a character.

Similar approaches to the human subject and its representation in theatre carried on to the nineteenth and twentieth centuries, particularly foregrounded in psychological realism and naturalist traditions, where the mode of characterization is usually based on the representation of the human as a three-dimensional individual with psychological depth. The naturalist notion of character offers a consistent and recognizable representation of the human as an individual with true human 'actions and [. . .] feelings [that are] linked in understandable ways' (Haring-Smith 2003: 46), and with a self-propelled nature liberated from the intervention of external forces. There are numerous examples highlighting the naturalist, liberal-humanist character, ranging from Henrik Ibsen's *A Doll's House* (1879), illustrating 'a *liberal humanist* belief in moral progress' (Fergusson 1996: 247; emphasis in original), to George Bernard Shaw's social dramas portraying self-governed characters with an awareness of the social structures they live in.

Half a century after Hegel, Friedrich Nietzsche argued against the Romantic devotion to 'inwardness', and 'the metaphysical conception of the subject as something isolated and independent' (Houlgate 1986: 184) and, relatedly, against naturalistic characterization. Following Nietzsche, the symbolists, whose criticism of liberal-humanist discourse was adopted by such playwrights as August Strindberg, destabilized the idea of character as the representation of a unified, stable and autonomous individual. They redrew characters as 'glimpses of human figures' (Haring-Smith 2003: 47) through allegorical representation. For instance, in Strindberg's symbolist and even in some of his naturalist plays, the characters are allegorical figures, 'conglomerates of past and present stages of culture' (Strindberg 1998: 60) patched together from 'scraps of humanity' (Strindberg 1998: 60), problematizing the notion of coherent, unified characterization.

The critique of liberal-humanist ideals and naturalistic characterization became more pronounced in the twentieth century partly in response to the prevailing disillusionment of post-Second World War, industrialized

Western societies. Playwrights, most notably Bertolt Brecht, reconsidered characterization in order to find ways to address the changing notion of the human within the socio-economic, political milieu. Drawing on Marxist philosophy, Brecht viewed character as a sum of gestures and acts in conversation with the sociopolitical, economic environment. Brecht's approach to characterization directly shaped the actor's role. Destabilizing the firm representational connection between character and actor, Brecht defied figurative acting and argued for a 'demonstrating actor' rather than an 'acting actor' (Brecht 1964: 136). The Brechtian actor therefore does not aim to mimetically represent a character and 'tidy away the inconsistencies in a character' (Shepherd and Wallis 2004: 181). Instead, she keeps the character at some distance, which is visible to the spectator, by demonstrating the contradictions in the character. The Brechtian actor comments on the role with gestures through her social experience and knowledge of human behaviour, and illustrates the socio-economic and political significance of the action. However, despite being liberated from the interpretive limitations of mimetic illusion, the Brechtian character and actor still reflect the human as a representational connection to the world and, hence, do not mark the demise of the naturalistic view of character. Characters are still placed in the framework of dramatic representation. For example, Grusha in *The Caucasian Chalk Circle* (1944) or Galileo in *The Life of Galileo* (1938) are recognizable, detailed representations of 'real' or lifelike people and are agents of dramatic narrative.

Besides Brecht, Samuel Beckett's plays, among those of other writers of the Theatre of the Absurd such as Eugene Ionesco and Jean Genet, show inventive approaches to characterization involving the use of language as an autonomous presence, disjointed from existentially ambivalent characters. Beckett's characters represent human existence often in abstract and intangible forms such as the torrent of words the mouth delivers in *Not I* (1973). Such innovative configurations of the human subject gesture towards further critical challenges to the liberal-humanist subject as new technologies have pervaded our everyday lives and have shaped how we perceive and experience the world, and position ourselves within it. In the highly technologized, late capitalist context of mediatized culture, where media technologies as ideological, cultural structures have radically influenced human existence, the idea of the human as a sovereign individual has become more problematic than ever. Likewise, theatre's response to the emerging subjectivity and the demise of the liberal-humanist project has generated new ways of thinking about character presentation in text and performance.

The rethinking of character has concurred with the changes in theatre practice and theory in general. Theatre has moved away from traditional dramatic form based on the representation of the world as a unified fictive cosmos with recognizable plot and characters, and on a unified relationship between character and language, character and actor. The dramatic mode of representation is replaced by a challenging mode of theatrical expression, a self-referential world of texts speaking to other texts, destabilizing the unity of character and actor and, by extension, the representation of the self as a unified whole. This also suggests a move away from character as the main point of emphasis, from its sovereign position in the dramatic narrative. Such changes have aroused the question of whether the character is dead. Although my intention is not to investigate whether character as a category exists or discuss its evolution in theoretical depth, it is relevant to highlight that the crisis of character suggests, as Elinor Fuchs argues, the end of the *humanist* conception of character rather than the category of character as a whole. It is the stable concept of character that has shifted towards the idea of character as a malleable, multifarious and decentred category.

Likewise, Gerda Poschmann coins an alternative term to identify the non-humanist character model. Marking the playtext as a 'Sprechtext' ('text to be spoken') (cited in Barnett 2005: 141) and the stage as 'Sprechraum' ('speaking space') (cited in Lehmann 2006: 31), Poschmann defines characters in no-longer-dramatic theatre texts and postdramatic theatre stage as 'Textträger' ('text bearers') (cited in Barnett 2005: 141) – characters that are deprived of their individual subject point and voice, and responsible for delivering the text as 'an associative piece of communicative material' (Barnett 2008: 21) rather than embodying and interpreting it. Discussing the incapacity of the figurative form of dramatic theatre in relation to the media age, Hans-Thies Lehmann reflects on the new forms of performance that challenge the theatrical portrayal of the world as an absolute totality and the human subject as a unified, consistent individual. In line with the notion of *Textträger*, the postdramatic approach destabilizes the position of character as the originator of meaning and the product of its own autonomous decisions and in-built talents. Moving beyond Brecht and Beckett, postdramatic theatre, as discussed, rejects the fictive text-cosmos as the central tenet and refuses consistent and easily identifiable characters situated within coherent and plausible dramatic plots. Instead, the theatre works restructure character as a fluid, multiple and decentred being with limited agency often by disrupting character's sovereign position and relationship to language as well as the unified character–actor relationship. The actor is liberated from the representational limitations of dramatic characterization and her subservient relation to the text. She is no longer the single logos or individual centre of the theatrical performance. Acting in postdramatic theatre is more 'presence' than 'pretence' (Lavender 2002: 189). Viewed in terms of Jacques Derrida's *différance*, the actor's resistance to a single logos leads to performance as 'a productive non-presence' (Auslander 1995: 60) that continually differs/ defers. The idea of a knowing subject, the character/actor as the central source of truth and representation of a unified self are all called into question.

Nevertheless, these new approaches to characterization do not suggest that these works have no characters or proclaim the death of the character. Character as a reflection on the human subject and subjectivity still persists in these critical conceptions, yet, rather than individual autonomy and a unitary state, character 'evokes the impression of functionality' (Pfister 1993: 160–1).[2] Defying the historical understanding of character as a recognizable, stable representation of human beings, Patrice Pavis underlines that the 'character is not dead; it has merely become polymorphous and difficult to pin down' (1998: 52). These new configurations propose a model of subjectivity that is fluid and multiple, a heterogeneous site of disunity and fragmentation, a hybrid of the human and the technological – aspects central to the current understandings and experiences of subjectivity that I identify specifically with the ontology of the mediatized subject. This specific perspective on characterization is in evidence in, for example, the fragmented snapshots of characters in Caryl Churchill's *Love and Information* and the unidentified speakers in Martin Crimp's *Attempts* that are disjointed from the sovereign language. The ways in which character relates to mediatized subjectivity can sometimes be buried in the aesthetics of character with no obvious reference to the constructions of subjectivity in a media-driven social ecology. Sarah Kane's *Crave*, in which the characters identified with letters (A, B, C, and M) are not fully knowable, or the self-reflexive, performative character formation destabilizing the character–actor relation in Tim Crouch's *An Oak Tree*, and Mac Wellmann's *Bitter Bierce* and *Jennie Ritchie*, where there are no character titles but characters constructed as a blend of discourses, all relate, albeit implicitly, to the heterogeneous, hard-to-pin-down, hybrid subjectivity in the media age.

Without doubt, the common tendency is to read these dramaturgical features with reference to poststructuralist, postdramatic and postmodern theories. Without forsaking those approaches, my aim is to look at the changes in the dramaturgy of character in contemporary plays specifically in relation to our mediatized culture because, whether the plays directly refer to them in their form and content or not, the writing is inevitably influenced by the wider social environment. It is important to explore how these new dramaturgical formations speak to our subjective position in the contemporary mediatized environment, whether they make a critical intervention into our ingrained understandings of subjectivity, widely shaped by new technologies, media culture and the power structures behind them. And, if they do, what do the interventions tell us about theatre and our ontology in a media-driven culture? To explore these questions, I will explore Simon Stephen's *Pornography* and John Jesurun's *Firefall* – plays whose thematic contents are not specifically or visibly focused on mediatized culture but whose formal engagements with characterization critically speak to our subjectivity in a world pervasively shaped by technologies. My analysis of each play will focus on three aspects of mediatized subjectivity and how these are treated through the form of character presentation: deindividuation, posthumanism and social disintegration.

Pornography: 'Being' in 'pornographic' times

Pornography depicts a landscape of terror and social alienation, with the 7/7 bombings in London as its main backdrop. The world of *Pornography*, identified with CCTV cameras, iPods, eBay and email, is a media-saturated one, in which society, human lives and relationships are shaped considerably by media technologies and the culture they have generated. The setting is a week, largely in London, when the Live 8 concert, the G8 summit, the 2012 Olympics announcement and the 7/7 bombings happened. The temporal setting gathers, yet does not unite, the lives of eight people: a female solicitor, disclosing trade secrets to her boss's rival; a pupil in love with his teacher; two incestuous siblings; one of the 7/7 bombers coming down to London on the day of the bombing; a university lecturer and his student; and a lonely widow, watching online pornography and craving human connection. Although every character in this mosaic of human lives brings different fragments of stories, the themes of deindividuation, fragmented subjectivity and social disintegration connect their narratives.

The play's title metaphorically hints at these themes. According to Stephens, '[w]e live in pornographic times' (cited in Gardner 2008) where people objectify others not very differently from 'the process of objectification that goes on in the production and consumption of pornography' (cited in Gardner 2008). Human beings in today's highly technologized, mediatized culture perceive and connect to the world and other humans beyond their physical experience through media technologies. This state of 'virtual proximity' and the consumerist culture ingrained in the mentality of the individualized subject leads her to judge other humans 'after the patterns of consumer objects by the value of pleasure they are likely to offer, and in "value for money" terms' (Bauman 2003: 75). In a similar way that the human body in pornography becomes an object of desire and satisfaction, people beyond the screens become images and experiences to consume. It is this change in perception, enabled by processes of individualization and, relatedly, deindividuation, intensified by media-saturated culture, that *Pornography* addresses through direct references to the mediatized environment and through inventive formal strategies. The play comprises seven scenes that are, like the lives it pictures, disconnected: there is neither a linear storyline nor a logically constructed plot uniting the fragments in an easily recognizable order. Only the temporal and spatial structure forms a common ground for the disjointed stories, yet the shared setting does not move beyond an impression of unity, nor does it generate a coherent narrative and an ontological core.

One of the most striking aspects of *Pornography* is the lack of character names that would traditionally identify the dramatic text with specific bodies and voices. Instead, Stephens eschews attributing individual names to the text, even to mark the change of speakers.[3] As mentioned in Chapter 3, unattributed text is not a new dramaturgical device or form. Plays such as Sarah Kane's *Crave* and Martin Crimp's *Attempts on Her Life*, or some of those written by Heiner Müller and Peter Handke in the German tradition, use similar formal strategies. Nevertheless, Stephens's play deploys unattribution in a way that foregrounds our mediatized subjectivity and puts it under a critical light.

The liberal-humanist character is being destabilized here. The characters in *Pornography* appear to be silhouettes without names. Even though we immediately have access to some aspects of the characters, which may initially create the impression of them as knowable and individual, we do not actually have detailed information about their personalities, backstory, intentions or psychological development. For example, scene 1 zooms in on a female character, albeit only briefly. Here, unlike a filmic zoom, which elaborates on an aspect of the character or the situation, we merely gather bits of information: she is a mother and a solicitor who is revealing her boss's business secrets to his rival. Stephens provides no further information about her motives or her past, leaving her as a snapshot within the limits of this fragment of a scene.

However, this is not a *characterless* or *subjectless* play. These unnamed speakers do still have some individual features and distinct storylines within the overall, mostly disjointed, plot. For example, while in one scene we encounter a student in love with his teacher, in another scene we see a university lecturer and his student having an affair. However, the scenes and the characters are contextualized specifically enough that we know that these are different people in different settings. Nevertheless, despite some individual traits, the characters cannot be considered as fully developed and recognizable dramatis personae. Instead, the characterization is purposefully incomplete and superficial. The lack of names intensifies this process of deindividuation that is emblematic of our contemporary subjectivity, which I will return to shortly. Moreover, the portrayal of the human as a subject with limited distinctive individuality and narrow information about the depths of her subjectivity generates the idea of *bite-size characterization*: characters that are not fully knowable or identifiable in the sense that we used to identify with the liberal-humanist characters. We can consider the entirety of the characters in the play as a collective character, signifying London-based British society; the individual stories seem to be intentionally brushed over and given as easy-to-consume fragments as opposed to in-depth and complete stories of individuals. *Pornography* puts London at a specific time under a kaleidoscope rather than a microscope, flattening its inhabitants' differences. Surely, one of the reasons behind this is to provide various perspectives on the social backdrop and the bombings yet, simultaneously, the mode of characterization suggests deeper critical connections to contemporary subjectivity beyond the play's historical and spatial focus. The withholding of information about the characters, at first glance, contradicts the info-rich age we live in. Yet, when considered more thoroughly, we can see the connections with the contemporary sociocultural environment, inundated with information and its fast-paced dissemination, consumption and disappearance into the depths of the web. In this environment we tend to pay attention to and process information about the world and others mostly superficially. The bite-sized characterization in *Pornography* reflects on the contemporary subject not only as deindividuated but also as objectified – I will return to this later in relation to the final scene.

Scene 5 furthers the epistemological uncertainty hitherto developed in the monologue form by switching to a dialogue between undefined characters. At the beginning of the conversation, it is not clear how many characters there are or who they are. The dialogue continues for a while without attaching a clearly identifiable individual voice to the speakers; then it implies that the speakers are siblings: 'You decide. Have you seen Mum and Dad?' (Stephens 2009: 231). This relationship becomes more evident later in the conversation when one of the speakers says: 'You're my sister' (Stephens 2009: 239). Nevertheless, the scattered bits of information about the speakers do not lead to any definitive picture of their characters, nor provide the reader with anything approaching an in-depth understanding of their identities. On the contrary, as the scene moves forward the sense of uncertainty becomes more intense due to the fragmented and discontinuous flow of the conversation:

You were absolutely mad last night. But it is.
–
What do you want to do today?
Go out.
Where do you want to go?

*

> She was a cleaner in St Pancras, at the train station. She found out she was pregnant. This was a hundred years ago. She came here. She spent all her money on getting a room. Threw herself over the side of the stairs. All the way down into the lobby. I've never seen her. People talk about her all the time. That's why they built the handrail. How did you find out you could get in? (Stephens 2009: 234)

Besides the discontinuity of the conversation, a hyphen in place of the character's response potentially indicates a silence or a pause, increasing the sense of uncertainty about the subject matter of the conversation, how the speaking character responds to the other, or how this might affect the narrative and so on. In addition to limiting what we know about the characters and their stories, this generates a sense of absence of an individual voice. Similarly, the asterisk before the abrupt change in the topic and mode of the narrative suggests a shift or pause; however, it is not clarified earlier through a stage direction. This adds to the uncertainty, drawing the reader into a guessing game about the identities of the speakers and their fragmented, intentionally incomplete stories.

Stephens underpins the limitations of individualization by challenging, through unattributed text, dramatic characters' once firm relation with and control over language. In *Pornography*, the text stands alone and the characters are detached from it, operating as its means rather than its originators. This sense of disjointedness between the characters and the words they speak does not suggest a total rupture between them or a loss of meaning. Rather, it suggests a separation of language from character as its autonomous creator, destabilizing the self-directing, liberal-humanist character as the representation of the only or main form of subjectivity. In other words, the unattributed and fragmented mode of the play generates a sense of text that exists before its speakers. Hence, the characters do not seem to be the sole source of words and meaning, nor does the language suggest the singularity or sovereignty of the characters. Nevertheless, the dialogue and language are realistic; thus, a director would have to address and indicate the speakers' status in performance. Despite the characters' limited agency, Stephens's unattributed text does not entirely divorce the characters from the language and deprive them entirely of individuality. Rather, every character presents some, albeit limited, personal traits and offers personal anecdotes through his/her monologues and dialogues. Nevertheless, at the same time, in the absence of fully formed, recognizable and stable characters, the decentred, unidentifiable mode of characterization prevails. It challenges the model of subjectivity as we know it, and offers a different perspective and mode beyond liberal humanism and capitalist individualization – one that corresponds to our deindividuated, multiple, protean subjectivity in these mediatized, globally networked, late capitalist times.

Along with the contemporary context of the play, the unattributed language undermines the idea of a sovereign subject, and the presentation of the characters with limited insight into their motives and identities speaks to the process of individualization – a process challenging our agency and individuality. Stephens's characterization evokes what Anthony Giddens defines as a common experience of all authors dealing with subjectivity in capitalist systems: 'feelings of powerlessness in relation to a diverse and large-scale social universe' (1991: 191). In contrast to the liberal-humanist subject, who believes herself to be substantially in control of the influences shaping her life, in late capitalism, 'the individual cedes control of his [sic] life circumstances to the dominating influences of machines and markets' (1991: 191). What is considered self-propelled or individuated has become or has always been a product of external agencies and symbolic structures, promoting individualization and, as a result, leading to deindividuation.

Let's pause here briefly and think about what this means in relation to our everyday lives. In today's pervasively technologized and networked societies, the details of our lives, identities and relationships are constantly transformed into and stored as data by media conglomerates such as Facebook. Every day we leave digital footprints behind us; we, as Lev Manovich argues, 'turn our own lives into an information archive by storing our emails, chats, sms (short message services), digital photos, GPS data, favorite music tracks, favorite television shows, and other "digital traces" of our existence' (2008: 335). Media technologies and platforms, as agents and symbolic mechanisms of late capitalism, seem to provide us with rights and options, telling us that we have autonomy and choice and are sovereign individuals (e.g. Google letting us decide on our advertisement preferences). However, under the guise of this discourse these platforms restrict the individual's agency and independence. As Bruce Schneier explains in relation to Google, we actually 'have no rights to delete anything [we] don't want there' (2015: 23). The ways in which Cambridge Analytica worked with the Donald Trump campaign in 2016 is a striking example of capitalist individualization and the role of media in shaping our subjectivities. The company provided the campaign with the data of millions of Facebook users, who did not give their consent to the use of their personal data for this or other political agendas, to influence their political thoughts and choices with campaign material and advertisements. To return to *Pornography*, the dramaturgy of character that shuns individual names, specified identity traits and detailed insight into personal stories does not merely reflect on our increasingly deindividuated, mediatized subjectivity. It also puts forward an act of resistance and opens up a critical space for dissident thinking, by challenging our accepted norms of subjectivity, and offering a non-humanist conceptualization of our position in the world, outside the boundaries of the neoliberal, individualized subject and its counterpart in dramatic text, the identity-based, fixed character.

The rethinking of the contemporary subject as one that is not fixed or unified also undermines anthropocentric understandings of the human. In *Pornography*, this view is replaced by a subjectivity that is protean, fragmented, multiple and with limited sovereignty. This aesthetic treatment of subjectivity speaks to another aspect of the mediatized subject: posthumanism. The characters, whose perception, words and actions are shaped by symbolic structures, suggest a mode of subjectivity that is an amalgam – a hybrid of the self-driven and the external-driven, the self and the symbolic, the organic and the machine. And this mode of subjectivity and characterization does not serve as the central, cohesive originator of meaning and identity. Rather, the subject is considered and presented here as part of a larger signifying landscape in which she exists without entirely losing her agency, but does merge with the structures around her. We experience this multi-ontological state in our pervasively mediatized lives – when we use wearable technologies such as smart watches, post a comment on Facebook or Twitter, or share a selfie on Instagram. In each scenario, we go beyond the singular self, we multiply, we fragment the whole and we become a hybrid of self and technology, flesh and data, organic and symbolic. *Pornography* does not overtly thematize this as, for example, Caryl Churchill's *Love and Information* or Jennifer Haley's *The Nether* does. Nevertheless, Stephens's play hints at the posthumanist aspect of our subjectivity, mainly through the separation of the speaker from the spoken, presenting language, namely, the symbolic (particularly in the last scene), not as the character's creation, but as an ontological component of her subjectivity. This mode of characterization suggests that the words indeed originate from a wider symbolic system such as the news media in the final scene, and presents the human as a semiotic construct that is no longer ontologically fixed or homogenous.

Besides what it means to be human in a mediatized context, the dramaturgy of character in *Pornography* also reflects on the intersubjective relations of the mediatized subject. Each character within the non-linear, fragmented plot structure is confined to one scene alone and has no direct, immediately perceivable relationship to the other characters or storylines in the play. The characters are related to one another through shared instances of time and space; nevertheless, neither they nor their stories link or develop together to form a coherent dramatic narrative, as we know it. This disjointed composition and positioning of the characters as disconnected from one another, living in their own bubbles, generates an overall sense of social disintegration and alienation. Their isolated narratives create the image of a society where the experience of community and togetherness is diminishing and the absence of a meaningful relationship to other humans is deeply felt. Considered in line with the play's contemporary context and the implicit references to media culture, one makes the link between this dramaturgical aspect and our globally connected, yet increasingly more isolated, social environment.

This critique via aesthetics becomes more pronounced in the scene where a lonely old woman talks about watching television, sending emails and using the internet, and defines the latter as being pulled 'towards the world that is there, on the other side of [her] screen' (Stephens 2009: 270). Throughout the brief fragment we gather that, through her own choosing, the character is living an isolated life: 'I don't see anybody. I don't speak to anybody. And God, the fucking horror if I were forced to' (Stephens 2009: 269). There is no clear explanation as to why the character feels such social anxiety or misanthropy, yet this does not appear as a shocking trait to us in a culture where we tend to prefer text messages to phone calls. However, despite her lack of interest in other people, there is an underlying reference to her longing for human bonds – *real* connection that does not depend on socio-technical tools. This becomes most clear towards the end of the scene when she smells barbecued chicken from a house while walking home on the day of the bombings and knocks on the door to ask for a piece of chicken. Finding this request strange and intrusive the characters think that she is 'fucking retarded' (Stephens 2009: 274). After whispering among themselves, which the reader cannot see as the lines are left blank, they give her a piece of chicken and ask her to leave with no sign of interest or sympathy for her. This rather absurd scene presents an uncanny glimpse of our social apathy towards another – a consequence of Margaret Thatcher's 'there is no such thing as society' and the rise of individualism. These themes run throughout the play and are emphasized every single time the characters attempt, yet fail, to move beyond isolation.

The presentation of characters as detached beings in a landscape of iPods, surveillance cameras and television evokes the increasing frailty of intersubjective relations and social unity – something that late capitalism (soft individualism) and its technological tools promote to monitor societies more effectively. The rise of social apathy, in line with the rise of late capitalism, the digital age and our media-driven social environment, has manifested itself in various sociopolitical situations such as the Syrian refugee crisis or the environmental crisis we are facing today, where social media lets us feel engaged as we react through 'shares', 'likes' and 'petitions'. At the same time, we are fed bite-sized, virally spread information quickly and superficially, keeping the popular imaginary distracted, which consequently prevents any enduring social solidarity or mobility that would lead to wider social, political, economic change.

Doubtlessly, none of these accounts denies the fact that we live in a world that is more widely connected than ever before as new technologies facilitate instant communication in ways that have been previously unimaginable. They also do not suggest that the core of human relationships has collapsed, or that we are entirely disengaged and apathetic with no hope for social solidarity. Technological advancements and the culture they have generated have shifted our intersubjective relations and social engagements in a positive way too. We communicate globally and instantly, we form groups and communities across the globe and work for our shared objectives or ideologies, we learn about and connect with different cultures around the world and so on. As mentioned earlier, social movements (e.g. #MeToo, #WomensMarch) have benefited from the internet and particularly social media as these platforms have promised a fast, accessible space of engagement that is open to all. However, despite this positive and at times revolutionary aspect of digital media, social activism via digital platforms also begs the question of to what extent hashtag activism and protests generate social change in the real world, who tells the story and how, especially when '[p]latforms like Facebook and Twitter, once the darlings of digital democracy, were suddenly on the defensive for their role in promoting fake news' (Schradie 2019: ix). In the mid-1990s, Sherry Turkle hinted at some of these concerns: 'If the politics of virtuality means democracy online and apathy off-line, there is reason for concern' (1995: 244). In her 2011 book, *Alone Together: Why We Expect More from Technology and Less from Each Other*, Turkle moves from this speculative position to a more dystopic one, arguing that new forms of technology distort human relationships and deplete our intersubjective, intimate experiences. *Pornography* tends towards this more apocalyptic social criticism, since the play thematically and formally, albeit implicitly, reflects on contemporary society in terms of social alienation – an outcome of a late capitalist system and how it uses technologies rather than the technologies themselves.

Pornography's last scene critically reflects on the theme of social disintegration through a focus on the objectification of the human subject by the media and its concurrent repercussion in social indifference. The mode of characterization here differs from the rest of the play. The scene consists of fifty-two separate, fragmentary descriptions with no speech prefixes. Each piece of utterance is numbered and provides information about each of the fifty-two victims of the 7/7 bombings. Numbering the victims, as opposed to naming them individually, speaks to a culture of institutionalized and objectifying individualization. Considered particularly in tandem with the references to the media-saturated cultural context (e.g. CCTV cameras, television), the numbering deprives characters of their individual identities and dehumanizes them as pieces of information rather than individual human beings. Some of the numbered lines echo various media-related discourses, styles, and indirectly refer to media culture:

13   The twenty-six-year-old, an engineering executive from Hendon, was killed on the number 30 bus after he was evacuated from King's Cross. [...]
24   She attended the mosque every Friday, but loved Western culture and fashions and regularly shopped for designer clothes, shoes and handbags. She worked as a cashier at the Co-operative Bank in Islington. [...]
43   – (Stephens 2009: 276–9)

Like the scenes preceding them, the numbered parts are disjointed glimpses taken from a wide variety of perspectives. They present a mosaic of diverse discourses – mainly in an impersonal tone and with no clearly identified source. These descriptions, albeit covertly, evoke the way the media presents people. For example, the impersonal and formal tone of number 13's description evokes the tone and style of broadcast journalism. Number 24's description gestures towards consumer capitalism and cultural assimilation, with a focus on the cliché binary of Islam and Western culture. Highlighting the superficial characteristics of a victim killed in a tragic event connotes the discourse of human-interest television programmes, the way the media treats people as a means to attract audience-consumer attention, foregrounding the sensational or polemical aspects of their stories to attract interest. Number 43, on the other hand, is the only number with no commentary. The absence of information suggests several meanings (e.g. a reference to an unidentified victim), but its presence as absence merely poses a question and resists an answer. The presentation of the 7/7 victims through anonymous, impersonal and brief fragments mirrors the flickering images on television, reducing their lives to superficial fragments of information or even to silence or nothingness ('43: –'). The composition of this final scene responds to the increasing and ironic frailty of human relations in a globally connected landscape.

Pornography transgresses the traditional, familiar mode of character presentation, and offers a new way of thinking about our intersubjective position in society – a position that does not replicate the late capitalist, seemingly connected society. In so doing, the play opens up a crack in the normative, *sensible* order. By extending our understanding of the self and the other outside the frame of a so-called homogenous social system, which does not allow for dissident or antagonistic thinking, the play, through a shift in its own machinery and hence its internal politics, offers a move, even if just on the cognitive level, towards social change. One wonders how the aesthetico-political focus of Stephens's playtext, and the formal–critical interventions it makes, shapes the conversation between text and performance, and what meanings *Pornography* on stage generates, reinforces or discards.

Pornography on stage

Despite its 'Britishness' in terms of setting and references (Luton Airport, Fitness First backpacks, the Olympics), *Pornography* premiered in Germany as a co-production between the Deutsches Schauspielhaus in Hamburg and the Festival Theaterformen at the Schauspielhannover in October 2007, directed by Sebastian Nübling. *Pornography* made its British debut in summer 2008 at the Edinburgh Fringe Festival before transferring to the Birmingham Rep in September. It is important to look at both productions because, although German theatre is outside the context of this book, Nübling's production is the first interpretation of the text in performance and provides an interesting reference point in relation to the British production.

At its world premiere, *Pornography* presented the audience with a city in ruins, a setting with implicit references to the contemporary world as a socially, politically and financially crumbling place. Nübling set the stage against a vast, fragmented image of Pieter Brueghel's 'Tower of Babel' as an unstable edifice, 'like a huge unfinished jigsaw puzzle with half the pieces lying around the floor' (Hamburger 2008: 541). The presentation of Brueghel's painting as a fragmented mosaic on the stage resonated with and foregrounded the play's disjointed structure, and visualized the disintegration of contemporary society and the destructive effect of 7/7 and other terrorist attacks.

Nübling accentuated the anonymous form of Stephens's text. He situated all the actors simultaneously on the stage, sometimes attributing multiple roles to them and refusing, for the most part, to identify them with individual names. Nübling seldom used props to physically transform the actors into characters, even though there were a few instances where he used props and accessories to indicate an actor's change of role from a previous scene. For example, he used high-heeled shoes to imply one of the male actors was enacting the role of a female teacher. Nevertheless, despite such correspondence between some actors and characters, the discontinuity of the narrative and the disconnectedness between characters did not allow for dramatic representation as such.

Nübling took advantage of the freedom of anonymity the playtext offers, and proposed alternative interpretations of some characters by deploying actors who did not fit the role in terms of their physical appearance or gender. In scene 6, we have a pupil, Jason, who falls for his teacher, Lisa (two of the rare characters with names). Onstage, however, Nübling presented Lisa using a male actor. Likewise, the interpretation of scene 5 differed from Stephens's text, which suggests that the characters are siblings having an incestuous relationship and that one of the characters is the sister. Instead, Nübling employed two male actors, making the incestuous relationship even more transgressive. Besides the uncertainty about the characters due to the unattributed, fragmented form of the play, Nübling's technique put forward a form of disparity – yet not a complete separation – between the characters and actors. The performance furthered the destabilization of the liberal-humanist characterization and presented characters and, by extension, humans as fluid, deindividuated subjects. Nübling did not use technology in the production to offer a direct link between the characters and a mediatized environment, but the mode of theatrical expression and verbal references to emailing and eBay suggested a critical link between the form of character presentation and the form of *being* in contemporary society, between aesthetics and ontology. Nübling's interpretation also highlighted the play's portrayal of the disintegration of intersubjective relations by situating the actors separately on the stage. While the actors in a given scene delivered their lines and performed, the other actors remained on stage, yet showed no interest in the ongoing action. They neutrally wandered around or gather pieces of Brueghel's mosaic. Their indifference to one another and to the world outside their personal microcosm generated a sense of disconnectedness. Furthermore, despite their trials, the performers failed to gather the pieces and complete the painting. This image symbolically spoke to social alienation and fragmentation in contemporary late capitalist, highly technologized societies, despite the desire for genuine human connection and community. Nübling's production presented a compelling interpretation of *Pornography*, exploiting its aesthetic dynamism and critical depth, and highlighting the text's deliberate opacity as a critique of mediatized culture that was able to reach beyond the theme of British society and the bombings.

In the first British production of *Pornography*, the set design foregrounded and amplified Stephens's references to the media-saturated landscape. The stage was a 'big mess of TV screens, stereo speakers and exposed lights [. . .] all connected up somehow by a riot of wires and extension cables that stretched out from the auditorium' (Cooper 2008: 1519). Drawing directly on

Stephens's text, Holmes presented a microcosm of London in the week of July before the attacks, as 'the faint sounds of Coldplay mix[ed] with the electric drone of a hot summer' (Gardner 2008, *The Guardian* Online).

Holmes staged the play in episodes; however, rather than individual episodes connected to a narrative arc, the production cut between different stories. Holmes's staging amplified *Pornography*'s fragmented structure and produced a sense of disengagement, suggesting the fragmentation of social relations. The intensified disjointedness enhanced the theatricality by exposing the workings of the performance and overexposing the seams between the fragments of scenes. This challenged the audience's expectations of a 'well-made' narrative, raising their awareness of the theatre as a construct and their position in it. Besides, the epistemological instability created through the unattributed and fragmented speech invited the audience to fill in the uncertainties and form their own interpretations. Holmes's production, therefore, encouraged the audience to engage with the meaning-making process and its critical implications.

The production involved an ensemble of eight actors, all present onstage at once. Following Stephens's characterization, Holmes gave a glimpse of the characters rather than a detailed, psychologically motivated, figurative representation: a randy schoolboy, the incestuous brother and sister or a jaded lecturer (Cooper 2008: 1519). Unlike Nübling, Holmes did not exploit the incongruity between the characters and the actors; however, he did not create completely unified individual characters either. Rather, he staged what the text proposed: superficially connected, but essentially unspecific characters, by refusing to give individual names and characteristics to the actors, merely gathering them, instead, in the same temporal space (the day of the bombing) without offering a unifying narrative. Moreover, following Stephens's text, Holmes did not present characters/actors in communication with one another outside the scenes they took part in. Instead, as in Nübling's version, they remained detached from each other and indifferent to each other's narratives.

Given the Britishness of Stephens's playtext and Holmes's production being the first British staging of the play, one might argue that this production failed to represent the bombings or their social implications. Joyce McMillan's review reflects on the production: 'the piece fails to convince [. . .] the portrayal of the bomber, in particular [. . .] Stephens has suggested the play is a serious exploration of four British men driven to attack the very heart of the society that raised them, but it hardly even makes a start on that vital task' (McMillan 2008, *Scotsman* Online). McMillan would be correct if the 'critical' and the 'social' in contemporary theatre involved only *direct* thematization of real-life events; *Pornography* refuses to give a fully developed representation of the bomber, or of any other character. However, this reading overlooks the critical inferences of Stephens's conscious refusal to generate dramatic certainty or to represent the world and subject as a unified totality. As my analysis suggests, the form allows *Pornography* to critically reflect on the darker elements of contemporary society – aspects that can no longer be fully surveyed and represented through traditional dramatic structure and the direct engagement of conventional political theatre. Instead, the aesthetic engagement with issues such as subjectivity and intersubjective relations in a mediatized culture, as illustrated in *Pornography*, are in fact acts of critical engagement. Through the form of character presentation, which challenges the conventional structures of characterization, Holmes's interpretation engaged politically with the play's central theme beyond its specific setting.

The stage interpretation of the final scene with the numbered lines in both productions offers thought-provoking perspectives on mediatized society and subjectivity. Holmes set the scene as a text scrolling up the wall/screen after the curtain call, evoking the credits at the end of a film. With this analogy in mind, the text could be read both as a memorial to the victims of the 7/7 attacks and as a critical reference to a media culture that reduces real lives to pieces of information and dehumanizes people, through filmic conventions, as mere lists of names or collections of images. In his conversation with Aleks Sierz, Stephens mentioned how some audience members had not even noticed the scene and left the auditorium.[4] This suggests Holmes's production created an unintended reflection of how the fast-pacedness of contemporary society reduces our attention spans and how becoming accustomed to rapid consumption leaves us increasingly indifferent to one another. In Nübling's production, the actors began eating apples expressionlessly as they listened to the pre-recorded text about the victims – a representation of social apathy more overt than Holmes's. The last scene in both productions enhanced the critical scope of *Pornography* by aesthetically engaging with the question of social apathy and objectification of humans. Stephens's strategies confer performative openness upon the text, allowing the audience to create their own associations, bounded only by the productions' own thematic concerns.

Pornography may at first seem to be only about the 7/7 bombings and British society. However, as my analysis suggests, beyond the historical details lie compelling techniques as critical tools that map aspects of culture and subjectivity through a link between the mode of theatrical expression and contemporary human condition. Thus, *Pornography* goes beyond its direct thematic concerns towards an analysis of the mediatized, late capitalist culture and its focus on deindividuation, social isolation and the objectification of human life. The dramaturgical structure, here, does not argue for the death of character, nor bemoan the lack of an already defined image of the 'human being' (Lehmann 2006: 18). Instead, it ruptures and reconsiders the representation of the contemporary in theatre and proposes inventive ways of mapping the phenomenology of living in today's world. In so doing, *Pornography* takes theatrical boundaries beyond the existing rules and expectations and enhances audience's critical horizons while inviting them to reflect perceptively on their own subjective position.

Firefall: Multidimensional reflections on 'homo media'

The writer, director and designer John Jesurun, whose writing has been greatly influenced by media technologies, captures various aspects of our lives in a mediatized, globalized world through the form and content of his theatre works. Jesurun's pieces offer, as Bonnie Marranca puts it, 'a portrait of *homo media*, an ontology of the mediated character: how the human being exists linguistically, visually, spatially, and digitally in our global age' (2010: 24). Marranca's concept is significantly similar to the notion of mediatized subject; they both theorize and identify the ways in which human beings exist in a highly technologized culture of global capitalism. Besides his interest in media technologies and their sociocultural and cognitive influences, Jesurun emphasizes the fluid nature of language in his texts and performances, constantly reshaping, reformatting and adapting it to new media forms, spaces and environments. The written text is a significant aspect of Jesurun's works, yet it is always on an equal footing with other elements of performance such as technology, space, body and so on. Through a multidimensional integration of text, media technologies and performance, Jesurun's works reflect on the angst and displacement of the contemporary subject. However, rather than telling a linearly structured, cohesive and identifiable story that is closed off from reality and gives a fixed perspective on it, Jesurun subverts dramatic design in text and performance to question the aesthetics and politics of theatrical expression and perception, and their relation to the contemporary world. While capturing the contemporary, Jesurun's works not only tell stories of and for the mediatized, late capitalist age, but they also consider the potential meanings underlying the ways in which we tell and understand stories today. However, Jesurun refuses to tell unequivocal stories. The focus in Jesurun's theatre is not on a story's meaning, and this is often the reason why readers and audience find Jesurun's pieces inexplicable and hard to fully pin down. Instead, the focus is on *how* the story is constructed, told and received, and what the form of storytelling suggests with regard to our lives, as Jesurun himself underlines: '[my work] is not about understanding a story; it's about seeing how stories are understood' (cited in Fried 1985: 72). Rather than providing his audience with directly familiar, unambiguous stories, Jesurun's works dig deeper and expose what is left outside, in-between or buried under the visible, the audible and the representable in an age of image- and info-saturation.

Jesurun's 2009 play *Firefall* meditates on our mediatized subjectivity and intersubjective relations; it tells the story of the contemporary self in ways that critically speak to the mode, meanings and politics of our ontology as homo media. *Firefall* has an interesting setup because the playtext, which is written before and for the performance, is activated and continually modified through the live use of the internet during the performance. If we consider the playtext as one of the many layers or dimensions, another is a website structure which consists of music clips, notes, images, video material and so on, generated through rehearsals and expanded through the performance run. Related to the main website, each character has a personal webpage which appears in a different configuration in each performance. Through their personal pages, performers access the archived material on the website which they use to add or take out material during the performance. Also via their personal laptops, the performers surf the internet, and concurrently integrate these found materials into the live performance. Additionally, they also use an online chat forum to communicate with one another on stage. All of these actions are simultaneously made visible to the audience through projectors reflecting on the wall-screens. Both the playtext and the omnipresent website are open texts which expand and alter through each performance. The playtext, in this context, acts as a starting point and an outline for the computer-generated live performance. The form of *Firefall*, as Bonnie Marranca herself explains, can be identified with 'mediaturgy' – a notion that refers to works that situate media at the core of their composition (something I will return to in Chapter 6) (2010: 16). In what follows, I will first explore Jesurun's playtext and then its performance particularly in relation to its characterization.

The playtext comprises eight characters, identified either with letters (R, F and K) or with pop-cultural or biblical names (Noseworthy, Peewee, Iscariot, Mary and Jesus). The anonymity of the letter–characters and the hyper-familiarity of the stock names both emphasize the restricted individuality of the characters. Surely there does not have to be individual names to generate individual characters. For example, in Samuel Beckett's *Not I* (1973), we merely have a mouth presenting the story, yet despite the lack of an individual name, the story the mouth tells us is deeply personalized and individual. In *Firefall*, however, it is hard to pin down the characters' identities or reach an in-depth understanding of who they actually are. This is the case with the characters that have symbolic names which suggest cultural and religious connotations; rather than three-dimensional individual dramatis persona with psychological depth, these characters seem to be more like stock characters. They are flat, lack depth and individuality, and they are ambiguous, as they are not connected through a consistent and recognizable storyline. Instead of endowing the characters with individual characteristics and roles, and locating them within a coherent narrative that would generate an easily identifiable theatrical representation, Jesurun provides each character with a directive about their comportment in the play: while Peewee is introducing chaos and Mary is introducing false information to change the perceived reality and create a new order, R is trying to preserve the status quo and Noseworthy follows and executes the rules (Jesurun 2009: 167). These instructions may at first seem to provide the characters with distinctive roles. However, two things happen here that immediately subvert the possibility of an individuated character with agency and personal voice. First, the directives are not self-chosen or self-shaped roles, but are given and constructed by an unidentified person or system. Second, the directives do not form an understandable story. By carrying out the instructions, the characters contribute to a total sabotage of any consistent, definitive narrative.

Firefall may seem different from *Pornography*'s unattributed form. However, the letters and symbolic names, particularly in relation to the unidentified storyline, time and space, which are more specifically delineated in Stephens's work, do not generate recognizable, consistent characters. Rather, they are presented as clear constructs – following the given roles without questioning the rationale behind their words and acts. The moment a character attempts to challenge the status quo, others interfere – preventing opposition and keeping them doing their 'job'. Peewee and Iscariot are the characters with directives that suggest a sense of questioning albeit their different aims. As Peewee mentions, the characters are given the directives and work for what is hinted to be an upper layer within a class system that rules and dominates the other strata in society for their own interests and gains (Jesurun 2009: 170). Iscariot refuses 'to accept [to] be a part of the harmonious harmony of acceptance [. . .] to believe in anything but the strength of [his mind] and its own singularity' (Jesurun 2009: 172). In response, Noseworthy, who 'follows the rules and executes them' (Jesurun 2009: 167), pressures him saying that they 'are going to have to rewrite you [Iscariot]' (Jesurun 2009: 180). The content of the directives are telling in relation to this implicit contextualization of power relations. Apart from Peewee, Iscariot and Mary, who prioritize their individual interests when they challenge the current system, the other characters seem to be constructed in a way that is based on either following the rules (Noseworthy), preserving the status quo (R) and finding a balance between chaos and status quo (F), or apathy

(K). The characters, whose identities are composed through instructions from an unknown upper stratum, have limited individuality. This mode of character presentation speaks to the contemporary subject's continual and often imperceptible regulation and shaping by the dominant system and its tools. Jesurun challenges our accustomed ways of understanding the subject, outside our comfortable humanist, mediatized gaze that considers subjectivity in line with capitalist individualism.

The directives that constitute the deeds and language, and therefore the identity, of the characters challenge the liberal-humanist concept of character. Instead, they produce a mode of characterization that is closer to Poschmann's text bearers who are not the originators of the words and meaning, but are mainly responsible for delivering the lines. The following dialogue illustrates how the directives in fact shape the language and subjectivity of the characters. Here, as the directives suggest, Iscariot is in doubt, F tries to find a common ground between status quo and doubt, R tries to preserve the status quo, Mary asks questions to subvert the ongoing situation and create doubt, Peewee intervenes and introduces mischievous chaos while Noseworthy follows the rules:

> **ISCARIOT** If I believe, I loose myself among you. I prefer to doubt.
> **F** That's not so bad.
> **R** But don't you find yourself in the comfort and familiarity of the group?
> **ISCARIOT** Don't want to be. [...] Give up what I was born with – my independence.
> [...]
> **MARY** Were you born with it?
> **PEEWEE** Maybe you learned or acquired it.
> **R** Only to have it broken here?
> [...]
> **ISCARIOT** Must you say those things?
> **NOSEWORTHY** It's our job. (Jesurun 2009: 175)

As the characters speak in accordance with their directives, it is hard to grasp to what extent their words are originally theirs or are based on the instructions. Words do not seem to be a creation or an expression of the subject speaking them; they do not seem to be instigated in the character's thoughts. Hence, the characters' subjectivity, agency and identity are all majorly an effect of the constructed, controlled language. This language appears to originate from various familiar sources and texts such as novels, songs, myths, fictional characters and so on. As the playtext continually introduces and throws in odd references to various texts, ranging from *Anna Karenina* and Lou Reed's 'Perfect Day' to the story of Jesus, the Apostles and Mary Magdalene, we become increasingly more convinced that the language is based on 'a databank of readymades' (Marranca 201: 23) rather than originating from an individual character:

> **PEEWEE and ISCARIOT** (*Singing over the track of 'In the Rain', by the Dramatics.*) 'I wanna go outside the rain,' etc.
> **ISCARIOT** Koizumi releases stress with legendary lewdness, (*Recites first verse of 'Atlantis', by Donovan.*) 'The continent of Atlantis was an island which lay before the great flood in the area we now call the Atlantic Ocean,' etc. (Jesurun 2009: 183)

The world of the play is based on this found language which is replicated by the characters and overtakes personal voice and experience, leading to ever-shifting identities. At times, some of the characters turn into animals such as donkeys and monkeys. Through these absurd changes, characters gradually lose their individual characteristics and become a part of the group. In addition, the characters' language is penetrated with phrases, commands and terms from computer-speak such as 'delete', 'fact check', 'search', 'trash' and 'rewind'. For example, if a character undermines and jeopardizes the story, namely, the status quo, another character can 'delete' this character. Likewise, any image, text and information can be 'erased' from the story or 'trashed' in a similar way that we edit texts in our computers (e.g. with reference to Tolstoy's *Anna Karenina*: 'Strike the author's name, it's not important'; 'Trash that' (Jesurun 2009: 197–9)). Or, if the conversation veers off track, one of the characters may instruct the others to 'rewind' in order to return to the story. Despite the seeming agency suggested by these imperative instructions, the characters speak a media-generated language – one that reinforces the operation of the directives. The computer-speak refers to the website and goes hand in hand with the sporadic incorporation of various layers of texts, images and information into the performance. On a textual level, before the play is activated through a live performance, the fragments of accumulated information, which derive from the internet and a vast body of sources, culminate in an unspecified, multifarious media-langscape (see Chapter 3) rather than a recognizable coherent story. The characters' speech vertiginously shifts from one topic to another: one is talking about a lost child, another about a dog, while another character is telling us about power relations. The mode of characterization with limited agency over language and deeds speaks to the ways in which we think, speak and be in a media age that saturates our minds, everyday lives and subjectivities with information to an extent that we no longer question the ideological and systematic undercurrents of our mediatized culture.

Nevertheless, having limited autonomy over language, thoughts and actions does not suggest that the characters do not have any sovereignty at all. Despite their limited agency, and their continual struggle to communicate through expressive dialogue, the characters still show the self-directed desire to question their existence and make sense of who they are in the world of the play in order to create a narrative that they can believe in:

> K   What are we talking about? Who are we? What are we doing here?
> NOSEWORTHY   Didn't they tell you?
> K   No.
> ISCARIOT   Who are we, and what are we doing here?
> [. . .]
> K   Why do I exist?
> PEEWEE   If you really existed, you wouldn't ask such a useless question.
> K   You mean we're not characters? (Jesurun 2009: 179)

This metadramatic moment indicates a sense of self-awareness and independence. However, it does not lead to the liberal-humanist model of character that we are used to seeing in drama and theatre. Despite their attempts, the characters do not find answers to their questions about identity, whether they are real or fiction, where they are, who they are, what they are doing, who have given them the directives and so on. There is a Beckettian and Pinteresque uncertainty and tension about the characters' identity and their job – the orders coming from above:

> ISCARIOT   Can I please explain my directive to you?
> NOSEWORTHY   Who gave you that directive?
> ISCARIOT   I can't remember.
> F   What matters is not who gave it to you, but that you received it.
> (Jesurun 2009: 198)

When characters attempt to challenge this intentional unknowingness around their character and move beyond the given directives into a state of individual subjectivity, their sovereign action is considered as a threat to the unidentified larger system:

> K   I have appeared to go unnoticed in this group of donkeys. Disguised as a fellow donkey. But I am not a donkey. It seems to

be what I am being told to be . . . by myself. I think. But I thought all the others talked to their own well-meaning selves about such things. But they don't. They are instead their own self-informants on the Website. I don't recognize the tender parts of my face even when it is so convincing. I don't recognize myself. [. . .]
PEEWEE   Why did you reveal that? What are you talking about? Yourself?
MARY   Now we have to get rid of you. (Jesurun 2009: 186–7)

Their dependence on directives, ready-made language and found texts, albeit their self-governed attempts to create recognizable story and characters, speak to the state of the deindividuated subject in the late capitalist, mediatized age. Jesurun's aesthetic subversion of the liberal-humanist character is a political act. Through directive-based characters as text bearers, Jesurun exposes what is often invisible to contemporary subjects inundated with information and bewildered by global capitalism that diminishes, if not erases, a sense of individual autonomy while creating a rule-abiding collective character. In other words, instead of reproducing our accustomed definition of the human as a self-governing individual, *Firefall* exposes the clandestine machinery of the hegemonic subjectivation processes, and the constructedness of the institutionally, socially and culturally individualized subject. By subverting the prescribed narrative of subjectivity engineered by rampant global capitalism and mediatization, the play invites us to question our subjective positions in unorthodox ways.

Jesurun's characterization also considers the connection between *homo media* and the *posthuman*. At the heart of *Firefall*'s architecture lies the omnipresent website – a conceptual and technological structure that shapes the entirety of the piece, as the performers and Jesurun himself mould and use it during the rehearsals and the performances. The website, however, is more than a stylistic tool, conceptual resource or a techno-specific space; it is, as Jesurun emphasizes, 'a character to be dealt with' (Jesurun 2009: 167). The website as a character is partly symptomatic of our decentred, fragmented, multi-layered, datafied state as posthuman subjects. It is constructed and regulated by multiple authors. It is made up of layers of information that are not gathered, used or stored in a linear manner that would otherwise generate a unified, easily identifiable entity. If we take the accepted definition of character as portrayal of people, we can partially relate the website–character to our mediatized being and consciousness. Also, since the website is a structure formed of and based on data, which exists within and is used by a larger information network, it also appears as a *datafied* entity – one that symbolizes the ways in which our personal lives and information are turned into data forms by media corporations and ourselves alike, whether consciously or not, and used for surveillance, marketing and ideological encoding.

Having personal pages on the website gives the characters an online, disembodied presence besides having a live, visceral existence in performance. In this design, the characters' subjectivity extends to a state beyond the actor's embodiment, but that combines the material presence with an existence in pre-recorded and live online platforms through the website. This hybrid mode of characterization evokes the posthuman subject – that is, a protean combination of the organic and the informational, the material and the virtual. In the playtext, this hybrid characterization is shown openly through stage directions:

> *Performers and author can continuously add material to the 'character' sections. These 'character' sections have the potential of spinning off into their own Websites. [. . .] The original text is the basis for a form that is growing in all directions. The text itself is open-ended and will expand and change as well.* (Jesurun 2009: 168)

This overt explanation highlights that the characters are not merely based on and formed of given directives, but are also shaped in line with an ever-changing media landscape that affects the overall aesthetics of the playtext and characterization. However, the textual indication – for example, stating that a character will appear on camera – merely signals the co-presence of the live and the mediated. The posthuman is communicated in the playtext by the non-linear, disjointed and instruction-based form of the text that refuses to provide a recognizable representation of the world and the human subject as a coherent, stable and uniform totality. The conversation often quickly jumps from one topic to another – in one moment it is about grief for a lost child, then it is about a dog called Lucifer, then it moves to the song 'Perfect Day', while continually referring back to earlier fragments of information and found text. Also, each time a scene or a conversation ends, it does not lead to a graspable conclusion or a tangible connection with earlier scenes and conversations. Through unstable language and unidentifiable character presentation, Jesurun presents a space of uncertainties and hard-to-pin-down moments, purposely avoiding a firm structure that would otherwise allow us to locate characters and narrative. These aesthetic choices are political ones that critically speak to our perceptual encounter with a mediatized world and how we are positioned as subjects in it; namely, how we have become over-stimulated, info-loaded, short-attention-spanned, multi-sensorial beings.

The computer-speak that the characters use also tells of posthuman subjectivity in *Firefall*. It suggests a critical connection to how our perception of reality has changed with our use of new technologies – for example, in our information-obsessed culture we constantly seek and consume information; we 'cyber-stalk' people; we enter personal information onto the internet and become 'editable' and, surely saleable, information assets. The fact that characterization is constantly created as the actors add information onto the website and to the characters' sections also corresponds to our online identities which are an extension and part of our subjectivity. The idea of the human subject as information structure or cybernetic organism beyond its organic, material body can be inferred in certain moments as when a character suggests that they will 'delete' another character, or, when characters hint at their disembodied presence: 'PEEWEE: So we're just wandering voices trying to connect to disembodied bodies?' (Jesurun 2009: 192). Characters appear to be disembodied, impermanent corpora of data, a hybrid of the material and the informational, representing our speedy consumption of information, our fast-paced social communication, as well as our objectification of others.

Throughout *Firefall*, the characters' interpersonal relations speak to how we perceive the *I* and the *other*, and how our relationality has evolved in a mediatized environment. To elaborate, the characters are not connected through a recognizable spatio-temporal context. However, the co-presence of the characters in the virtual realm (e.g. they can delete or edit one another on the website) insinuates a relationship among the characters communicated through and shaped by the logic of new technologies. The hybrid ontology suggests a layered mode of intersubjective relations – embodied and disembodied – that signifies relationality beyond a physically shared environment. This form reflects on our widely networked society, our digital connectedness to one another through the internet without having to be in the same space. *Firefall* offers more than a mere reference to our mediatized relationships. In both spaces, the characters are fundamentally related to one another through the directives, which to an extent objectify and even dehumanize them as instruments or constructs within a system – cogs in the machine. Their interactions, as a result, are majorly based on the given instructions that define their ontology and, hence, are devoid of intimate, individual, self-created relationships. Similarly to the characters in *Pornography*, Jesurun's characters seem to be indifferent to one another outside the context of their roles, their direct and online communication with each other notwithstanding. The play opens with a reference to this sense of apathy and social fragmentation. Here, Mary talks about how a wannabe writer used her and the death of her child as artistic material and ended up in politics: 'The idea is to take someone and make something out of them. For yourself. Making something out of someone else's soul. That's why she ended up in the city government' (Jesurun 2009: 169). This scene is a thought-provoking take on how we objectify other humans – an act normalized and reinforced by capitalist individualization and media sensationalism which promotes the dehumanization of others outside the egocentric subject or self-interested group.

The majority of the characters continually refer to the idea of being a group with an unspecified job they need to fulfil. They often identify their sense of togetherness in relation to comfort, familiarity and belief: 'R: But don't you find yourself in the comfort and familiarity of the group?' (Jesurun 2009: 175). Nevertheless, despite the initial and surface solidarity this connection may suggest, the underlying scenario reveals that the familiarity, comfort and group belief are all based on an unquestioning consent to the given directives, the unknown job and the subordinate position they are put in. At times, ISCARIOT and PEEWEE attempt to question this homogeneous, subservient state:

> **K** Cover your ears. That's what I do.
> **ISCARIOT** Isn't that what you do all the time to maintain your group belief?!
> [...]
> **R** You've tainted the air of belief, the very nature of ...
> **MARY** ... submission.
> **F** Love, devotion, and surrender.
> **ISCARIOT** My mind will not change. Can you break it for me?
> [...]
> **R** If we do it, it may maim you, and you will go around limping like us.
> [...]
> **MARY** ... But believing all the same.
> **ISCARIOT** You have to submit willingly.
> **PEEWEE** And be a pawn and a fool like you. (Jesurun 2009: 176)

Considering particularly ISCARIOT's resistance to be a part of the group – 'Don't want to be. [. . .] Give up what I was born with – my independence' (Jesurun 2009: 175) – we gather that opposition and dissidence are not acceptable. We know from before that a character who does not comply with the group belief or the directives can be *rewritten* or *deleted* from the website, the group and supposedly from the play. ISCARIOT eventually 'give[s] [his] mind to the belief' (Jesurun 2009: 180). Performing his directive – '*changes sides as is convenient to his own interest, which is being on the winning side*' – that already makes him a part of the system and the group (Jesurun 2009: 167), he shifts to the dominant side: 'I believe, and find myself among you' (Jesurun 2009: 180). This scene hints at the deliberate exclusion of dissensus from the dominant social order. In our post-political world, where we are continually deceived into the idea that consensus is democracy and that there is no alternative to the contemporary mode of globalized capitalism, the intersubjective relations in *Firefall* sarcastically suggest that '[a]cceptance creates strength and certainty' (Jesurun 2009: 180).

Jesurun's characterization rethinks our subjectivity both as individuals and as relational beings, and reveals what is often invisible in our liberal-humanist understanding of the subject as a self-directed individual, maintained by late capitalism and its metaprocesses. In this respect, the play redefines our subjectivity as deindividuated, posthuman and objectified, and also uncovers the connection between this mode of subjectivity and the globally mediatized, late capitalist system. The form of characterization on a textual level along with the references to the website and internet/computer aesthetics functions as an aesthetico-critical tool accentuating how media technologies and our mediatized existence are a fuel and instrument of this sociopolitical structure. In so doing, the text as the source for performance initially offers a rupture in the accustomed paradigm and representation of subjectivity from within the mediatized state so as to disrupt and transgress it. Relatedly, this critical space, inviting unconventional thinking about our selfhood, challenges the dominant ideas of subjectivity and points at alternative perspectives on our collectively agreed-upon mode of being. The live performance of Jesurun's playtext elaborates on these alternative outlooks.

Firefall: Performing the 'homo media' on stage

Jesurun's playtext, as stated earlier, is a foundational element of the intermedial performance that enhances what the text offers through the online and offline collective work of the actors and the director. Therefore, the entirety of the performance can be considered as an outcome of the 'co-evolution between writing, forms of performance, and technology' (Jesurun 2012: 121). *Firefall* opened at the Dance Theater Workshop in New York in 2009 after being developed in collaboration with students from the New School in New York City in 2006. On stage there were seven performers, excluding the eighth performer who appeared as JESUS and only on video. The set created the feeling of an office: all the performers sat at tables with individual laptops in front of them through which they drew pre-recorded and live material from the *Firefall* website and from various others, and communicated with one another via iChat. Characters–performers managed their individual webpages; they added and took away material and live-streamed numerous texts such as music videos and news clips. All the computer-based activities were made visible to the audience via eight screens. For example, the audience saw the online chat windows and the characters' communications in one screen, while, at the same time, they could see *New York Times*' headlines or read 'murder of a lawyer shocks Russians' on a different news media website. In addition to the vast eight screens behind the performers onto which pre-recorded material and live images from the performers' laptops were projected, there was also a live camera and two video projectors. The projections were divided into four images drawn from live and pre-recorded sources, creating a fragmented, patchwork-like visual backdrop – somewhat similar to how Nübling used Brueghel's painting in *Pornography*. While some of the images remained static during the onstage action, others were moved – a character scrolled down a page or did research online. When a video played on a screen, the live performance on stage *froze* – in a similar way that an image freezes on our computer or television screens when we press 'pause' – and the audience were exposed to another fragment of a scene, an old recording of one of Muhammad Ali's boxing matches or a news report on current affairs in Australia. The entirety of *Firefall*, with the patchwork of images incorporated into the live performance of the pre-written text, acknowledged the combined reality we live in, our fragmented and multi-perspectival consciousness and attention, and our posthuman subjectivity.

Throughout the performance, the multi-layered, disjointed design refused a sense of narrative depth or coherence. Instead, the composition was a 'live collage' of images that flowed without forming a unity as '[n]one of these sites relates to each other but they exist as the actors' own research and files saved on their laptops as well as new ones they are browsing during the performance' (Marranca 2010: 18–19). Furthermore, in line with the overall design, the idea of linear time and specified space was disrupted, problematizing a recognizable, logical relation to reality, as we know it from traditional dramatic representation. Jesurun's composition offered a theatrical landscape and experience that defied '"authored" realism, [namely] presenting a fake reality', and 'show[ed] what it is like on a stage to create meaning in the moment' (Collard 2017: 13), particularly in the current highly technologized environment. In relation to this, the production undermined the familiar notion and experience of subjectivity and challenged the known ways of representing individual and social ontology. It explored meanings of the subjective and the intersubjective in a mediatized age in which our lives and consciousness are too inundated with technologies and their socio-cognitive, political repercussions to consider our individual position from without.

Figure 6 *Firefall*. Photo credit: Paula Court.

Drawing from multiple sources throughout the performance, which sometimes led to a vertiginous number of projected images to grasp, the characters did not merely generate a collage of information on stage. But, through their online–offline presences, namely, their moves in and out of the website and the internet, all of which were intermingled in the here-and-now of the performance, the characters also oscillated between various states. While at one point a character might be talking about her dog or their unidentified role in this enigmatic setup, in another minute she might present a piece of news from a news broadcasting website or play a music video on YouTube. Considered in line with the non-linear design of the playtext, the fragmented form of the intermedial performance (including the characters' live on-screen presence) emphasizes the fluidity and multi-layeredness of identity in relation to constant mediatization. In addition, the repeated references to recognizable texts such as songs, novels and news material suggest the idea of identity in the making, that our subjectivities are constructed through our exposure to and engagements with cultural, social, economic and political realities. This is certainly not a new discovery about our subjective position. However, *Firefall* particularly stresses how our sense and experience of selfhood have become increasingly multi-layered, hybrid and changeable. Additionally, even though the characters on stage had control over their own webpages and what online or pre-recorded material they chose to incorporate into the onstage action, their actions and decisions were still based on the given directives. The character was not a recognizable individual with psychological depth and unique personality, nor was the actor an identifiable embodiment of this character on stage. On the contrary, both were, to some extent, devoid of individuality and agency, objectified into instrumental entities, into 'positive, useful objects' (Jesurun 2009: 194) as the character F identifies. The fact that the characters can be modified, rewritten or deleted also underlines the idea of the human as no longer an individual with full autonomy, but a being whose subjectivity constantly shifts in line with the media-driven environment she lives in. This emphasis on the condition of the contemporary human, the *homo media*, is particularly relevant in the context of our contemporary overexposure to images and information that *Firefall* aesthetically and thematically captures.

The use of technologies in *Firefall* offers both a semiotic hybrid of the live and the mediatized, and also an ontological one that evokes our posthuman subjectivity. The individual webpages are extensions of the characters/performers that suggest that the on-stage body oscillates between and merges the material and the mediated, the organic and the technological. This hybrid subjectivity destabilizes the liberal-humanist view of the character and actor with reference to the contemporary human through continual emphases on a disembodied, mediatized subjectivity. For example, fact-checking and rewriting a character indicates a state of *being* that is no longer ontologically stable and permanent, but immaterial and virtual. This was in evidence when characters decided to delete JESUS, who appeared on screen, and turned the screen off. As the image of JESUS disappeared, he was no longer present in the virtual world or the here-and-now of *Firefall* – as a character or an image. Such instances play with the idea of subjectivity as material and organic and point to the multidimensional aspect of our beings in the age of media. The portrayal of the mediatized subject as posthuman was also visible in the use of the website not only as an extension of the characters but also as a character in itself – an artistic response to and engagement with the disembodied, technologized, cyborg aspect of the posthuman subject. The camera and the screen projections were the visible, material extensions of this cybernetic character. Creating a website and taking its use beyond a mere dramaturgical and scenographic instrument to another level of semiotic and critical presence, which is reminiscent of such contemporary realities as artificial intelligence, virtual avatars and online collective memory, Jesurun draws attention to our inevitable posthuman state without offering or indoctrinating a specific understanding of it.

The connection of the characters through the internet and their computer-based communications with one another are directly suggestive of our intersubjective relations in today's networked world. What was striking about the media-based interactions on the stage was that the characters often communicated with one another through the internet even when in the same physical space. This mode of mediated communication between live performers on stage produced intriguing images: a character speaking to an image of another character on the screen, or the other way around, a disembodied character such as JESUS speaking to the embodied characters on stage. Moreover, throughout their conversations, the characters only occasionally looked at each other and made eye contact and, even when they did, their gestures and facial expressions were dispassionate and indifferent. It is interesting that one of the rare moments that the characters interacted physically on stage was when they held hands and virtually replicated an online group chat, fact-checking data and editing the text in line with their directives. What this setup suggests is not very alien to our everyday lives where people are too immersed in their phones at tube or dinner table to have a conversation or make eye contact, or where we prefer texting our friends and family instead of calling because phoning someone is perceived as more demanding and intimate. Symptomatic of our mediatized social ontology, Jesurun's design provides a rather disconcerting, yet at the same time, thought-provoking picture of our increasingly deindividuated and alienated subjectivity – a picture about who we have become as an *I* and as *we* in the mediatized age.

Conclusion: Resistant aesthetics of characterization

Pornography and *Firefall* present a model of characterization that reflects on the human subject as deindividuated, posthuman and socially alienated. While engaging with this theme, *Firefall* makes the connections between subjectivity and mediatization clear through a media-based dramaturgy, scenography and performance. On the other hand, *Pornography* offers more implicit, and perhaps unconscious, links to our media-saturated culture and, relatedly, our media-driven subjectivities. Nevertheless, whether they engage with mediatized being explicitly or implicitly, both plays undermine traditional dramatic representation and the liberal-humanist concept of character that has become increasingly redundant in relation to the fluid, protean, hybrid and multiple subjectivities we experience in mediatized culture.

Destabilizing our accustomed idea and expectations of what a character is through a no-longer-dramatic, non-humanist design, these plays subvert and call into question our subjectivity. As they offer a different aesthetic logic through nameless and directive-based characters with limited agency or psychological depth, and through dispassionate intersubjective state and language use, these plays do not suggest the end of 'character', nor 'bemoan the lack of an already defined image of the human being' (Jürs-Munby 2006: 18). Rather, they reconsider the representation of the human in theatre and propose compelling possibilities for addressing our current state as homo media. They expand our definition and understanding of who we are and how we relate to the self and other beyond the boundaries of the capitalist, liberal-humanist notion of subjectivity. They expose the intricacies of our individual and social ontology, and how they are radically shaped by new technologies, media culture and the late capitalist order.

Through their subversive aesthetics, these plays open dissident, critically engaging vistas for thinking about the mediatized environment we are perceptually, ontologically and experientially immersed in. This suggests a rethinking of and resistance to the consensual idea of the human subject within liberal-humanist, capitalist social structure from within the very same structure and by using its technologies and discourses. This formal gesture from within is a political act, a dissident intermission, that is embedded within the internal politics of the plays in a way that negates its own traditional structures and, therefore, allows us to have an alternative view on the self and the other, or the society in general, both in theatre and in real world. In relation to this, one wonders how playtexts further such questioning from within through the entirety of their composition, namely, through plot structure, and what meanings they would offer if and when subversive internal politics accommodates a similar antagonistic intermission.

5

New designs for the mediatized world

Plot structure

Plot: The shape of reality – from perception to reflection

Plot structure forms a play's overall design and encompasses the other theatrical pillars such as characterization, theme and language under its architecture. The *form* of a plot reflects on the *form* of reality, namely, on the organization of our perception of the world we live in. Hence, like the other components we have explored thus far, plot evolves through history and in relation to the changing sociocultural, political and technological conditions and structures through which we identify the world and our existence in it.

In his seminal essay, 'The Work of Art in the Age of Mechanical Reproduction', Walter Benjamin writes: 'The manner in which human sense perception is organised, the medium in which it is accomplished, is determined not only by nature but by historical circumstances as well' (1969: 5). The technologies we have created throughout history have been one of the crucial factors shaping our historical, material conditions. Today, where media technologies develop more rapidly and are more pervasive in our lives than ever before, our view of and relation to reality is different from how it was organized by the social and technological conditions of the 1980s and 1990s, for example. If you saw the iconic *Back to the Future* films at the cinemas or on analogue TVs and VHS players in the 1980s, you will remember that headsets, handheld tablet computers and videoconferencing technologies represented in the film seemed like distant future dreams. It was hard for us to comprehend what the world would be or feel like if, like Marty's future kids, we could wear headsets to watch TV, or could video call anyone anywhere in the world, let alone having a computer as small as a book and accessing global news and other information instantaneously through it. A sharp personal memory confirms this view: during the *hot* days of the Gulf War in 1990–1, which was troubling nearby countries like my homeland Turkey, we used to gather around a radio in the classroom and wait desperately for the news about the war. Information sources and communication technologies were more limited than they are today, and a globally networked world or self-broadcasting on personalized, social media was distant, if not non-existent in our minds. We perceived and related to the world differently – geographical and cultural distances were bigger, life was slower, we had longer attention spans, spent more time with each other than on our personal technologies, and our understanding of surveillance did not involve the self-surveillance (sousveillance) that we experience in today's selfie culture. Almost forty years on, the landscape of our socio-cognitive existence has radically changed with the increasing ubiquity of digital technologies, and the fast-paced, information-loaded, globally networked environment they have produced – a point I will return to later. Where our access to information about the Gulf War was restricted in the 1990s, we are now bombarded with information to the extent that it has become difficult to discern which is accurate. For the 'digital natives' – the young 'who were born into the digital era and are growing up exposed to the continuous flow of digital information' (Dingli and Seychell 2015: 9) – these technologies and socio-cognitive changes are integral parts of their everyday existence. For those of us that could easily identify with the scene I presented above, they have produced a new worldview that we have adapted to. Nevertheless, without doubt, regardless of whether one is a digital native or immigrant, how we identify reality in the contemporary moment is radically *mediatized*, rendering our being and consciousness unintelligible and unrepresentable outside this greater *form*.

To return to the concept of plot, one wonders: if the *form* of the reality perceived has transformed in line with the technologies of today, how has the *form* of the stories we tell in theatre about this world, these technologies and their sociocultural, cognitive repercussions changed? To what extent do contemporary plays, following the Aristotelian plot structure, relate to the mediatized contemporary? What are the formal and critical implications of the no-longer-dramatic plot design, and how does it respond to our media-saturated environment? The previous chapters have hinted at these questions and pointed towards the focus of this chapter: *mediatized plot structure* – its aesthetics and critical implications. In what follows I scrutinize Douglas Maxwell's *Helmet* (2002) and Caryl Churchill's *Love and Information* (2012). While the plot of the former draws overtly on the computer game format of the time, the latter presents a less explicitly formal engagement with specific technologies. Besides their directly and implicitly mediatized plots, the plays also offer disparate aesthetic approaches to plot composition – dramatic and no-longer-dramatic – that suggest different modes of engagement with the outside world and, relatedly, different critical implications. After analysing the plot structures of these mediatized plays on a textual level, I consider the ways in which the media-centred or mediatized design of the text translates to the stage design and action, and what meanings these onstage formations offer. To this end, I will explore the plays' first productions: *Helmet* by Paines Plough and Traverse Theatre at the Traverse in 2002, and *Love and Information* directed by James Macdonald at the Royal Court Theatre in London, 2012.

Helmet: Dramatizing computer games

Theatre has become increasingly more interested in the genre and aesthetics of computer games with the rise of digital technologies. Recently, various theatre practitioners have used games as central constituents while devising work, such as Blast Theory's *Can You See Me Now?* (2001) and Rimini Protokoll's *Best Before* (2010). Both of these productions use the computer games' interactive design features as a tool to involve the audience in the performance process. For example, *Best Before* transfers the multiplayer computer game structure from a virtual space to the intimate setting of the auditorium by giving the audience gaming controllers with which they direct their avatars in response to the questions asked. In *Can You See Me Now?*, which takes place simultaneously in the virtual realm and on the streets, players from all over the world play the game online in a virtual city against the members of Blast Theory, while actual players/actors on the street are tracked by satellite and guided by the online gamers. And yet, while theatre companies and performers have explored and implemented game aesthetics, there has not been much evidence indicating playwrights' interest in this genre.

Douglas Maxwell's *Helmet* is possibly one of the early examples of a playtext that overtly remediates game aesthetics through its plot structure. The story revolves around two characters: Sal, in his mid-twenties, is an Indian man who has lived in Scotland all his life. He owns and runs the computer game shop Zone, which he considers his last chance to show his father that he can be as successful as his brother. However, Sal fails in this as he has recently bankrupted the shop. Roddy (aka Helmet) is a teenager obsessed with computer games and regularly visits the Zone to escape the bitter memory of his brother's death and the hardships of his dysfunctional family.

The play opens in the Zone; Sal is closing down the shop as Roddy comes in and tries to keep the shop open for longer. Roddy, who is infatuated by computer games to an extent that he experiences outside reality through the lens of games, treats the shop's closure as another challenging 'game', and accordingly tries his best to 'survive' in the Zone as long as possible, even if this means taking dramatic steps. Noticing this, Sal repeatedly tries to convince Roddy to get a 'real' life like other children, to go out and play 'real' sports rather than their simulated versions in the games. Nevertheless, Sal is Roddy's idol; he wants to be the owner of the shop. At the play's opening, he also wants to buy the updated version of a game – a 'new and flashier' one (Maxwell 2002: 39). As the play moves forward, we see that Roddy's obsession with games is an act of escapism from his unhappy household which is haunted by the death of his brother; meanwhile, Sal becomes more paranoid about his wife's potential affair with his brother and resents himself for not having followed his dream of becoming a stand-up comedian.

Helmet inventively presents this story through a plot design that remediates the form of computer games. Every scene is a level and there are five levels in total; each character has three lives. Every so often, the characters lose lives, or their energy levels drop when, for example, they become upset about something said or implied. Also, they gain lives when they feel happy or satisfied about something. When one loses a 'life' the action halts, and then reverts to a few minutes earlier. The characters then pick up where they stopped as if nothing has happened. Each time a scene is replayed, the narrative moves on a little further, but with different outcomes. There is a continual play-fail-replay-succeed sequence; until the characters make a successful manoeuvre, the level remains incomplete and they cannot move onto the next one. Before analysing *Helmet*'s mediatized plot structure in detail, it is useful to grasp some of the key aspects of the computer game genre and aesthetics, and briefly consider the connections between dramatic structure and game design.

Computer games can be defined as 'any form of computer-based entertainment software, either textual or image-based, using any electronic platform such as personal computers or consoles and involving one or multiple players in a physical or networked environment' (Frasca 2001: 4). They are based on a representational system that generates a virtual make-believe world, a simulation imitating real-life situations. Similar to ancient societies, which 'regarded games as live dramatic models of the universe or of the outer cosmic drama' (McLuhan 2001: 257), videogames often contain insights into sociocultural, political circumstances. Some examples are games simulating the Iraq War or the American-led 'war on terror' in Afghanistan, or games representing celebrity fetish culture as in *The Sims: Superstar*, which allows gamers to become celebrities next to the simulations of real-life celebrities such as Marilyn Monroe and Jon Bon Jovi. The virtual world of games is complete and self-contained as a structure in that it is based on predetermined rules and narratives, generally centred on a conflict or puzzle to be solved by the players by associating themselves with characters through role-playing and achieving tasks. The narrative moves forward as the player manoeuvres, overcomes obstacles and achieves the ultimate goal, indicating a linear narrative and structured time, developing towards a logical finale. Hence, computer games are interactive media forms. Players are at the core of the action as it is their input – manoeuvres, flaws and achievements – that determines the course of the game within the boundaries of the game's design. Besides their interactive parts, games also contain non-interactive segments such as cut-scenes, breaks or intermissions, requiring little or no player input. Along with their interactive and non-interactive layers, games also have a multi-plot structure. Often, through the 'replay' pattern, players can experience multiple possibilities, plots and alternative realities and discover and map these potentialities.

Computer games have roots in the age-old traditions of make-believe, narrative and, hence, drama and theatre. The concept of drama has continually been brought into play in game design and studies: 'games, as the word "play" reminds us, are intrinsically dramatic, enactments of life situations at varying levels of abstraction' (J. Murray cited in Dixon 2007: 601). Games are constructed through a similar framework to that of Aristotelian drama. Drawing on Aristotle's *Poetics*, in *Computers as Theatre*, Brenda Laurel underlines this aspect and argues that the 'Aristotelian paradigm is more appropriate to the state of technology to which we are trying to apply it' (Laurel 1991: 36). Aristotelian theatre is based on mimesis, the creative imitation of action with a linear plot structure; the coherent unfolding of a conflict towards the climax and then resolution; unity of action, time and space; and identifiable characters. Aristotelian theatre also aims to draw the audience into the heart of this representational world through identifying with the characters. Computer games aim to generate a similar experience. The audience's identification with the character here is a central distinguishing feature since, as Steve Dixon argues, it is 'closer within a videogame than in traditional theater [. . .] the audience is the participant, the participant is the player, the player is the character' (2007: 601). *Helmet* and its game-based plot structure, as we shall see shortly, repeat the Aristotelian aesthetics that traditional drama and the game genre adhere to. To what extent could this technologically inspired play with a traditional dramatic plot design reflect on the ways in which we perceive and experience the world in a mediatized age? What are the meanings generated through the form of the plot in relation to how our perception of reality is organized?

At the opening of the play, Maxwell provides some 'Instructions': the setting is 'The Zone', a half-empty computer games shop. It is the end of the day. Maxwell explains the structure of the play in a way that a computer game would be introduced before the player starts the game: there are five levels to the game, some of which are for two and others for a single player; there are power-ups, special effects, graphics and so on. 'The Story' – another element of game design – summarizes the narrative of the play, and exactly as it would happen in a computer game, the 'Instructions' section ends with a 'Good luck' note, emphasizing the game aesthetics at the heart of the playtext we will soon read, and partly suggesting that the target readers (potentially the performers) are the *Helmet* game's players. Although stage directions are often not considered in relation to plot structure, here Maxwell extends the mediatized design outside the plot. This not only presents an early entrance into the play's dramatic world but also underlines the game format that is embedded in, remediated and adapted through *Helmet*'s composition and content. This direct and explicit mediatization that we see before the play begins continues consistently throughout *Helmet*.

The five levels of the play are built within the linear framework of two hours: Level 1 starts at 7.05 pm and the final level ends at 9.08 pm. Apart from Level 4, analysed later in this section, each level contains a number of replays leading to the 'appropriate' instance which facilitates the 'player' moving to the next level. The play opens with Sal 'performing [the] last rites' of closing the shop at 7.05 pm on a Tuesday evening – he switches off the screens, sets safety alarms and does all the final checks. This scene is interrupted when Roddy enters, surprised at finding the screens off. Sal tries to persuade him to leave the shop, and upon Roddy's refusal, becomes violent and kicks him out of the shop. At this point, the stage directions indicate: '*RODDY dies. Death noise, blackout, life lost on screen*' (Maxwell 2002: 22). What follows this scene is its replay; it is again 7.05 pm, Sal carries out exactly the same closing ritual, Roddy enters and they bicker, this time with more insistence and resistance from both sides. Then, as Roddy loses energy, he asks where Sal's wife is, which reminds Sal of his paranoia about his wife's adultery, and he 'dies'. The following scene shows the time as 7.11 pm; it opens with Roddy's question to Sal, this time with a different answer and attitude, changing the direction of the action. This scene is followed by two others, the latter finishing at 7.25 pm, with Sal insisting that Roddy leaves, giving him 'a long hard look of disgust as the lights go down to blackout' (Maxwell 2002: 29). Level 1 repeats parts of the same scene five times with different outcomes each time, leading to a different restarting point, until every replay reaches the ideal point for the dramatic action to culminate in the predetermined ending before moving to Level 2.

Helmet is filled with such scenes with the replay feature. Nevertheless, the beginning of Level 3, using the same plot tool, is particularly important and worth exploring here because of its critical thematic content, a point I will return to later in the chapter. Level 3 starts at 8.45 pm: Sal and Roddy are having a discussion about an upcoming game with Sal criticizing the media industry's bombardment of individuals with new and flashier products. Roddy, on the other hand, seems to have earned the necessary money for this new game. However, as the dialogue moves forward, it turns out that, rather than earning it, Roddy stole it from a woman after punching her in the street. As Roddy reveals this, *'as if telling the punchline to the world's funniest joke'* (Maxwell 2002: 43), Sal freezes with confusion and phones the police. The scene halts. The pause at this instance hints at the moral function of games, which inculcates their players with certain values, here warning at an amoral act. The next scene starts at 8.50 pm from the point where Roddy is about to talk about how he punched a woman and stole her money. Yet this time, instead of exposing the ugly truth about the source of his money, he changes his mind and moves the story in a different direction by telling a story about how his brother died in a fire when he was one year old. At this point, the level ends and the next level starts which focuses on Roddy's sad memory of his little brother.

The replay pattern at the core of the plot seems to generate a multi-plot narrative as opposed to a one-dimensional plotline. The succession of scenes does not appear to occur in the conventional consecutive manner, whereby the initial point leads directly to the second and then to the third with complete consistency. Rather, the plot is structured in a looping manner, so a scene stops, starts over, moves forward, halts, starts over again and finally moves forward. This game design element, however, does not suggest a deviation from a linear construct. Even in the most seemingly non-linear games, there are a finite number of levels, manoeuvres and plot variations. The looping time structure does not entirely violate linearity and coherency, yet expands the temporal dimension to the extent that the linear timeline coexists with looping time, the constant possibility of a rewind and restart. No matter how many different plots a gamer creates, the 'successful' action leads to the 'next' point in the narrative, and the game finishes in designated ways that are fundamentally similar. Likewise, in *Helmet*, the time is structured in a linear manner and action is unified. The replays always lead one scene to the next, chronologically and thematically. In other words, the story still evolves and time moves forward as shown in the numbered titles (levels) of the scenes, with an indication of the elapsing time continuum. Hence, the replays follow a well-structured dramatic plot in which every resetting or mini-plot serves the dramatic illusion and the dénouement, the 'game over' point. Considering this, although one might initially think that the resets in *Helmet* undermine the unified, chronological sequence of events we know from the traditional

Aristotelian form, the play actually reproduces the traditional dramatic form through its mediatized plot structure.

In addition to replays, *Helmet* remediates 'cutscenes' – an element often seen in computer game design. Cutscenes are predetermined, fixed and non-interactive narrative components of a game. They are 'embedded narrative element[s]' (Salen and Zimmermann 2004: 408) which are essential to narrative-based computer games. In Maxwell's composition, cutscenes can be associated with certain dramaturgical elements such as the 'Instructions' section at the very beginning of the play, the stage directions indicating the energy levels (projected onto the screen on stage), and the monologue-based narrative in Level 4. The Instruction part, for example, 'fills the role of both prequel and epilogue' (Salen and Zimmermann 2004: 408) and serves to guide and inform the reader. Level 4, on the other hand, pauses and expands on the dramatic action, in the gameplay format, as it presents background information. Here, Roddy narrates his childhood memory about his little brother's death, thus revealing the underlying motive for his escapism from the real world into the virtual world of games. The cutscenes in *Helmet* function as descriptive tools, facilitating the flow of the dramatic narrative rather than disrupting it. Like the resets, the cutscenes serve to create a manageable and identifiable representation of the world with certainty and entirety. They reinforce the uniformed, coherent plot composition and recognizable characterization, space-time and language. Therefore, while remediating game aesthetics through the plot, the play carefully remains within the boundaries of traditional Aristotelian model and reproduces the key aspect of dramatic theatre: the mimetic representation of the outside world as a unified fictive cosmos, and accordingly, of our perceived reality as a uniformed, coherent one.

Besides the mediatized composition, the play also thematically engages with the contemporary world with a focus on consumer capitalism and the connection between disillusionment and virtual reality. Maxwell particularly thematizes consumer capitalism and commodity fetishism through Roddy's constant desire to buy the new version of a game and the struggle that Sal's shop, which mainly has older technologies and games, is facing due to shops with newer, flashier products. In one of the climactic and most shocking scenes in the play, Roddy confesses he attacked a woman and stole her bag to get the money to buy the new version of a game. The callousness of Roddy's attitude and his perception of violence as an acceptable behaviour evoke not only mindless consumerism but also the normalization of violence in the hands of certain media. This particular scene presents an aspect of the prevailing social reality of consumer capitalism where a woman Christmas shopping used a pepper spray on other shoppers or a man died of a heart attack on

Black Friday, and people stepped on him and didn't call 911 (Crockett 2019: The Hustle website). In addition to denoting the wider social phenomenon of consumerism, Roddy's act also addresses individualization and, in parallel, people's indifference to one another. As consumer capitalism promotes self-centred progress and profit rather than collective solidarity, it inevitably leads, as Zygmunt Bauman argues, to a certain degree of indifference to the fate of others. Accordingly, this leads people to perceive even their most unethical acts as acceptable, as Roddy coldly does. The presence of computer games both as the setting (the shop) and the plot device emphasizes the game industry's role in perpetuating neoliberal capitalist ideology. Games are often a key factor in building global markets – merchandising new products embellished with recent technologies, and transferring them into other media products, such as the film and television industries. Similar to other media, games contribute to the 'update culture', the constant release and promotion of new designs, which consequently leads the consumer to update her products by buying their new versions.

Helmet also engages with the mainstream financial success-oriented narrative of 'progressive' capitalism. We learn early on in the play that Sal has bankrupted the shop and, as opposed to his successful, rich brother with a car, house and so on, Sal is identified by himself and by society as a failure. Roddy confirms this social reality: 'He's got an ace car your brother. It's like something from Gran Turismo Two. Miles better than your car. Bindi was talking about him the other day. Says he's rich and he's got a big house, but you have to stay with your mum and dad even though you're married' (Maxwell 2002: 205). This kind of social definition of what success is and how a person should live and behave in line with the dominant social order may lead to disillusionment, as we see in Sal's case:

> **SAL** The real world is rubbish, Helmet. [. . .] I've seen the real world and I give you my word – it's not worth seeing. The real world is vile and horrible and boring and fatally depressing. You just play games and don't let anyone tell you it's wrong. It's not wrong. It's right. That's my problem, that's always been my problem, I actually pay attention to those idiots that bang on about money and jobs and relationships and responsibility. Effort and concentration! (Maxwell 2002: 54)

The discontent that Roddy experiences may at first seem to originate from a different cause: a dysfunctional, unhappy family and the loss of his young brother due to parental negligence. However, albeit not identified distinctly, Roddy and his story evoke the hardships of the working class for whom access to financial and educational success, and monetary security is profoundly difficult, if not purposely prevented. *Helmet* reflects on such disillusionment caused by the demands and living conditions of capitalism which pressurizes individuals, particularly the young who are trying to be successful and start up in life, and often leaves them in a vortex of underprivileged living conditions with psychological repercussions that are not easy to surmount. Disenchanted with the real world, the characters escape to the alternate reality that computer games can provide.

For Roddy, the virtual world becomes an alternative reality that allows him to 'drop out of real life' (Maxwell 2002: 193) and 'makes the time go quicker' (Maxwell 2002: 46). Because of his utter and constant immersion in the game world, it also becomes the lens through which Roddy sees and relates to outside reality – it is the fictional, virtual world that makes the real one bearable and graspable. There are multiple instances where Roddy defines an experience as if he was playing a game rather than having a real-life experience; in the following, he talks about the day he found out about his brother's passing and, panicked, tried to find his father:

> **RODDY**   I was in the car. I sat in the car and thought about Gran Turismo. The screens slowly fade in again. There's two hundred and fifty cars in Gran Turismo and full motion video replays. You have to get different licences and it's dead hard to get the A licence. There are no cheats available. When I got home I had to see a counsellor. He let me play games in his office, but he never played. Except once and he couldn't do it. He didn't even know how to hold the controller. (Maxwell 2002: 527)

He often finds it hard to grasp reality beyond the alternate reality that he submerges himself in:

> **SAL**   That's a game. That's a golfing game for the Playstation. It's not a sport.
> **RODDY**   Golf's a sport.
> **SAL**   Golf's a sport yes, but golf on the Playstation is not.
> **RODDY**   I don't understand this. (Maxwell 2002: 567)

Towards the end of the play, Sal decides to stay with Roddy and play a game. The virtual environment is a landscape away from the roles, norms and values Sal is expected to conform to. The form of escapism here is not the mindless entertainment associated with an unquestioning flight from reality. Rather, it means getting away from the normative roles and values of capitalist society

Sal has been struggling to meet and has decided to leave behind. This sense of escapism evokes a similar pattern in contemporary society caused by our fast-paced, info-loaded, progress- and performance-oriented everyday lives, which the leisure and advertising industries use to promote recreational activities and products that allow for a break, an escape. In Sal and Roddy's case, they seek and find the comfortable 'zone' in the virtual world of games that is away from the unfair conditions of the real world. The escape into virtual reality represents an aspect of our contemporary lives; whether it challenges the underlying material realities and how they condition us remains in question.

Helmet's engagement with computer game design contributes to the increasing conversation between technology and theatre. However, unlike most other plays, *Helmet* incorporates media aesthetics into the heart of the playtext's architecture. The play also intriguingly marries the mediatized plot with a critical focus on themes such as consumer capitalism and the media-shaped perception of reality through the story of two disillusioned characters in a game shop. While addressing important aspects of our mediatized environment through an innovative plot structure that directly adopts and adapts game aesthetics, *Helmet* adheres to the traditional dramatic construct, characterized by recognizable causality, linearly structured time and unity of action. Representing the world as a unified, closed-off totality may be an attempt to make sense of and bring order into a world that is faster, smaller, info-saturated, media-driven and increasingly more precarious than before. However, the traditional tenets of dramatic theatre based on Aristotelian unities, which are still central to many contemporary dramas in the Anglophone theatre practice, no longer comprehensively relate to and critically engage with the socio-cognitive conditions of the age we live in. Plays written in the tradition of dramatic theatre may give a surface glimpse of the sociocultural and perceptual realities of the outside world, mainly through a thematic reference, yet representing this world and how we perceive it as a unified totality seals the play's world off from it. To be more precise, mediatized dramatic representation reproduces the dominant ideology – the homogenous, consensual and static culture of late capitalism that promotes a homogenous perception of reality through media technologies, and hence, obstructs possibilities for critical spaces for dissensus and antagonism. As a result, rather than critically reflecting on and challenging the prescribed narratives of the dominant social order by revealing its machineries and calculated social impact, the mediatized dramatic mode of *Helmet*, similarly to that of Ravenhill's *Faust* and Haley's *The Nether*, imagines the contemporary in an easily identifiable and consumable way. In doing so, the play allows limited openings for subversive views and alternative meanings regarding our perception of the world and its conditions. One wonders what meanings

Helmet on stage would offer and whether the performance of the mediatized plot can go further than the logic and aesthetics of dramatic theatre and offer a critical view of our mediatized culture.

Helmet on stage

Helmet was first staged by Paines Plough and Traverse Theatre Company in 2002 under the direction of John Tiffany, and with the collaboration of a team of digital animation and game designers, a movement director, and sound and lighting designers. Tiffany and the team designed the show within a vast computer game picture frame. As the audience entered the auditorium, they saw the title sequence projected onto the huge white screen showing the names of the two companies and cartoon versions of the characters, similar to how computer games begin. After the title sequence, the middle section of the screen was rolled upwards, while the frame surrounding the screen remained and enclosed the set of the shop, where two actors took the roles of Sal and Helmet. The box-like stage, encircled by the frame, made the set 'look like the inside of a screen with its rapidly receding perspective' (Scott 2002: 626). Energy levels, power bars and bonus points in the shape of hearts were projected onto this digital frame on either side of the stage.

Tiffany's production, in accordance with Douglas Maxwell's plot composition, approximates the computer game format, environment and the gameplaying experience. It remediated some of the major elements of game design such as the rewinding/replaying format, characters with multiple lives and cutscenes. For example, each time a character died on stage, the action stopped and the screen faded to black and then the action looped back to a few minutes earlier. The spectators saw the same scenarios enacted in a different way each time. Thus, the resetting of scenes on stage enacted the replay structure of Maxwell's play. The theatrical performance followed the text's traditional dramatic plot structure and its filtering of 'the old certainties of narrative and dramatic development through a new medium with different rhythms' (Cramer 2002: 372).

Tiffany's production focused on realizing the text in a three-dimensional setting and embedded the game form fully into the dramatic configuration of live performance to an extent that the new medium was indistinguishable from the fictive cosmos and the form of theatrical representation. The remediation process in Tiffany's interpretation served to generate something similar to what J. David Bolter and Richard A. Grusin call *transparent immediacy* (1999: 14) by erasing the mechanics of remediation, representation and making the viewers forget the presence of the medium within theatre. Maxwell accentuated this point and the representational aesthetics underlying the play when talking about his expectations for the production: 'The important thing for me is that while the audience get a buzz from the exciting way the story is told, all the flashing lights and gubbins, it shouldn't act as a barrier to the heart of the characters.'[1] Likewise, the connection between the live action on stage and the computer-generated world of the game, operated along with the logic of immediacy. There was a harmony between the actors/characters and the roles they played in the game. That is, when one of the characters, embodied on the stage by live actors, lost energy or gained lives, the bars on the screen on both sides of the stage concurrently showed this change in their physical and emotional conditions. Also, if a game character lost a life, the live actor on stage would enact dying by collapsing in a stylized way, doing break-dance moves inspired by Tiffany's videogame experiences. After this, the scene would restart. The digital images here functioned as a virtual other to the live actors. Tiffany has indicated this as one of the most ingenious aspects of the play: 'it was like the subtext of the play, what is happening *between* the characters was played on energy levels, projected through bars onto the screen' (Tiffany interview).[2] The juxtaposition of the live and the mediatized not only manifested the coherent plot structure of the play and its mediatized content on stage but also portrayed our media-saturated lives where virtual reality has become a part of our lives and social relations.

The uniform presentation of the two states and ontologies, however, does not speak to the complexities of hyperreality, the inseparable coexistence of the two different states, and how this alters our consciousness. Although there are references hinting at how Roddy saw the world through the lens of games, the production does not tackle this idea through the form of the performance. Rather, the production situates the mediatized within the borders of the fictional world of theatre and creates transparent immediacy as opposed to a critical perspective on hyperreality. The production, as both Maxwell and Tiffany individually underlined, aimed to get rid of anything that was a barrier to 'the audience's love/belief of the characters' (Maxwell interview), to the spectator's empathy with the characters and the represented world. Given that the mechanics of remediation were wiped out to create a sealed-off fictional cosmos, the audience was drawn into the heart of the theatrical illusion. Thus, the idea that the remediated game aesthetics may have defamiliarized the audience due to its presumed difference from theatrical representation is misleading, as Tiffany states: 'people often think that [the play] is alienating, but actually I don't think it is true at all. I actually think it pulls you more into an intimate and honest experience' (Tiffany interview). 'Honesty' in this context refers to naturalistic representation that generates a superficial rather than a critically sensitizing performance and the identification of the audience with the fictional world rather than a self-conscious experience, awakening the spectators to social reality.

Maxwell's explanation of his motives illustrates the play's dependence on traditional dramatic representation and the underlying reasons for the production's adherence to the form and logic of dramatic theatre:

> There is a character, a story, something I want the audience to hook into and love and that's the centre. [. . .] The structure of the story, the way it is told, is thus just the sparkle, the hook. [. . .] I want my audience to love the play. To feel for the characters. [. . .] I want the audience to take them as REAL. I'm not looking to make a point beyond that of these guys' lives. No grand political narrative or analogical pattern lies beyond their story. Their story is all there is. This is about Sal and Helmet and how they feel, not what they mean. (Maxwell interview)

Nevertheless, Maxwell's play does more than telling the story of two characters. The incorporation of game aesthetics into the play's plot composition and thematic context offers intriguing observations about the contemporary sociocultural environment – both on page and stage. The play acknowledges media's influence on our lives with a specific focus on computer games, which could be extended to the context of other media forms such as social media and news-sharing social networking platforms. While addressing mediatized culture, the play adheres to the boundaries of dramatic representation and the sociocultural, ideological conditions this model repeats in the theatrical platform. It reproduces the given and agreed-upon viewpoints of the dominant power structures and, relatedly, affirms the prescribed Form – the structure of the world and our perceptions of it. Therefore, although Maxwell's play undoubtedly represents an innovative experiment with an unusual media form as well as reflecting aspects of contemporary social landscape, its traditional architecture remains limited in offering a provocation that challenges our accustomed views of and relations to the world around us. Caryl Churchill's *Love and Information* offers such a conversation through its plot structure which reflects on the connection between theatrical and contemporary societal form instead of sealing the former off from the latter.

Love and Information: The shape of information age on the page

Information is the prevailing social, political, economic and cognitive base of our current society. It is the very condition and backdrop to our technogenesis, our being, relationships and perception. In this information-rich, widely connected environment, however, exposure to a torrent of information does not always or certainly culminate in a better-connected, more knowing human society. The more we are loaded with information and the more multimedia-tasking we have become, the shorter our attention spans, the more fragmented and fast-paced our perception, and often the weaker our human connections have become. Information overload has brought with it an emotional underload and an increasing sense of apathy as we cannot make meaning of and relate empathetically to the sheer volume of information. Hence, we experience information fatigue, information pollution, information anxiety and the desire for techno-detox. Equally, therefore, we find it hard to engage deeply with and respond to information, for example, about climate change, the migration crisis and Brexit because there is too much for our minds to process, manage and responsibly sympathize with. We feel connected to the stories and we identify with them, yet only for a short fraction of time until another bite-sized piece emerges for us to consume. In this ecology, where we are bombarded with and also love and depend on information we, at the same time, tend to feel a rising sense of loneliness, disconnection and the need to connect with and love other people.

Churchill's *Love and Information* reflects on the shape of the information age, namely, on the shape of our perceptions, relationships and subjectivity that have evolved as a result of our info-driven lives. In relation to this, it considers isolation, betrayal, loyalty, desensitization, disinformation, memory and identity, and weaves them together with the central focus on information to consider how we respond to and evolve as a result of the information overload we are subjected to. In dealing with this considerably complex subject, Churchill displays various aspects of the big picture rather than giving a straightforward, single-sided answer. While, in some scenes, the characters are invigorated and satisfied by language, in others they are numbed or confused.

The play has seven sections, each of which has approximately seven individually titled scenes. Churchill asks that these seven sections be played in the order given yet provides flexibility in terms of the order of the scenes within each section. There is also an additional section titled 'Random' with nineteen optional scenes – apart from the item called 'Depression', which Churchill stresses is a central part of the play that should be integrated into any section. Each of the seven sections meditates on a loose thematic context – while one deals with memory, another focuses on getting information or on the ethics of information sharing. Nevertheless, there is no unity of action, characterization or space through the seven sections and more than sixty discrete scenes; no scene, situation or character returns; and no dramatic backbone unites them under a uniform universe. Each scene – short, disconnected and incomplete – presents a single situation with generic, recognizable faces ranging from parents and scientists to lovers and colleagues, and with a shared desire for connection and belonging and engaging with the world that is prevented by limited attention. In one scene, we encounter celebrity-obsessed fans revealing meticulous information about a celebrity, in another, two people talk about not being able to sleep because 'head's too full of stuff' (Churchill 2012: 12), then nameless 'spies' discuss the disinformation and political manipulation of information about the war on terror. There are no speech prefixes or detailed information about any of the characters (overall, more than a hundred); and the places are as non-specific and transient as the speaking figures: gym, bedroom, doctor's office, lab and so on. Similar to Christopher Brett Bailey's marathon of words in *THWD*, *Love and Information* bombards our minds with a flood of information, yet in a considerably more disjointed, achronological and multi-layered manner with numerous characters. The scenes flow at high speed, evoking the information overload we experience on a daily basis as we rush from our smartphones to laptop screens to smart watches, or as we surf the internet, clicking on a page, then another one, and then another one, often engaging with the information rapidly and superficially before moving onto another page. The fast-paced and disconnected plot composition purposely leaves little time for the audience to grasp or reflect on a scene before the next begins. *Love and Information* overthrows our attempts at connection, meaning and deep knowledge, engaged perception and focused consciousness.

Churchill, known for her inventive dramaturgical experiments that always relate and respond to sociopolitical subjects, structures the plot here in a way that suggests a profound relationality to the form of the outside world and our perceived reality. Let's consider the intriguing aspects of *Love and Information*'s dramaturgical backbone vertebra by vertebra. The overall architecture of the play is based on a non-linear, non-chronological, fragmented plot: seven discrete sections unfold independently from one another without culminating in an easily identifiable, unified meaning or a representation of the world as a cohesive totality. Instead, the composition of the sections with the appendix puts forward a patchwork of numerous disconnected contexts with different characters, places and conversations that we never encounter again in a different section or scene. The discontinuous and fragmented structuring of the sections that defies a sense of unity of action, space or characterization is emphasized by the suggested integration of fragments from 'Random', particularly from the scene 'Depression' which contains ten lines. The disjointed, non-causative design of the sections hints at various aspects of our information-loaded society and consciousness, particularly speaking to our social alienation and fragmented perceptions. As Churchill stresses with the 'Depression' scene, a key part of the play, this leads to collective and individual depression and to a need for connection – a feeling that the design of the sections persistently hinders.

The scenes push fragmentation to its breaking point: individual scenes flood in, one after another, and each time with new characters, situations, voices and places without ever returning to a previous setting. As I mentioned briefly earlier, the characters, spaces and situations in the scenes are not alien to us. For example, we know of the teenage fans possibly cyber-stalking and obsessing about a celebrity, as well as of the couple or friends who cannot sleep at night and go online. The generic characters are in generic places in the scenes – such as an office or a bedroom. Behind this recognizable picture, however, there is no in-depth information available about who these characters actually are, where and when they are, and what the story is behind their situation. What is it that keeps them awake? Are they men or women? How old are they? Are they a couple or siblings? Putting forward merely surface snapshots of the socio-cognitive landscape and patterns of the information age, these discrete and non-cohesive scenes reflect on some aspects of our mediatized existence – on our fragmented perception and, relatedly, our increasingly superficial engagement with the world and other humans. Ironically, the more we have access to instant and vast amounts of information, the less we know of each other. Information overload has made our realities less intelligible and our intersubjective positions shallower. Furthermore, the brevity of most of the scenes (e.g. 'Keys': 'You don't know where I put the car keys, do you?' (Churchill 2012: 76)) also speaks to our mediatized existence in the late capitalist West, namely, our shorter attention spans and fast-paced lives in a soundbite culture where we have become increasingly accustomed to the experience of the world being broken into intelligible and easily consumable bite-sized pieces (e.g. Twitter posts, sitcoms, web-browsing). Other plays such as Suzan-Lori Parks's *365Days/365 Plays* (2006) present a design that challenges the traditional plot structure through non-causative architecture and short disconnected scenes. Parks's play is based on a combination of 365 plays written everyday throughout a year to be performed in different parts of America. The short plays are not connected through a unified storyline but offer glimpses, snapshots of scenes, speaking to a similar sociocultural reality to that of Churchill's play.

To return to *Love and Information*, besides its fragmented and non-linear plot, the rapid pace of the scenes generates, if not intensifies, the limited and superficial engagement with the content and, therefore, suggests a connection between the form of the plot and the form of the outside world. The short and discrete scenes that appear abruptly one after another without clear logical and temporal order or any in-depth plot development generate the sense of quick snapshots. For example, in Section 5, we swiftly jump from the scene 'Maths', in which a couple debates seeing their friends with whom the male speaker disagrees about maths, to the shorter scene 'Sex' that identifies sex and love as information, and then to 'God', a discussion about the meaning of existence and the questioning of the belief in God as the source of meaning. There is no break between the scenes, but a continual and fast move from one to another. In addition to the speedy flow, the scenes feel incomplete, having neither a clear beginning or end within themselves, nor connecting to one another to generate a linearly developing whole or the unfolding of a unified narrative. This mode of plotting produces a pace that resonates with the rhythm of the digital, our everyday, media-saturated lives in the neoliberal capitalist order where we rush from a video call to multiple screens on our laptops, then to social media platforms and to our smartwatches.

With this pace, the play speaks to the rewiring of our perceptions, represented by our increasingly shorter attention span and weaker memories as a result of high-speed technologies, information overload, and our fast lives in a global information age. Relatedly, it reflects on the fact that we do not deeply or fully engage with, or emotionally and intellectually respond to the information that bombards us. Therefore, although the plot structure evokes a perceptual state and pace that we can recognize, it deliberately defies the possibility of this familiarity leading to a fully identifiable and easily consumable story. We recognize the rhythm – the swift jumps from one snapshot of a scene to another; we also recognize the contexts in the fragments of scenes and conversations: the celebrity-obsession in 'Fan', the desire for and at the same time the anxiety about a technology-free environment in 'Remote', and the stressed, overloaded mind of the contemporary individual and the quick escape to the internet as a solution to insomnia in 'Sleep'. However, none of this leads us to an easily recognizable and tangible epistemological certainty since we cannot generate a whole from the parts with a definite meaning and homogenous view of reality. We do not fully and instantly identify with these characters, their stories and histories, their place and time and so on. Instead, we end up frustrated due to our inability to connect deeply with these stories. Similarly to the flow of social media – a torrent of emails, status updates, newsfeed posts or tweets – the play's short, fragmented and fast structure deprives us of our known, accustomed rhythm of emotional response. Instead, as the play suggests, despite the benefits of this widely networked and information-rich world of ours, the social ecology of 'too much information' has, more often than not, led us to emotional detachment, estrangement and social apathy. Hence, the thinness of the plot structure is beyond a simple mimetic device. It is a critical instrument that questions the socio-cognitive aspects of our information-loaded environment by first reproducing its rhythm and promises, and then subversively unravelling its buried social and perceptual repercussions.

The relationship between characters in the play is telling of this growing social alienation. Any dialogue between characters is superficial; characters appear only once; there is no sense of growth in their relationships. Throughout, we encounter characters that long for a sense of connectedness and belonging, and yet they are obstructed by their inability, inattention and apathy, as well as by the plot's speedy, fragmented form. For example, in 'Climate', one of the characters is incapable of processing the information about climate change, engaging emotionally and critically with the sheer reality of it or taking it seriously:

> There were those emails those scientists, I can't remember the detail
> no it didn't make any difference in the end
> no I think you're right, most scientists all agree it's a catastrophe.
> The question is how bad a catastrophe.
> It's whether they drown or starve or get killed in the fights for water
> I'd choose drowning.
> Are you really not going to take it seriously?
> I don't know how to.
> I don't know how to. (Churchill 2012: 54)

This sense of feeling lost, uncertain and unknowing within an info-rich landscape evokes how media's overload of information – which is often disinformation – about issues such as the refugee crisis, Brexit and climate change results in the majority of people looking away in a state of collective apathy. In addition, even when there is a glimpse of intimacy between characters in scenes such as 'Sex' and 'Virtual', these intersubjective positions are pictured as generic, superficial or automated, or 'liquid' to use Zygmunt Bauman's idea – relationships that are easy to enter and exit and to consume with the mere touch of a button (2003: xii). The supplementary 'Depression' scenes, which are highlighted as an essential part of the play (with the suggestion that they be scattered throughout), in which depressed people are addressed but do not respond, underlines the same collective psychology, weakly connected social ties and increasing indifference in an information-saturated, widely networked social ecology.

Love and Information's reflection on the mediatized age, however, is not a condemnation. Instead, the play offers a cautionary critique of our media-saturated lives and our existence and consciousness in a technologically driven culture of fast and excessive information without overlooking its potential.

The fact that *Love and Information* problematizes dramatic representation while presenting a kaleidoscopic view of our lives in an information-soaked age, and that it defies a risk-free, easily consumable and forgettable portrayal of it, shows that the play does not leave our perceptions unchallenged. Instead, by pushing the *form* – both of the represented and mediatized reality – it positions us in an unknowing and uncertain state. Furthermore, within this plot, the play bombards us with information while continually withholding knowledge, keeping us in a state of wondering, and ambiguity, encouraging us to reflect on our desire for knowledge and meaning-making. The transgression of familiar modes of representation reveals how our being and thinking are sculpted by technologies and the culture these technologies have engendered. In Caryl Churchill's plays, sociopolitical concerns and formal experiments go hand in hand, as Elaine Aston and Elin Diamond highlight in their recent work: 'For Churchill, dramatizing the political is not just a question of content, but also of form. With the renewal of form comes the renewal of the political: new forms and new socially *and* politically relevant questions' (Aston and Diamond 2009: 2). In this respect, the play's resistance to the representation of the world as a unified totality is not merely a formal criticism of dramatic theatre, but also a critical and political reflection on our perception of reality today which is profoundly shaped by pervasive technologies and mediatized culture, and therefore, can no longer be thought with traditional dramatic forms. This formal composition, as a result, situates us in a critically engaged position, allowing for dissident thinking outside the accustomed ways of relating to the world, and challenges how we think about the greater Form that shapes our lives and the stories we tell. Through its plot structure, the play presents a design for a world that is less surveyable and manageable than before as it is based more on multiplicity, fragmentation, changeability and uncertainty than unity and continuity. The subversion of the causative architecture of dramatic theatre, opening inventive cracks in narrative and style, offers an epistemologically and aesthetically challenging design for theatre-makers and audience. The cracks and pores in the dramaturgy of *Love and Information*, framed within certain instructions for performance which we can consider as 'liberating constrictions', to use Duška Radosavljević's idea (2013: 151–8), opens the text to various interpretations on stage and encourages makers and spectators to engage with their social, political and cognitive reality.

Performing *Love and Information*

Churchill's complex playtext was premiered at the Royal Court Theatre in 2012 under the direction of James Macdonald. The stage was constructed as a clinical, open-fronted, white-walled cube and framed behind a screen that closed at the end of each scene with a sudden blackout and opened again for each new scene. The closing and opening of the screen was abrupt, resembling how a camera-shutter closes and opens back up again while taking a snapshot, or evoking how we jump from one page to another when we surf on the internet, flicking through Instagram or Twitter, or simultaneously engage with multiple media platforms, from Pinterest to Gmail to Facebook. Scene changes are also marked by a projected number, and between some of these scenes, we hear sounds such as birdsong, an iPhone ringtone and footsteps. These audio-scenes enact some of the 'Random' scenes Churchill presented at the end of the play. The set design for each scene was minimalistic with bare use of costume and generic props that, like the white-box set, evaded particularities while creating easily identifiable spaces: a couch for a living room, a patch of grass for a patio, a bed for a bedroom.

The set design suggested an intriguing contrast with the personal context of most of the scenes as well as the 'love' in the title. This contrast between dispassionate information structures and humans as emotional beings whose intimate interpersonal connections and subjectivity have been shaped by these structures reflects on the datafication of the personal and on our technology-, information-, media-dependent lives and relationships which render us 'anxious about intimacy', and lead us to 'look to technology for ways to be in relationships and protect ourselves from them at the same time' (Turkle 2011: xii). While designing the performance of Churchill's text, which does not overtly identify any space or location, Macdonald's production interpreted the intentional uncertainties or lack of definition and information in a more precise, naturalistic manner. The scene 'Sleep' took place in a bedroom while 'Lab' took place in a clinical room and so on. Although these onstage places were generic, they generated meanings and cohesion rather than resisting them as in the text. Similarly, Macdonald deployed sixteen actors to embody Churchill's anonymous and non-specific characters, which are not identified with name, age or gender, in a more definitive style. The actors on stage, performing more than 100 characters in 57 self-contained scenes, were easily recognizable: scientists, office workers, lovers. Rather than pushing the limits of dramaturgical uncertainty offered by the text, the production tied down and anchored meaning into a limited number of structures or patterns.

 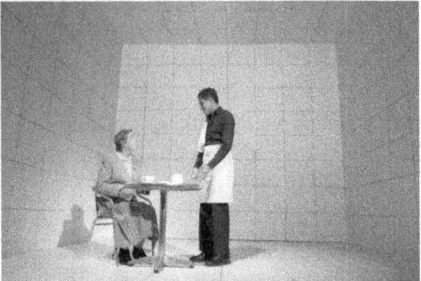

Figures 7 and 8 *Love and Information*. Photo credit: Geraint Lewis.

The coherence of Macdonald's self-contained scenes, however, was undermined as he adopted and adapted the fragmented, disconnected, fast-paced aesthetics of the playtext. On stage, snippets of scenes flowed with no sense of unity or direction; each time after a blackout, the frame-screen rolled up and disclosed another discrete context and conversation between new characters who did not relate to the previous or the following ones. The nonstop, swift staging of one individual scene after another during an uninterrupted two-hour performance, with no connection between the scenes, rendered it impossible for one to arrive at a single, unified meaning or recognizable characters to identify with, and did not allow for the emergence of slow responses. The performance's fragmented form, which continually asks the audience to focus on new content, is hard work: we try to pay attention and grasp the potential meanings while the piece resists our desire to make unified meaning. This mode of staging leaves us no space to think, absorb or fully engage with the content. As individuals living in a media-saturated, info-driven culture, we recognize the pace and the situations that pass rapidly in front of our eyes. The pace is neither alien nor shocking; we, consciously or not, live in and through this tempo of life – sitting in front of the television hopping through the channels and spending a few minutes on each before we switch to another one; emailing someone while on the phone; or checking Facebook on the laptop, while scrolling through pictures on the phone and speaking into a headset at the same time.

However, the familiar tempo and context in Macdonald's production, as Churchill structured it in the text, did not lead to a representation of the information-rich, fast-paced world we live in as a unified whole and our perception of reality as a definite and easily intelligible totality. We *notice* the images and contexts and processed the information in a blink of an eye before we shift to another and then another – putting us in a vertiginous, info-saturated state where a solid, ultimate meaning and knowledge is hard, if not impossible, to arrive at. It is this inability to fully grasp, stay focused on and deeply connect with stories, characters and feelings that invites one to question the implications and meanings underlying the complex, hard-to-digest form and content the play presents. Nevertheless, one may choose to consume the pieces as we might a Facebook post, a tweet or an Insta-video. Yet, albeit this option, *Love and Information* demands critical reflection and emotional engagement when our racing minds and eyes acclimatize to outside reality again after witnessing numerous disjointed images in a flipbook style performance. It creates the desire to *slow down* and think critically about how we tell stories today and about the meanings buried under the avalanche of information.

Conclusion: Dissident plot, de-forming the form of reality

The mediatized plot structures of both *Helmet* and *Love and Information* address our everyday lives and the form of our perceived reality in the contemporary, profoundly shaped by media technologies and by their sociocultural and cognitive repercussions such as information overload, acceleration and fragmentation of perception, and social disintegration. However, as discussed in relation to other dramatic theatre texts such as *Faust, Closer* and *The Nether*, which are based on the dramatic logic of causality and unity, *speaking about* aspects of mediatized culture or incorporating media aesthetics into well-made Aristotelian plot structure does not necessarily involve *speaking to* or critically questioning and emotionally engaging with its complex structures and ramifications.

Maxwell's *Helmet*, which portrays the world as a stable totality – knowable, representable and easily consumable – is based on a vision of reality that can only limitedly reflect on the cognitive and social aspects of contemporary culture that it contextualizes. As mentioned earlier, the play undoubtedly acknowledges certain issues in our current social environment through its narrative content. Nevertheless, the dramatic form of the plot structure, based on order and certainty, does not fundamentally correspond to the form of outside reality, namely, the epistemologically unstable environment of contemporary hyperreal, media-saturated culture, an environment that the use of game aesthetics and motif of virtual reality, as well as the play's content, hint at. The incorporation of game design therefore works mainly as a contextual accessory, adding to the dramatic composition. *Helmet*, in an Aristotelian manner, recoups a notion of order from the increasing uncertainty, multiplicity and even chaotic state of the human condition and consciousness. This sense of absoluteness seals off the play from the actual conditions of contemporary reality rather than relating to it, and therefore closes the text to critical readings, to alternative ways of thinking about the world we live in and how we perceive it. In so doing, the dramatic mediatized plot structure reproduces and retains the image of the outside world as fashioned by the dominant power structures and maintained by the most pervasive of ideological apparatuses, namely, technologies. Reproducing the dominant sociocultural and perceptual patterns through the traditional ingredients of dramatic theatre and using game aesthetics in line with the unitary dramatic framework, the play portrays not the actual, underlying machinery of our reality but a particular way of perceiving the world that adheres to the discursive certainties of late capitalism and defies dissensus against them.

Dissensus is possible in a plot design, be it explicitly or implicitly mediatized, that questions and undermines the status quo and shows its workings, which have become imperceptible to our accustomed minds. Churchill's *Love and Information* presents such an unorthodox composition while addressing the *Form* of our perceived reality – how it is constructed and disseminated through structures such as media – as it refuses to seal off the plot from the world we experience and to treat it as an intelligible and complete whole. In other words, although the play recreates aspects of the information age, it does not reproduce the prevailing social patterns and perceived reality as they are constructed by the dominant ideology and its mechanisms. Instead of a dramatic replication of the outside reality through an easily identifiable, consumable frame, the play's no-longer-dramatic form and thematic reflection on the contemporary push the boundaries of representation, fragmentation and pace, and present a hard-to-digest look into the machinery underlying our perceived reality. As the play problematizes dramatic representation and our accustomed ways of representing the world around us, it also destabilizes our familiar ways of seeing the world that is often shaped and fuelled by capitalism's design to eliminate the possibility for dissidence. The more information we are exposed to, the less we engage with the content of the information, the less political awareness and critical capacity we have to question the system we live in. The play puts such dynamics under a microscope, and goes beyond our surface construction of reality towards the deeper reality of our socio-cognitive and political state, throwing our perceptions and narratives into question. In doing so, it allows us to make the connection between the form of reality presented and the form of reality perceived without uniting them in a definitive meaning or a closed fictional cosmos, opening up cracks in the traditional representational and perceptual structures to allow in critical, dissident viewpoints. While playtexts as we know them have evolved in form and content in relation to mediatized culture, as we have discussed thus far with a focus on various dramaturgical ingredients, there has also emerged a new kind of playtext whose entire dramaturgical formation process and overall form are based on a specific technology. The following and final chapter focuses on such novel plays that I call *mediaturgical plays*.

6

Mediaturgical plays
Writing for theatre through media

Throughout the long history of human storytelling, we have consistently adapted how we tell and shape our stories to the changing environment and techno-ecology. From the cave paintings in the Lascaux Caves, the epics of Gilgamesh and the Bible, Renaissance paintings, and the photo-storytelling of Hiroshima or the Tiananmen Square protests, to digital storytelling on social media today, methods, mediums and forms of storytelling have altered. And, as a part of what I define as our sociocultural technogenesis – *how our cultural expressions change in accordance with technological developments in our society* – the practice of playwriting has likewise changed in relation to prevalent technologies and their social, cognitive impacts. While, as I have discussed thus far, the dramaturgy of plays evolved in relation to mediatized culture, an intriguing change also occurred in the means and medium of writing in relation to the prevalent use of digital technologies, particularly of interactive, participatory services such as social media. Playwrights have written plays *through* such technologies, incorporating the techno-aesthetics of these media into the heart of the plays' composition. These social media-based plays indicated a transformation not only in the fashion and medium of writing for theatre in the 2010s but also in the form, meaning and performance of playtexts, generating a novel aspect of mediatized dramaturgies yet to be explored. This chapter looks into this aspect and advances my study of playtexts in a mediatized culture by reflecting on David Greig's *The Yes/No Plays* (2013–14) – a play that was written via Twitter, shaped in line with Twitter's design and then edited into a live performance piece. I call playtexts such as Greig's *mediaturgical*.

There is a connection between mediaturgical plays, which have digital technologies and their socio-cognitive effects at their core, and the notion of postdigital culture and performance. Matthew Causey identifies the 'postdigital' not as a notion referring to digital technologies and our engagements with them as *bygone*, but one that now preconditions our current cultural praxis. He emphasizes 'the overdetermined relations, circulations, and exchanges of those phenomena [...], a recognition of the many flows and distributions' (2016: 432) of data structures on the internet which define power relations, consciousness and communication. And the idea of the postdigital is, of course, closely connected to the phenomenon of mediatized culture. The former differs from the latter in terms of its specific focus on digital technology and its pervasive sociocultural and cognitive effects, as opposed to the less medium-specific umbrella concept of mediatization. Nevertheless, both notions relate directly to late capitalist society and its metaprocesses. Causey argues that artists who are 'conversant with the language and conceptual frameworks of the digital are thinking digitally in order to respond, engage, and critique the systems of control inherent in the omnipresent networks' (2016: 431). Causey identifies the art work, formed with a consciousness of the digital technologies and ideological machinery within which it resides and from and against which it operates, as a *postdigital performance.*

Although Causey's focus is on performance, the concept of the postdigital is relevant to the study of mediaturgical plays that follows here. Some of these digitally composed texts incorporate not only the technologies but also the sociocultural, perceptual and ideological bearings of the digital, which we as audiences are often too entrenched to engage with critically. Certain mediaturgical plays undermine these phenomena and environments from within. As I shall explore, Greig's *The Yes/No Plays* takes a postdigital stance through its integration of the aesthetics and machinery of Twitter into a no-longer-dramatic form which interrogates our known modes of perception, being and relations – all, to a great extent, regulated by power structures and control systems. By using digital technology along with a no-longer-dramatic design, *The Yes/No Plays* refuses to reproduce the prescribed narratives and viewpoints of the dominant social order. In so doing, it disrupts our accustomed frames of perception – immersed in and inundated with media technologies and the underlying capitalist structure – and offers a multi-perspective, porous view of the contemporary through which it opens up space for critical engagement with our systems of perception and representation. Not all mediaturgical plays use digital forms and platforms with the motivation of critiquing the ideological meanings and machineries underlying these technologies. Adhering to the logocentric paradigm and implications of the dramatic theatre fashion, other playtexts, based in and shaped through digital media, reproduce what is given as rational or normal in an orderly manner and mould differences and uncertainties into an easily identifiable and consumable, homogenous order. Jeremy Gable's *The 15th Line* (2010) was one such playtext – an early instance of Twitter drama and a play that deploys the same micro-blogging technology as Greig's *The Yes/No Plays*, but in a different way and to a different effect.

In this chapter, I will explore mediaturgical plays and their aesthetico-critical workings with a focus on *The Yes/No Plays*, which, I argue, incorporates the form and context of Twitter into its structure in a subversive manner and challenges our mediatized systems of perception and representation. Throughout my analysis of Greig's play, I shall also refer to other mediaturgical plays such as *The 15th Line* and Chris Goode's *Hippo World Guest Book* (2007) to illustrate different takes on digital social technologies, environments and behaviours. In the rapidly evolving age of digital technologies and social media, Greig's and Gable's Twitter plays serve as early examples of dramatic writing engaging formally with social media. While analysing these early formations, we should bear in mind that playwrights and theatre-makers have continued to explore and adapt to the changing features of social media platforms, engendering new modes of texts (textual mediaturgies) – something I will come back to in the concluding chapter.

From mediaturgy to mediaturgical plays

Before analysing these plays, it is necessary to theoretically define the key terms: 'mediaturgy' and 'mediaturgical plays'. Bonnie Marranca originated the term 'mediaturgy' to suggest a shift from a text-centred performance dramaturgy into a media-inspired composition that 'embeds media forms in the performance' (2010: 16). The notion suggests a modulation in critical attention to media aesthetics and language embedded in the composition and delivery of theatre performances that speak to our contemporary media-saturated lives. Nevertheless, in a similar vein to postdramatic theatre theory, the concept of mediaturgy does not suggest a complete break from the dramatic text and its textual traces and meanings. Rather than being anti-text or non-textual, mediaturgy extends dramaturgy to enable us to concentrate on the new language of performance, and those elements which are not a part of the narrative but embedded in or foundational to it, without excluding or hierarchizing the textual elements and overtones. Marranca illustrates this approach with reference to John Jesurun's *Firefall* (2009) and the Builders' Association's *Continuous City* (2007). Marianne Weems, the founder of the Builders' Association, thinks of mediaturgy as an interweaving between the dramaturgy of their shows and 'the Builders' media design – the screens, the network, the space, the video and sound – [that] is both the material and the metaphor' (Jackson and Weems 2015: 384). This method of composition is both the container-maker of meaning and the meaning itself. It presents a cultural critique of 'the complex relationship between media and personhood in the twenty-first century' (Jackson and Weems 2015: 384).

Marranca's term has since been used to focus on the study of live performances, not playtexts. Although this focus is justified, the same approach, focusing on the embeddedness of media aesthetics in performance, can be used to study playtexts and their mediacentric architecture. This is not to suggest that we privilege the textual component and return to the kind of dramaturgical thinking which Marranca moved away from. Instead, it is to expand mediaturgy as a methodology to understand how a media aesthetics that is profoundly embedded in the formation process, composition and meanings of playtexts shapes the idea and role of a playtext in contemporary theatre, and the meanings and effects it produces in relation to our media-driven culture. In line with this, while I have used the notion of 'mediatized dramaturgy' to study the structure of plays in a mediatized cultural, social, political setting thus far, in this chapter I use 'mediaturgical plays' to refer to playtexts that are written, composed, shared and presented through media technologies, often before they are performed live on stage, if they are at all. Mediaturgical plays, by nature, are mediatized since they are shaped by the technologies that inundate and fashion our lives, perception, relationships and cultural expression. Nevertheless, the ways in which they interact with and address contemporary culture and technologies differ from what I call 'mediatized plays'. Media technologies and their formal and sociocultural characteristics are at the very heart of the material, making, architecture and reception of mediaturgical plays. In this emerging category, elements of dramatic form such as characterization, plot and dialogue remain central, but all these aspects are shaped in relation to the media form in use, be it Twitter or Facebook, through which they are produced, structured and presented. For example, as we shall see in Greig's play and as we see in other Twitter-based plays such as Jeremy Gable's *The 15th Line*, the brief form of language use in the micro-blogging platform shapes the language, narrative and characterization in these plays as the plot has to be developed in a succinct manner. The form of media in use, as a result, is not a mere container or vehicle for the text. Rather, it is the very material, process and metaphor that are embedded in the ontology of the text and have always already been connected to the contemporary sociocultural, perceptual environment.

There is a direct historical correlation between the emergence of mediaturgical plays and the rise of popular use of social media. It is not only the case that theatre has adapted itself to digital environments and digital reality – mediaturgical plays also represent a new form of engagement of theatre with the public domain. Platforms such as Twitter, Facebook and blogs are often at the root of these plays. Furthermore, as Patrick Lonergan in *Social Media and Theatre* (2016) and Bree Hadley in *Theatre, Social Media, and Meaning Making* (2017) outline, social media itself has a theatrical quality: the computer interface acts similarly to the stage. There are performers and audiences. In this virtual realm we create digital identities as avatars of our true selves or as imagined characters, and we tell stories about the contemporary whether they are fictional or in response to real events. In addition, social media, based on web 2.0 technology, is a user-generated, public platform that is, more often than not, open to everyone. For example, Twitter is an open virtual domain where anyone can become a user and contribute to feeds. The collective, apparently egalitarian quality of social media, allowing for self-expression and interactivity,[1] creates the possibility for user-audiences to act as actors, writers and directors – something that resonates with the interactive and participatory aspects of some contemporary theatre. Mediaturgical plays are written in various ways, either solely by a playwright or collectively by participants and a writer. While Greig's play illustrates the former, other plays such as Chris Goode's *Hippo World Guest Book* (2007), based on Goode's edited version of the comments people from all over the world posted on a blog, or Brian Lobel's *Purge* (2016), which incorporates the messages and comments of his Facebook friends and the decisions of the audience members about which friend to keep/delete, exemplify the latter – although, as I note below, the line between writing and performance in these works is far from stable, meaning that the definition of 'play' is itself made problematic.

Mediaturgical playtexts engage with various themes without always having to address the technologies they deploy and inhabit or the mediatized culture that they are a product of. Nevertheless, even if they do not comment on the digital, they comment *through* these technologies. This contextualizes them within the sociocultural, ideological and cognitive system of the mediatized society, whatever theme they focus on – be it the Scottish Referendum, as in *The Yes/No Plays* – or the love for the hippo in *Hippo World Guest Book*. Superficially, Goode's play is simply about hippo lovers around the world expressing their love on a blog. However, when one scratches the surface a little and considers the aesthetics and politics of the digital, one sees that the play at its heart reflects on the workings of online culture with its democratic as well as abusive, violent and commercially motivated machinery (highlighted starkly at the end of the play where the website becomes a void filled with neglected casino spam). The lack of any direct reference to contemporary events or politics, however, does not render Goode's play any less capable of critically engaging with the contemporary. On the contrary, the play invites us to consider the mechanics of mediatized culture through a remodelling of theatrical expression and representation with a critical awareness of how media shapes our perception.

Another important aspect of mediaturgical plays is the relationship between text and performance. In the case of mediaturgical plays, this relationship can be rather complex due to a double-layered structure. First, writing that takes place via a media platform can be interpreted as a digitally live performance, witnessed by the users of the specific media. Next, the text as a finished piece is performed live on stage, drawing upon the digital writing-as-performance. This double-layered structure is evident in Goode's *Hippo* – on one level, the participants posted their comments online and read and responded to one another's writing, on another level Goode edited and curated these posts into a playscript drawing on the aesthetics of blog posts and netspeak. As I shall analyse in detail later, Greig's *The Yes/No Plays* was written online in real time, and audience-users experienced and participated in this process which simultaneously acted as a virtual theatrical stage onto which the characters and action emerged. Following this, an edited version of the play was performed live on the Traverse stage. The evolving use of playtexts in the theatre does not represent an entirely new textual form but rather an expansion of the notions of playtexts and playwriting, as we know them. In addition, while mediaturgical plays such as Greig's piece are completed as texts and handed over to the directors and actors, they may not be published subsequently as material texts and become part of a body of dramatic literature mainly due to their yet unknown, unidentified status – something that this chapter opens to discussion.

Alongside the original plays written and presented through specific digital media forms, such as these works by Goode and Greig, there has been an escalating trend in adapting canonical plays, for example, by Shakespeare and Henrik Ibsen, to digital media forms by using their specific formal characteristics. The most popular and well-known examples have been adaptations of works for Twitter – ranging from Brian Yorkey and Tom Kitt's musical *Next to Normal* (New York, 2009), which adhered to the main narrative with little editing, to Shakespeare's *Romeo and Juliet* (Mudlark Productions and the Royal Shakespeare Company, 2010), entitled *Such Tweet Sorrow*. This re-imagining of Shakespeare's play on Twitter deployed the aesthetics of the micro-blogging social media platform and used it as a stage. The adaptation took place via the *Such Tweet Sorrow* Twitter account where Twitter identities for Romeo (@romeo_mo), Juliet (@jlitcap16) and Mercutio (@mercuteio), among other characters, performed the play in real time over five weeks and occasionally interacted with Twitter followers. While followers could comment on the action and characters, they could not shape or change them. These mediaturgical adaptations invite intriguing questions about the dissemination and accessibility of traditional dramas, about authorship, and about audience participation in the writing and performance, cultural value, and politics of adaptation, among other topics. Nevertheless, in order to understand how mediatized culture is shaping playwriting practice and fashion in general, and how mediaturgical plays are composed and what their aesthetic and critical implications are in particular, we need to exclusively focus on original mediaturgical plays. My exploration of *The Yes/No Plays* is a bid to understand the form, context and performance of this newly emerging form of playtexts. In relation to this, I will also consider how the play responds and relates to the contemporary mediatized sociopolitical and cognitive landscape, and whether such plays reinforce or subvert the ways in which this landscape is structured, operated and maintained. Before exploring Greig's play in detail, it is important to contextualize and understand Twitter in relation to theatre – its commonalities with theatre and the main types of Twitter plays.

Twitter: Technology, theatricality and Twitter plays

The social networking and micro-blogging service Twitter has rapidly become the platform for sharing and accessing news in the last decade – predominantly as a result of its immediacy and its role in enabling individuals to self-publish. Twitter's initial prompt to its users was 'What are you doing?' However, noticing that the majority of Twitter account holders used the service not only to respond to the specific question but also to share information and report news, the company changed its motto to 'What's happening?' in 2009. Tweets are short texts containing a maximum of 280 characters (this used to be 140 before 2017). The Twitter feed is chronological; however, interactions and posts are intermittent and fragmented without necessarily developing in a linear, coherent order. Twitter offers a platform for public conversation where anybody can contribute and one can equally access information and news about a topic. The hashtag sign (#) is used to designate topics and categorize relevant posts, opinions and information (e.g. #icebucketchallenge; #metoo; #Brexit). Interactions vary from serious public opinion pieces on current affairs to pithy jokes and memes that gather as scattered, inconclusive commentaries.

The commonalities Twitter shares with theatre are hard to miss. Twitter, like theatre, is based on a real-time representation of and commentary on what is happening in the outside world. Twitter is a social medium populated by people (users) who are writers, directors and spectators all at the same time. Twitter users, similar to actors on stage, perform identities, be they realistic self-representations or fabricated, and they watch the Twitter stage and participate as audiences might do in a theatre, albeit on a highly individualized and individuated basis. In addition, the site's design resembles a playtext and comprises elements of dramatic writing. For instance, the Twitter 'handle' (username), which precedes each post, works in a similar way to speech prefixes (character names, letters, numbers, dash sign, etc.) used in dramatic writing to identify the author of the lines. Similar to stage directions in playscripts indicating to whom the character is speaking in a dialogue (*to Nora*), the '@' sign with the username (@nora _ibsen) is used on Twitter to address and respond to another user. Additionally, Twitter members use the hashtag (#) sign to classify certain topics and events; this categorization builds up a narrative context. The hashtag also works in a similar way to dramatic asides since they 'mark the messages as public speech from which we imagine some people are excluded' (Muse 2012: 56).

As a result of its widespread use and shared qualities with theatre, theatre-makers and playwrights have become interested in Twitter as a form, medium and milieu through which they can instantaneously respond to the fast-paced, bite-size culture in a comprehensible and accessible way and share their response with a global collective. As John Muse notes, Twitter-based plays have appeared in two main forms: single-tweet and multi-tweet plays. In the former, less common genre, an entire play is formed and presented within the limited space and duration of one tweet. Single-tweet plays are self-sufficient, and they can be written and published by various authors-Twitter users with ease – evidence of 'a publication landscape that is radically democratized' (Muse 2012: 44). On the other hand, in the latter, a series of Twitter posts, shared often by multiple characters over a period of time, constitute the play (Muse 2012: 43). One of the first examples of this category is Jeremy Gable's *The 15th Line: A Play of Brief Communication* (2010) which takes place in an unidentified city and tells the story of four characters (Patrick, Dustin, Seth and Angela) and their intersecting lives after an accident in an underground station. For this play, Gable set up individual Twitter accounts for each of the four characters and wrote almost all of the Twitter updates in advance himself before he, as the sole author and performer of the roles, shared the drama online over a two-month period. At the end of the eight weeks during which the Twitter followers watched the story unfold slowly yet coherently, Gable gathered and edited the posts and published them as an online playscript.

The Yes/No Plays: A Twitter play

David Greig's *The Yes/No Plays* took the form of the multi-tweet play in a different direction. It offered a series of Twitter-based vignettes that focus on the conversations between a woman and a man ('Y' and 'N') regarding the Scottish Referendum (2014). The choice of Twitter is telling since the topic was trending on social media for a consistent period of time up to the day of the Scottish Referendum on 18 September 2014, allowing space for various individual perspectives on the issue as opposed to the divisive, polarized discourses of the mainstream media and politics. The characters 'Y' and 'N' live together, and they have different opinions about the Independence debate and the Referendum. While Y, as an activist, vehemently advocates independence, N is sceptical about it and thinks in accordance with the London-based politicians and the Union.

Greig started writing and simultaneously sharing the plays, each of which consists of three or four tweets, via Twitter in December 2013. After approximately 475 Tweets, the playwright edited the plays and adapted them to an hour-long live performance that took place on the day of the Scottish Referendum in September 2014. The complete, revised text follows the digital one and adapts the Twitter aesthetics into an abridged playtext for performance. The Twitter account 'The Yes/No Plays' is used as the title of the edited script; the character names Yes and No remain the same; the tweet-scenes are separated with an asterisk (*) and follow the same chronological order with the addition of subtitles that group the related scenes under a topic (e.g. 'Scenes from life', 'Stirrings'). The analysis of Greig's playtext that I offer here takes into account both the original digital text developed throughout a year and the compact playscript he edited from these tweet plays.

The Yes/No Plays takes an important political event – the Scottish Referendum – as its frame and context. Its setting is generated through such

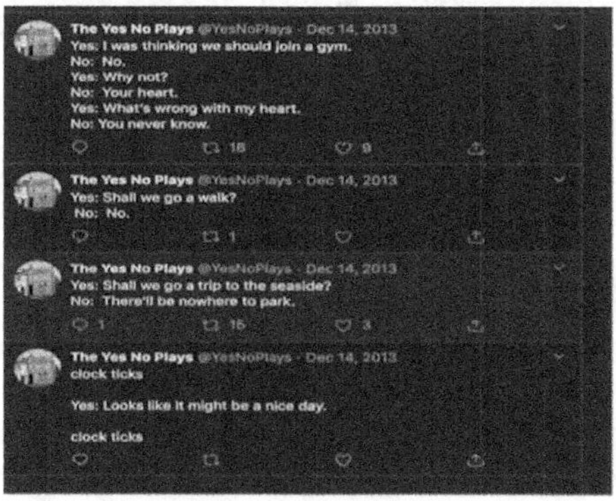

Scenes from Life

One

•

clock ticks

Yes: Looks like it might be a nice day.

clock ticks

Yes: Shall we go a trip to the seaside?
No: There'll be nowhere to park.

•

Yes: Shall we go a walk?
No: No.

•

Yes: I was thinking we should join a gym.
No: No.
Yes: Why not?
No: Your heart.
Yes: What's wrong with my heart.
No: You never know.

•

Figures 9 and 10 *The Yes/No Plays* (unpublished script).

cultural, social and political references as Andy Murray, Alistair Darling and the National Collective Devolution Max and functions as a connective tissue within the fictional realm of the play, gathering the scenes under a thematic umbrella. The outside reality is also deliberately present in the virtual domain of the Twitter play: Greig, a member of the National Collective of Artists and Creatives for an Independent Scotland, wrote the @YesNoPlays by using the play's title as the Twitter handle. This Twitter handle revealed an authorial presence behind the tweet-scenes without revealing Greig's identity at the beginning of the play. This approach highlighted the constructedness of this fictional-world-in-a-virtual-world instead of confining it within the boundaries of a fictive cosmos generated on Twitter and closed off from the external world. By contrast, in *The 15th Line*, each character held a Twitter account and was placed in a fictional landscape, where they communicated with one another via Twitter without reality leaking into this fictional–virtual realm. Greig refused such uniformity in his play and instead created a hybrid, intersecting the non-digital, real world with a digital virtual reality as well as with the fictional. He produced the tweet plays in real time and in line with everyday news and events. Moreover, outside reality made an entry into the digital realm of the play every single time the followers reacted to Greig's writing in real time. During the writing-performance of *The Yes/No Plays*, approximately 1,300 Twitter users followed the play, and some responded through liking or commenting on the scenes. Greig did not reveal his identity as the author of the piece for some time since he wanted the play to have a life of its own.[2] But Twitter users figured it out halfway through, and Greig then welcomed the connection and engagement with people about the Referendum via the play. The majority of the comments accordingly addressed Greig himself rather than responding to the fictional characters.

This response to the play on the part of audience members is a consequence of Greig's unusual way of using Twitter since, conventionally, each individual has an account through which she interacts with another user on the platform or comments on others' feeds. By using the familiar form differently, Greig, in a metatheatrical manner, highlighted the artifice of the narrative and sphere we are digitally present within, and brought our attention to the presence of the outside cosmos within the virtual and vice versa. That is to say, in the multidimensional composition of the play, intersecting reality, virtuality and the imaginary, external reality was not peripheral to a closed-off fictive cosmos, but an intrinsic component of the play's world. In addition, the digital was not simply a container for dramatic representation, but an integral part of the non-digital. Twitter here was an aesthetic and conceptual mainstay and a critical tool in the play's mediaturgical design, facilitating what Berry and Dieter call 'a hybridized approach towards the digital and non-digital, finding characteristics of one within the other, deliberately mixing up processes of making things discrete, calculable, indeed and automated in unorthodox ways' (2015: 6). The real and the virtual, albeit still familiar and valid categories, merged into each other more and more, generating a multidimensional sense and experience of reality where the virtual was not outside the real, but coexisted with it as a part of it, and vice versa. Causey explains this state as a part of postdigital culture and identifies it as 'the reality of the virtual' – a complex modality of the digital – '[which] indicates that the binaries of the biological and the virtual, the organic and the inorganic, the machine and the flesh, and specifically the virtual and the real are no longer useful in conceptualizing and performing within a postdigital culture' (2016: 434). *The Yes/No Plays* responded to this changing social environment and cognitive state not merely through its mediaturgical design but also and mainly through its no-longer-dramatic aesthetics. That is, the play's hybrid aesthetics, presenting a multi-reality experience and view of the world, undermined the binary footing of virtual reality and physical reality and disrupted the conventions of dramatic conflict and representation which tend to portray the world as a sealed-off and singular reality.

In a similar vein, Greig's approach to plot structure subverted the logocentric logic and form of dramatic theatre in a bid to explore the critical role and impact of resistance against accepted models of representation and, relatedly, of perception. The scenes unfolded in a chronological manner – an outcome of Twitter's real-time setup. However, despite the chronological order and the overarching thematic context, the play did not work through a causative, linear structure. Instead, similarly to how we share and follow information on Twitter and other digital platforms, the scenes were presented as short snapshots of the everyday life of its two characters in conversation with the real world of Twitter (the author and followers), as bite-sized vignettes more fragmented than unified, and more sporadic than causative. While a few tweet-scenes followed the same topic such as the first scene – 'Scenes from Life' – regarding Y and N's disagreement, overall the scenes did not follow one another in a consistent order to generate a single, linearly developing narrative. Greig likens the form of the play to daily cartoon strips in a newspaper. Each tweet is a frame, and three or four tweets together make up a strip that stands on its own and is 'completely unique to this moment' (Cited in Ferguson 2014). This aspect of *The Yes/No Plays* evokes the structure of various plays with mediatized dramaturgy such as Simon Stephens's *Pornography* (2008), in which disjointed scenes are connected through the context of the 7/7 bombings, or Caryl Churchill's *Love and Information* (2012) where the concise, free-standing scenes are not interlinked through a logical order, but merely through a broad thematic arch.

Greig's characterization added to the play's resistant aesthetics, disrupting our known modes of representation based in linearly organized narrative form with identifiable, psychologically motivated characters. The mode of characterization hybridized the fictional, digitally mediated realm of Y and N's everyday life and the outside reality where Greig wrote and Twitter users followed the play. In the fictional landscape, there are also other characters such as Y and N's neighbours, the Undecideds, who epitomize hesitant or indifferent perspectives on the debate, as well as personifications of real people such as the leader of the Scottish Labour Party, Jim Murphy (2014–15). Rather than three-dimensional, fully developed dramatis personae with individual idiosyncrasies, presented through personal Twitter accounts as in Gable's *The 15th Line*, Greig's characters are flat with limited information provided as to their personality, background or psychology, and presented under the shared Twitter account: 'The Yes No Plays @YesNoPlays'.

Such an approach to characterization suggests intriguing points about the form of the play and the meanings it produces. As mentioned earlier, the single Twitter account handle indicated an external authorial voice, belonging to Greig, which reaffirmed the presence of the real within the mediated, fictional, digital landscape. Here, Greig made it evident that he was the author of the words rather than illusively suggesting that the individual characters produced the dialogue and had agency over their thoughts and words. Greig's use of a single Twitter account as the frame and source of the fictional world underlined the constructedness of the experience on Twitter, subtly implanting in the play questions such as to what extent the content we encounter on social media is constructed, and who the actual speaker behind the posts is, both in terms of truth of identity and degree of agency. In addition to the metadramatic mode through which Greig creates the words, characters and the fictional world on Twitter, he, albeit on limited occasions, acknowledged and engaged with the Twitter account followers and responded to their tweets through dialogue-scenes between Y and N (see Figure 11). While emphasizing the hybrid form and the artifice of @YesNoPlays, the inputs of the Twitter followers, which appeared as comments often directed at Greig (not to the characters) and did not alter the content of the tweet-scenes, add to the question of agency. Greig's choice here was potentially a practical one as allowing the followers to shape the Y and N's interactions would have created a cacophony – doubtlessly an interesting one rich with meanings, but a less coherent experience, nonetheless. Nevertheless, the limitation also foregrounds a question about the politics of social media where we apparently freely express our opinions and make political gestures: whether we actually partake in the political discourse and changes, and

Figure 11 *The Yes/No Plays* (unpublished script).

whether our Twitter or Facebook activism in fact shifts the course of social, political events. Greig's mediaturgy does not provide a direct answer to this question or land on a definitive opinion on the Referendum – the characters were fashioned as emblematic figures presenting different perspectives on the Independence debate. But it invited one to engage with different voices and viewpoints and question who is able to speak and who is visible in this platform and outside in the sociopolitical landscape. Nevertheless, in the local context of the Scottish Referendum and *The Yes/No Plays*, Twitter undoubtedly helped to connect people and allowed them to have discussions beyond the mainstream media's prescribed narratives, although the majority of the artistic endeavours, including Greig's, were geared towards the pro-Independence campaign.

Given these aspects, the characters seem to act more as mouthpieces, or 'text-bearers' to use Gerda Poschmann's term (*Textträger*, cited in Barnett 2005: 140–1), responsible for delivering the dominant social reactions to the Independence debate on Twitter, rather than life-size, psychologically motivated representations of individuals with agency, critical depth and nuance. This mediaturgical choice speaks to how our perceptions and reactions are shaped by the media content we receive under the guise of the freedom to access and share information. What we consider as our free subjective choices and opinions are in fact greatly influenced, monitored and controlled by dominant power structures and narratives. The play, as stated earlier, did not leave us in a knowing, firm position with a definitive sense of subjectivity and agency. Instead, it disrupted the prescribed interpretation of social reality and subjectivity that would funnel us into a single and demarcated way of thinking. In so doing, it left us with the tension that uncertainty engenders. Adding to its overt political focus on the Referendum, Greig's play embodied mediatized being from within by using Twitter as a critical mechanism. In addition, by hybridizing the digital with the non-digital, the imaginary with the real, through fictional characters and real-time, real-world participants and a real-world author, the play engaged with our mediatized subjectivity, comprised of the organic and the technological.

Mediaturgy: Critical meanings and effects

The 15th Line and similar mediaturgical plays focus on updating drama through new media forms and platforms for the consumer's gaze without necessarily disrupting or revealing the mediatized state of perception and being, or the underlying ideological gist and socio-cognitive impact of such technologies. Unlike *The Yes/No Plays*, *The 15th Line*'s dramaturgical choices brought order to what is in fact a multidimensional, non-linear, unstable and fragmented communicative state. John Muse calls techniques like this "'virtual realism'" – realism that 'reproduces real-life experiences, characters, and relationships which are themselves increasingly virtual' (2012: 58–9). *The 15th Line* reiterated and reproduced the logic and discourse of neoliberal capitalism that we are too immersed in to view from a critical distance. Greig's play, on the contrary, refused to offer virtual realism and replicate our virtual interactions and evolution without engaging with its complexities and concerns.

Without doubt, we are familiar with and grasp the hybrid, multi-layered and fragmented design of *The Yes/No Plays* as it resonates with how we experience, perceive and relate to the world around us. That design ran counter to more traditional forms of dramatic representation deployed in works like *The 15th Line*. That is, *The Yes/No Plays*' hybrid, multi-layered and non-causative composition used the digital tools and environments of the everyday in a way that disrupted expected and known models of dramatic representation and destabilized the idea of the world as a stable, homogenous totality. Instead, it offered a view that was porous, multi-directional and changeable – a view that opens space for critical engagement with the reality we live in, how we operate in it, and how our consciousness is framed through it. In doing so, to draw on Causey's argument, Greig's play 'thinks digitally' in order to respond to and critique our mediatized world and its ideological underpinnings and effects.

The overtly thematized political moment of the Scottish Referendum lay at the heart of this reality in Greig's play. In line with the play's aesthetics, there was no unidirectional, unified representation of this matter through a traditionally realistic frame. Instead, *The Yes/No Plays* put forward a mediaturgically produced reflection on the contemporary mediatized culture with its multiplicities and refused to lean on a single viewpoint and engage with the world as an easily graspable, representable, consumable whole. It subverted and resisted the pervasive flow of mainstream media presentations and discourses by using Twitter as a *playground* for perspectives on different sides of the debate without prioritizing one view over the other or leading to a desired critical position. Instead, the play ended in an unscripted, open space, one rich with interpretations of the play and the world it refers to, and that offers a look beyond the *consensus* – 'the distribution of the sensible' (Rancière 2013).

The Yes/No Plays is an extension of, yet different from, the play script as we know it, namely, a material text written for and often before its live performance. The mediaturgical play as a text contains performative qualities owing to its media-based design, formation process and digital liveness. As much as *The Yes/No Plays* is a play written and presented via Twitter, it is also a performance. Similarly to live performance, the play is formed and performed in front of an audience in a shared real time, yet here in a digitally connected virtual world rather than a shared physical space. The fact that its writing happened live on Twitter shaped not only the ontology of the text as text-as-performance but also the experience of playwriting. In a conversation I had with Greig, he emphasized that the play was emerging and happening live on a digital platform and also in real time in line with what was happening in the world – which was often unpredictable. As a result of this unpredictability, which shaped the content of Y and N's dialogues, there was no fixed dramatic arc. Furthermore, Greig mentioned that although he had planned and created every scene carefully, he kept editing the scenes as he put them online due to digital liveness, turning the writing experience into one of live performance (Greig Interview). Considering the evolution of playtexts in relation to mediatized culture and technologies, such double ontology presents a fruitful viewpoint, surpassing binary dichotomies as well as suggesting another way of thinking about text and performance in theatre.

Besides its performative elements, the playtext on Twitter also has a continuing existence and evolution within the virtual realm as opposed to the ephemerality of performance and the completeness of dramatic writing. That is, although Greig finalized the play and edited it into a more compact script for performance on the day of the Referendum, he did not entirely *close the page*. Greig occasionally added more scenes to *The Yes/No Plays* after the Referendum; for example, in February 2016 he wrote new scenes focusing on the Brexit debate, and, in January 2017, on the reality of Brexit and Donald Trump's presidential victory. The mediaturgical play has remained digitally live and can evolve if and when there is an action and reaction in the virtual realm. Even if Greig does not add more new scenes into the world of the Twitter play, the caesura or inaction on the online platform does not suggest a full closure or completeness. Unlike a published playtext, the mediaturgical play always remains open-ended as long as the digital platform is active.

Considering *The Yes/No Plays* as a digitally formed, digitally shared and digitally live text, how might the mediaturgical play – a long piece composed of short, fragmented scenes and one that accommodates a fictional world and outside reality via the digital platform – be performed on a live stage, and what might it signify? Greig, as mentioned earlier, edited the original Twitter-based text for an hour-long piece of live theatre performed twice at the Traverse Theatre – the first before the results of the Referendum were announced, and the second after. The edited playtext followed a similar structure to its longer, digital counterpart. On stage, the play was structured as sets of concise scenes made up of three/four tweet-scenes. These were all connected through the same historical, sociopolitical context, yet they did not work through and towards a unified, linearly developing dramatic narrative. The scenes, each of which presented a scrap of story without a through-narrative, defied traditional dramatic representation. Despite this, one may consider the performance of the edited script as a work of dramatic theatre mainly because, within the aesthetic parameters of its physical liveness, the performance did not embody the duration, length and intermittent pace of the Twitter-based play – aspects that would attenuate dramatic representation. However, the lack of such qualities on the stage did not bring about a coherent and fixed representation of the world as a unified totality but provided a kaleidoscopic view of the historical moment for the audience. The sporadic, short and fragmented form of the edited playtext produced a porous dramaturgy as opposed to a firmly structured, cohesive one, and therefore offered various possibilities for live performance.

Greig's motivation regarding the timing of the two performances – one before and one after the results were revealed – was to share the year-long conversations about the Independence debate on the day of the Referendum, to respond straightaway to what felt like a monumental moment, and to reflect collectively on different sides of the debate as it was coming to a close. Both while writing the Twitter-based play and editing it for performance at Scotland's new writing theatre, Greig aimed to avoid the divisive politics that dominated the established media as well as social media platforms. What the audience encountered on the Traverse stage was the physical version of the shared forum on Twitter that did not exclude either angle of the discussion and offered a neutral discursive space to encourage dialogue about differences instead of agreement on the same viewpoint.

The play's production was more of a reading than a fully rehearsed and organized piece with detailed scenography, acting, lighting and so on. On a bare stage, Greig introduced the play and the cast to the audience. Five actors with Greig's edited script in their hands read and performed the lines: Frances Thorburn played the enthusiastic Y while Richard Clements presented the lines of N, and Louise Ludgate, Keith Macpherson and Callum Cuthbertson delivered characters such as Alistair Darling, Jackie Bird, as well as dispassionately communicating the stage directions, violating any possibility of dramatic realism. At the end of each scene, a generic announcement chime marked the change, and the actors read the title of the next scene as a chorus.

The bare stage added to the play's mood of aesthetic and ideological neutrality. As opposed to a three-dimensional set design, which would try to recreate the digital realm in a way Haley's *The Nether* attempted and would possibly take the critical attention away from the debate, the empty stage functioned as a blank canvas, an open space for a discussion of different perspectives. The actors appeared both in their roles and as performers (voters) with a distanced attitude towards the fictional world of the text. This oscillation between performer and character, reality and fiction, reinforced the theatre-ness of the event and foregrounded the stage as a self-reflexive, fluid and open forum that was not walled off from the audience but, rather, invited them to participate in the collective dialogue. Considering such aspects of *The Yes/No Plays*, theatre critic Thom Dibdin referred to the performance as not being 'a whole play in itself' (2014, AE website). This comment, which suggests a sense of aesthetic and thematic incompleteness, in fact demonstrates the dissident potential of Greig's play. Similar to its counterpart in the virtual realm, the play's live performance challenged the accustomed and expected form – a linearly organized, complete narrative with psychologically motivated characters in a three-dimensional, lifelike setting. Instead, the mediaturgical play on stage and on Twitter presents a crack, an opening in our agreed-upon idea of theatre and consensual, homogenous perspective that was in evidence in the dominant divisive politics and discourses of the Referendum.

The Yes/No Plays represents an aesthetic and thematic resistance against: (1) the representation of our mediatized consciousness and world (and its power structures) through the logocentric paradigm of the *dramatic*, based on the idea of the world as a unified totality, and relatedly, (2) the reproduction of the consensus rooted in late capitalism and its divisive, de-politicizing machinery. By placing the familiar digital platform and its easily identifiable qualities in a no-longer-dramatic architecture, the play, in a Brechtian way, makes our known ways of being and knowing strange and disorderly. Adding to this Brechtian frame, Greig presents different angles on the Independence debate. Nevertheless, neither these theses nor the image of mediatized culture and consciousness point at a definitive politics or a unified reality. Instead, by allowing these multiple perspectives, the play 'preserves the tensions between [these suggestions] as a dynamo of interrogative dramatic energy' (2016: 34), as Clare Wallace argues. By not favouring Yes or No, Greig also disrupts and interrogates Twitter's typical modus operandi: deliberately funnelling users towards polarized discourse in order to mine data from them – 'one of the most profitable raw materials yet discovered' (Seymour 2019: 25). In this way, *The Yes/No Plays* takes a postdigital stance and thinks digitally (Causey 2016: 431), using Twitter and engaging with its ideological machinery from within to deconstruct it. As a consequence, in our endeavours to arrive at a recognizable, final picture of our fast-changing media-saturated world in general and the Scottish debate in particular, we end up in a land of unscripted multiplicities that opens a gap in what we perceive as given or normal. The disruption in *the sensible*, to return to Jacques Rancière, subverts and opens divisions in 'what is given and [. . .] the frame within which we see something as given' (2010: 69). In this respect, this particular mediaturgical play's porous architecture offers a space for *dissensus* to engage with multiple perspectives and different discourses of the contemporary beyond the limits of *consensus*, fuelled by de-politicizing populism and the idea that there is no alternative to the neoliberalist model. Greig's play eschews the notion of a political alternative that would pose another definitive direction or perspective. Instead, it invites us to critically engage with the gaps and tensions in the play and to grasp the connection of the digital to the power relations and socio-cognitive environment of the contemporary late capitalist order.

Conclusion: Reflections on mediaturgical play

The mediaturgical playtext gives us a new perspective on the question of how playtexts have evolved in relation to mediatized culture and its technologies. Differently from the playtexts that employ a mediatized dramaturgy, this form actively engages with and accommodates the digital at the heart of its composition. While reconsidering the aesthetics of dramatic writing in relation and response to the technology it deploys, the mediaturgical play does not emerge as an entirely new kind of text in theatre that is different from playscripts, as we know them. Instead, what it suggests is an expansion of the known parameters and paradigm of plays written for theatre performance. As seen in the analysis of *The Yes/No Plays*, elements of dramatic writing such as characterization and plot are still relevant and play a significant role in this evolutionary process, albeit adapting to new technologies and a mediatized environment. One of the intriguing outcomes of this adaptation process is that mediaturgical plays, more often than not, combine text and performance as the act of writing, whether done by a playwright or along with participants, takes place on a digital platform such as Twitter in Greig's play or Facebook in Brian Lobel's *Purge*. Nevertheless, text-as-performance is not always a definitive characteristic of mediaturgical plays because sometimes the production of the text can take place before it is edited into a playscript or before it was put on social media. For example, Chris Goode's *Hippo World Guest Book* was largely based on posts of hippo-loving bloggers which Goode edited into a playtext, and in Jeremy Gable's *The 15th Line*, the Twitter-style drama came into being before it was shared on Twitter. The various states of the text, in terms of its performative ontology, offer a prolific ground for further research since the idea of writing-as-performance does not only shape the notion and role of playtext in theatre but also a playwright's relation to the text in terms of digital liveness. For example, as Greig highlighted in an interview I conducted, writing a short scene each day on Twitter, publishing it online and instantly editing it as it becomes digitally live suggests a practice that is new and possible through media-based playwriting. Furthermore, mediaturgical plays involve different degrees of agency on both the playwright's and the reader–audience's parts. While in Greig's and Gable's Twitter plays, the playwrights held the majority of the authorial agency and users could comment on the posts, in Goode's *Hippo* blog visitors were the main authors of the text and Goode became an editor and performer of the text. These examples indicate that, in this context, the audience has become a participant, echoing our contemporary experience of social media rendering us all as writers. These experiments, which I label as mediaturgical plays, demonstrate the strong desire in contemporary playwriting to adapt to mediatized culture and its ever-changing realities and how they engage with our technogenesis.

Conclusion

Mediatized dramaturgy and beyond: Texts in progress

'[I]t is necessary to pick out, amongst the machines, videos, technology and other computers, [. . .] some scraps of text' (2003: 191), argues Patrice Pavis, pointing out the tendency towards the perception of performance 'as visual and spectacular, thus non-textual' in view of the rising influence of media technologies in society and theatre (2003: 191). Pavis's thoughts here highlight a significant drawback in the conversations concerning new technologies and mediatization in theatre. Playtexts have often remained in the blind spot when we consider the theatre–media relationship. This book is driven by this limited attention to playtexts that I have noticed in various instances – ranging from conferences, academic research to conversations had with theatre-makers and scholars – in an age and stage saturated by media. This lack of attention came as a surprise to me particularly in the context of British theatre – a theatre culture that praises its plays and playwrights and supports its new writing scene. In response, with *Mediatized Dramaturgy* I want to draw attention to the fact that writing for theatre has always been in motion and co-evolves with the technologies we continually create and transform. Therefore, I argue, plays, whether we concentrate on them or not in our reflections on mediatized theatre, inevitably change in relation to our evolving existence, consciousness and environments, offering intriguing ways of thinking about the world, how we perceive and represent it. In *Mediatized Dramaturgy*, I hope to have initiated a conversation about playtexts in a mediatized culture and theatre landscape that moves beyond the common expectation and understanding of mediatized plays as scripts 'about' technology, towards a focus on the form of plays and their aesthetico-critical evolution in an age of theatre marked by mediatization and its possibilities.

Throughout the journey of this book, I kept returning to Cinna's question: What can words do?[1] I kept asking and exploring: How can dramatic writing in theatre – the place of seeing – make the act of seeing (perceiving) an active, critically engaging and felt experience on the textual and performance level beyond and against the obviously visible? In a world of overflowing images, of constant surveillance and self-representation, is it possible to *see* from a critical distance? When I started exploring this question, I expected that plays with mediatized dramaturgy, which deploy aesthetics of technologies and aspects of mediatized culture in their form and/or thematic content, would inherently reflect on the complexities of our media-driven society and consciousness and engage us critically with this reflection. However, exploring various plays written between the late 1990s and 2010s (such as *Closer, Love and Information, Pornography, The Nether, The Yes/No Plays* and *The 15th Line*), I have noticed that the depth and effect of a play's critical engagement with the mediatized age are profoundly connected to its approach to the aesthetics and politics of representation, rather than how explicitly it pictures technologies in its narrative. In tune with the current debates and trends in theatre, two dramaturgical models with differing takes on the dramatic paradigm – the philosophical category of the 'dramatic' as a representational design for a unified world – have stood out: the dramatic and no-longer-dramatic. These aesthetico-critical positions, I contend, offer different treatments of not simply and only the mode of representation in plays and on stage, but also of our mode of being and perception that is greatly shaped by media technologies and the culture these technologies have engendered. While dramatic mediatized plays strive to mimetically represent reality and, relatedly, reproduce the prevailing power structures and discourses in an easily recognizable, orderly way, no-longer-dramatic plays with mediatized dramaturgies disrupt the dramatic paradigm and the replication and uncritical consumption of prescribed ideological narratives and images in order to critically question the intricacies and implications of the mediatized, late capitalist order.

Plays that adhere to a traditional dramatic design and logic are by no means obsolete or bygone. They still populate the Anglophone, particularly British, theatre scene and certainly acknowledge aspects of our mediatized world and being. We have seen, for example, that *The Nether* addresses the ethics of virtual reality, while plays such as *Closer* and *The 15th Line* draw attention to the impact of emergent technologies on human relationships from the early stages of the internet to social media. However, these plays' dramaturgical conformism confines and filters the workings of mediatized, late capitalist culture into a set, recognizable and easy-to-consume representation, often repeating the images and discourses that we are too engrossed in to view and question with a critical eye. Similar to how various mainstream media platforms such as Facebook circulate the prevailing capitalist viewpoint and channel us towards a sense of consensus that basically eliminates differences and oppositions (as revealed, for example, in the case of Cambridge Analytica[2]), these plays' dramatic representation tends to replicate this constructed, homogenous perception of the world and portray it as a stable, rational whole with no alternative to it. These plays, as argued, certainly speak about timely and important aspects of our mediatized culture and lives, yet they do this often in a manner that confirms expectations and delimits critical discussion. They offer a look *onto* our experienced reality, yet without necessarily looking deep *into* its workings and effects and opening up spaces for us to see them from within and without.

On the other hand, mediatized plays that are not governed by the dramatic paradigm but instead defy it create a rupture in the perception and representation of the world as a homogenous whole. We have seen this unorthodox mediatized dramaturgy in plays such as *THWD*, *Attempts on Her Life* and *Firefall*. Instead of the unrecognized identification with the machinery and effects of the mediatized capitalist order and its uncritical consumption, as we often see with traditional dramatic representation, the nonfigurative sign usage in these plays does not allow for a fully attainable and easily identifiable, definitive view of the world as a knowable whole with a final meaning and ideological direction. Instead, they open up information gaps and irregularities and leave the audience epistemologically adrift – something ironic as well as provocative given the instantaneous accessibility and overload of information we have in our media-saturated culture. These dramaturgical fissures, formed through, for example, non-linear, fragmented plot structures or a rupture between character and speech, destabilize our accustomed and unchallenged perception and representation of the world and the self. They offer a space of unscripted multiplicities that allows for thinking differently about our subjectivity and perceptual processes beyond and against the prescribed narratives and viewpoints of the dominant sociopolitical consensus. Hence, the plays in this category incorporate media aesthetics and the socio-cognitive implications of mediatization into their architecture in a subversive manner and turn the often invisible, entrenched workings of late capitalist mediatized order against itself. In a post-political age of consensus where images of conflict and possibilities of opposition are omitted from the social, and therefore artistic, imagination often by means of pervasive media platforms, these plays offer a dramaturgy of uncertainty that accommodates multiplicities and differences and challenges passive viewing. The dramaturgical design resists 'the implicit promise of the medium' to keep us 'spectators/viewers [so that] the catastrophes will always stay outside' (Samuel Weber cited in Lehmann 2006: 184). Instead, it proposes a nonconformist and transformative perspective on the contemporary that disrupts the spectacle, confounds expectations and stimulates debate.

One of the challenges, as well as thrills of writing about mediatized dramaturgy, has been the constant and rapid development of new media forms and platforms, and relatedly, the continual emergence of new plays and dramaturgical experiments in relation and response to these technologies. Since the mid-2010s, Twitter has become even more widespread due to various reasons but most prominently because of its frequent use in global sociopolitical situations (e.g. protests, elections) and by politicians and celebrities. Picking up on this new popular language and stage, playwrights have produced what I have called in this book 'mediaturgical plays' – texts that have media technologies and aesthetics at the core of their structure and formation process such as the Twitter plays by David Greig (*The Yes/No Plays*) and Jeremy Gable (*The 15th Line*). My researching on mediaturgical plays has led me to some important remarks on this evolving aspect of contemporary dramatic writing and theatre. To begin with, these plays are not entirely new textual formations nor do they put forward a completely novel genre in theatre. Instead, they are fundamentally 'plays', as we know them, because mediaturgical plays use the known elements of dramatic writing such as plot structure, dialogue and characterization. Similarly to mediatized plays such as Simon Stephens's *Pornography* or Caryl Churchill's *Love and Information*, mediaturgical plays either adhere to the dramatic paradigm and logic or challenge it and open new vistas to think about the world we live in, how we perceive and represent it, as we have seen in Greig's play.

As a part of their mediaturgical design and ontology, these plays often remain in the digital sphere rather than being materialized and fixed as a published playscript. When considered strictly within the parameters of how we traditionally define dramatic writing, the fluid and immaterial status of mediaturgical plays may be confusing and leave them outside the category of playtexts. However, given how rapidly technologies and our lives are changing, it would be incongruous to stick to the traditional definitions and risk engaging with the new dimensions of these old categories. Mediaturgical plays draw on dramatic writing and expand and adapt its boundaries to new media and environment. In addition, while playtexts, written for and before a performance, offer a more straightforward relation between text and performance, mediaturgical plays display performative qualities in their formation process. As the plays come into being in real-time digital space, and the story and characters emerge and unfold while audience-participants watch this formation on their screens, the act of writing becomes a performance. Text and performance merge into each other on the digital stage. The state of text-as-performance suggests a double ontology as a result of which mediaturgical plays often offer an unorthodox, multi-layered, fluid relation between and definition of text and performance in theatre.

Last but not least, being thus far the most popular media form that playwrights have experimented with, social media platforms such as

Twitter and Facebook often render these plays interactive and polyvocal. While mediaturgical plays can sometimes be single-authored similarly to playscripts written by a single playwright, as seen in *The Yes/No Plays*, they are often the product of multiple authors as the social media users contribute to the playtext, if not entirely write it, as in Chris Goode's *Hippo World Guest Book*. Nevertheless, even when only a single author writes the play as Greig did, the comments and reactions of social media users are inevitable and still shape the digitally formed playtext and its live perception on the virtual stage – whether the writer includes these in the edited version for live performance or not. This mode of playwriting resonates with our recent technogenesis that has turned all of us into writers, and certainly suggests innovative, and continually shifting, views on authorship and spectatorship, challenging the idea of an unproductive audience interaction. Nevertheless, we should take the idea of social media as liberating platforms that give everyone a voice with a pinch of salt, because while being apparently free, social media (and other media forms) mine personal data from each user as well as monitoring what everyone is writing. This is no different from the multi-authorship and participation that take place in mediaturgical plays. However, the invisible control mechanisms underlying social media are more effectively critiqued at certain times than others – Greig's decision to not include participants' writing in the main body of *The Yes/No Plays* can be taken as a critical gesture, questioning power dynamics and individual agency in the digital age, for example.

Playtexts form only one aspect of the media-text relationship in the current theatre landscape. Other modes of texts have emerged in mediatized theatre and performance in addition to dramatic writing and have influenced the textual grounds of contemporary theatre. Among these mediatized textual dramaturgies we can consider theatre texts that are originally produced, found, patched together and edited in mixed media or virtual theatre performances, such as Blast Theory's app-based piece *Karen* (2015) in which pre-recorded film, gaming, interactive personality questionnaire and dramatic narrative are hybridized and form a multi-layered textual design.[3] There are numerous examples of these new kinds of texts in contemporary theatre practice, ranging from the works of the New Paradise Laboratories and the Plaintext Players to those of the New York Futurists, to name a few. Such textual formations, along with newly emerging mediatized plays since the late 2010s, represent new aspects of mediatized theatre, redefining the contours of what we consider a play to be, how we identify writing and text in contemporary theatre, as well as the role and position of playwrights – all yet to be explored in further research. Therefore, future studies may draw on and extend the scope of this book (late 1990s to mid-2010s) and its focus on playtexts towards more recent and different forms of texts to appreciate the changing form, role and critical gestures of texts and writing in the theatre of a rapidly evolving media age.

As I am writing this concluding part of *Mediatized Dramaturgies*, we are going through the unprecedented Covid-19 global pandemic that has locked all of us down in our living spaces and closed theatre stages for about a year now. But theatre, as a rapidly adapting organism, has adapted to this new reality and its intensely online ecosystem. Theatre companies and institutions such as the Wooster Group, Forced Entertainment, Imitating the Dog and Schaubühne Berlin have offered their archived performances online for free. The Old Vic Theatre in London, among others, has live broadcast performances (e.g. *Lungs*, 2020), while companies such as Coney have produced new work (*The Telephone*, 2020) for the interactive, digital stage, and theatre-maker/playwright Tim Crouch has adapted his play *I, Cinna (The Poet)* to the Unicorn Theatre's online Zoom stage. While online theatre practice is not a new phenomenon, the sheer number of companies, practitioners (theatre-makers, playwrights, actors) and institutions taking up to the virtual space surely signals a paradigm shift that is to be explored in the years to come. This emergent digital space that we currently inhabit more intensely than ever is not only altering how theatre is made and plays are written but also changing our perception of the world and understanding of narratives. In this new global context with its fast-developing technologies, how we write is bound to change, and in return it will change us, leaving one to continue wondering 'what words can do'.

Notes

Introduction

1 Please see such works as
   Auslander (1999),
   Auslander (2012),
   Bay-Cheng et al. (2010), Dixon (2007), Chapple and Kattenbelt (2006) and Giannachi (2004).
2 There are divergent discourses on and approaches to the question of 'liveness'. Such performance theorists as Michael Kirby, Susan Sontag, Matthew Causey, Michael Kustow, Patrice Pavis, Peggy Phelan and Philip Auslander have written on the subject. Here, I refer to some of these theorists since their differing approaches give an overview of the discussion.
3 I use media, media technology and technology interchangeably.
4 Theorists such as Bernard Stiegler and N. Katherine Hayles use the notion of *technogenesis* to refer to 'the idea that humans and technics have coevolved together' (Hayles 2012: 10). See Hayles (2012).
5 I investigate techno-texts through Blast Theory's *Karen*, for further information please see
   Ilter (2018).
6 This study only investigates original plays and does not consider the adaptations of canonical texts in new productions as *Mediatized Dramaturgy* focuses on the evolution of playtexts rather than of performance.
7 The mediatized dramaturgy of some of the plays resonates with Bertolt Brecht and Ervin Piscator's and Walter Benjamin's positive take on technology as tools that can bring art in sync with contemporary realities and generate a potential to resist and critically think about the techno-political machinery of capitalism. More on this in Chapter 1.

Chapter 1

1 Swedish media scholar Kent Asp uses the term 'medialization' to point to the impact of the media in political processes. See Kent (1990).
2 Sociologist John B. Thompson explores the media and modernity by focusing on symbolic forms, their modes of production and circulation in social sphere and the cultural transformation they bring about, which Thompson defines as 'mediazation of modern culture'. Here, the term 'mediazation' (without the 'ti') is not significantly different from 'mediatization'. It refers to the similar questions and concepts regarding the

impact of the media on society. For further information, see Thompson (1995).

3 Although mediatization is identified as a primarily Western phenomena, I contend that this has quickly changed as other societies and cultures in various developing parts of the world such as Africa are inundated with information and communication technologies which are greatly decisive in those cultures. Therefore, it is more accurate to consider the highly industrialized Western societies as the starting locale of mediatization, but through global capitalism it has reached most parts of the world.
4 See Flusser (2011).
5 See Couldry (2015).
6 Mark Fisher's *Capitalist Realism: Is There No Alternative?* is a key text to engage with in terms of postpolitics and 'the distribution of the sensible'. See Fisher (2009).
7 I will draw on aspects of Mathew Causey's critical frame while exploring mediatized plays, particularly the ones with media-based architecture in Chapter 6.
8 In the work of such scholars and theatre companies as Peggy Phelan, Philip Auslander, Michael Kustow, the Wooster Group, Forced Entertainment and Builders Association, the interest in the relationship between media and theatre focuses mainly on theatrical performance.
9 O'Neill (2015).
10 Allen (2012).
11 Wotzko (2012).

Chapter 2

1 What *Faust* puts forward in the late 1990s is indeed what we experience today in a world where our perceptions of current and historical facts are constantly fashioned by media – the ways in which Donald Trump and Recep Tayyip Erdoğan have been using mass media and social media platforms as propaganda tools to *bend* reality is just one example of this.
2 For more information, see such reviews as Alison Mercer's review in *The Stage*, 20 March 1997; Kate Basset's review in the *Daily Telegraph*, 6 March 1997, as well as Nicholas de Jongh's 'Review on *Faust is Dead*' (*The Evening Standard*), *Theatre Record*, 17 (1997).

Chapter 3

1 Please see Michel Foucault's writings on language, discourse and power, for example, Foucault (1972). Foucault (1980). Also, see works on M. Foucault, for example, Mills (2003).

2   There is a difference between mediatized language and media language. While the former refers to everyday language, whose form, discourse and content change in view of mass media technologies and media-saturated culture, the latter alludes to a rather more medium-specific or characteristic language and discourse particular to mass media use. These are, of course, not disconnected. On the contrary, there is a close interaction between the two since media language as a part of media technologies and culture affects daily language. Here I will focus on the mediatization of language and occasionally relate it to media language.
3   Info: 'In 1999, websites would lose a third of their traffic if they took eight seconds to load. By 2006, that had shrunk to four. Now, Google puts them on notice if it takes more than two' (Acceleration Book 5).
4   Colvile (2017) in Accelaration book, 11 - (Advertising slogan for the BlackBerry Playbook).
5   Apps such as Blinkist and Joosr are examples for this. Please see the news material on this subject here: https://www.theguardian.com/books/booksblog/2016/jun/23/condensed-apps-that-turn-books-into-15-minute-reads-joosr-blinkist
6   The notion of 'language as protagonist' (*Sprache als Hauptdarsteller*) is introduced by Gerda Poschmann qtd. in Barnett (2005: 140–1).
7   Various reviews of the piece made similar connections to such works, please see here for examples: http://statesofdeliquescence.blogspot.com/2014/07/break-on-through-to-other-side.html; https://synonymsforchurlish.tumblr.com/post/89196456338/lets-make-love-and-listen-to-death-from-above; http://postcardsgods.blogspot.com/2014/08/this-is-how-we-die-forest-fringe.html
8   For further information, see: Harvey (1990). Particularly see, Part III, 'The Experience of Space and Time', pp. 201–84.
9   For further information, see Giddens (1990).
10 For further information, see Jameson (1991); Jameson and Miyoshi, (2003).
11 Tim Albery chose to balance genders with four men and four women; in terms of nationality, he selected five British actors, a Portuguese, a Nigerian and a Serbian actor. The Nigerian actor was black; all the other actors were white.

Chapter 4

1   Gergen (1996: 127–41, 127).
2   Pfister (1993).
    Pfister identifies 'figure' as 'dramatic figure' in contradiction with 'character' while alluding to 'the ontological difference between fictional figures and real characters'. Alternatively, although I will refer to the artificial construct of 'character' in a similar way, I shall avoid delineating 'figure' as 'dramatic' to indicate its fictitiousness, since in the context of this chapter it might

confusingly refer to the use of character in the convention of naturalist tradition. Thus, I shall be using the term interchangeably with 'postdramatic character/actor', speaking figure or text-bearer.

3 There are only dashes in front of the lines in scene 2, which indicates the use of dialogue form. Stephens (2009: 273). All references to *Pornography* are taken from this edition.

4 The interview can be accessed through the TheatreVoice website: Aleks Sierz, 'Interview: Simon Stephens/ Playwright Simon Stephens on Pornography'. http://www.theatrevoice.com/audio/playwright-simon-stephens-on-pornography/ (accessed 13 July 2020).

Chapter 5

1 Subsequent quotations refer to the email interview I conducted with the playwright Douglas Maxwell in July–August 2010. This interview is unpublished and will be indicated as 'Maxwell Interview'.

2 All subsequent quotations refer to the interview I conducted with the director John Tiffany, on 10 August 2010. This interview is unpublished and will be indicated as 'Tiffany Interview'.

Chapter 6

1 It is important to note here that although social media platforms allow anyone with an internet connection to become a user and writer, this should not suggest that the service is actually free or the platform is based on egalitarian values. Every single time a user posts, shares, responds, searches, etc. on a social media platform, she shares data with the system. This is how the network of global corporations, media companies, political parties and so on make profit. Therefore, the idea that we are all authors and we can enjoy instant creative and expressive autonomy is predominantly a bait to enable mass surveillance and data mining. For further info, please see books such as Seymour's 2019).

2 Subsequent quotations refer to the phone interview I conducted with the playwright David Greig in April 2020. This interview is unpublished and will be indicated as 'Greig Interview' in the text.

Conclusion

1 As discussed in the Preface, Cinna in Tim Crouch's play *I, Cinna (The Poet)* questions the role and potency of words and writing (his role as a poet)

in the face of big sociopolitical events and harsh realities such as violent riots and police brutality that he follows via his mobile phone and laptop. Throughout the play, Cinna questions whether his words can change anything and have an impact on people's perception and society.

2 Cambridge Analytica – a private company that uses data mining and data analysis for election management and process – mined, analysed and used individuals' personal data (e.g. likes, profile pictures, contacts on social media platforms) in managing, marketing and manipulating Donald Trump's election and the Brexit (Leave) campaigns. Further information is available online: https://www.theguardian.com/technology/2017/may/07/the-great-british-brexit-robbery-hijacked-democracy; https://www.ted.com/talks/carole_cadwalladr_facebook_s_role_in_brexit_and_the_threat_to_democracy?language=en

3 For information on *Karen*, please see https://www.blasttheory.co.uk/projects/karen/ Also, see Ilter (2018).

References

Adorno, T. W. (2002), *Essays on Music*, trans. S. H. Gillespie, Berkeley: University of California Press.

Adorno, T. W. (2005), 'On the Fetish Character in Music and the Regression of Listening', in Andrew Arato and Eike Gebhardt (eds), *The Essential Frankfurt School Reader*, 270–300, New York: Continuum.

Allen, R. (2012), 'Earthbound: Strindberg's "Dream Play" Reimagined for the Era of Digital Media Convergence', *Scandinavian Studies*, 84 (3): 413–24.

Altheide, D. L. and R. P. Snow (1979), *Media Logic*, Beverly Hills: SAGE.

Aronson, A. (1999), 'Technology and Dramaturgical Development: Five Observations', *Theatre Research International*, 24 (2): 188–97.

Aston, E. and E. Diamond, eds (2009), *The Cambridge Companion to Caryl Churchill*, Cambridge: Cambridge UP.

Auslander, P. (1992), *Presence and Resistance: Postmodernism and Cultural Politics in Contemporary American Performance*, Michigan: Michigan UP.

Auslander, P. (1995), '"Just Be Your Self": Logocentrism and Difference in Performance Theory', in P. B. Zarrilli (ed.), *Acting (Re)Considered: Theories and Practices*, 53–62, London: Routledge.

Auslander, P. (1999), *Liveness: Performance in a Mediatized Culture*, London: Routledge.

Auslander, P. (2012), 'Digital Liveness: A Historico-Philosophical Perspective', *PAJ*, 102: 3–11.

Badiou, A. (2008), 'Rhapsody for the Theatre: A Short Philosophical Treatise', trans. B. Bosteels, *Theatre Survey*, 49 (2): 187–238.

Bailey, B. C. (2014), *This Is How We Die*, London: Oberon.

Barker, C. (2008), *Cultural Studies: Theory and Practice*, London: Sage.

Barnett, D. (2005), 'Reading and Performing Uncertainty: Michael Frayn's Copenhagen and the Postdramatic Theatre', *Theatre Research International*, 30 (2): 139–49.

Barnett, D. (2008), 'When Is a Play not a Drama? Two Examples of Postdramatic Theatre Texts', *New Theatre Quarterly*, 24 (1): 14–23.

Baudrillard, J. (1993), *The Transparency of Evil: Essays on Extreme Phenomena*, trans. J. Benedict, London: Verso.

Baudrillard, J. (1994), *Simulacra and Simulation*, trans. S. Faria Glaser, Michigan: Michigan UP.

Bauman, Z. (2003), *Liquid Love: On the Frailty of Human Bonds*, Cambridge: Polity Press.

Bauman, Z. (2012), *Liquid Modernity*, Cambridge: Polity Press.

Bay-Cheng, S. (2015), 'Virtual Realisms: Dramatic Forays into the Future', *Theatre Journal*, 67: 687–98.

Bay-Cheng, S., C. Kattenbelt, A. Lavender and R. Nelson, eds (2010), *Mapping Intermediality in Performance*, Amsterdam: Amsterdam UP.

BBC News (2015), *David Cameron Criticized over Migrant 'swarm' Language*. Available at: https://www.bbc.co.uk/news/uk-politics-33716501 (Accessed 5 July 2020).

Beck, U. and E. Beck-Gernsheim (2001), *Individualization: Institutionalized Individualism and Its Social and Political Consequences*, London: SAGE.

Benjamin, W. (1969), 'The Work of Art in the Age of Mechanical Reproduction', in H. Arendt (ed. and trans.), *Illuminations*, 1–26, New York: Schocken Books.

Bernstein, J. M., ed. (1991), 'Introduction', in Theodor W. Adorno, *The Culture Industry: Selected Essays on Mass Culture*, 1–29, London and New York: Routledge.

Berry, D. M. and M. Dieter (2015), 'Thinking Postdigital Aesthetics: Art, Computation and Design', in D. M. Berry and M. Dieter (eds), *Postdigital Aesthetics: Art, Computation and Design*, 1–11, Basingstoke: Palgrave Macmillan.

Billington, M. (1997), 'Review on *Attempts* in *The Guardian*', *Theatre Record*, 6 (17): 312.

Bolter, J. D. and R. Grusin. (1999), *Remediation: Understanding New Media*, Cambridge, MA: MIT Press.

Brecht, B. (1964), *Brecht on Theatre: The Development of an Aesthetic*, trans. J. Willett, London: Methuen.

Butler, J. (1990), 'Performative Acts and Gender Constitution: An Essay in Phenomenology and Feminist Theory', in Sue-Ellen Case (ed.), *Performing Feminisms: Feminist Critical Theory and Theatre*, 270–82, Baltimore: Johns Hopkins UP.

Callens, J. (2003), 'Staging the Televised (Nation)', *Theatre Research International*, 28: (1): 61–78.

Causey, M. (2016), 'Postdigital Performance', *Theatre Journal*, 68 (3): 427–41.

Chapple, F. and C. Kattenbelt, eds (2006), *Intermediality in Theatre and Performance*, Amsterdam and New York: Rodopi.

Churchill, C. (2012), *Love and Information*, London: Nick Hern Books.

Collard, C. (2017), 'Traveling at the Speed of Thought: John Jesurun in conversation with Christophe Collard', *PAJ*, 115: 12–23.

Colvile, R. (2017), *The Great Acceleration: How the World Is Getting Faster, Faster*, London: Bloomsbury.

Cooper, N. (2008), 'Review on *Pornography* in *The Herald*', *Theatre Record* (Edinburgh International Festival and Fringe 2008 Supplement to Theatre Record).

Couldry, N. (2008), 'Mediatization or Mediation? Alternative Understandings of the Emergent Space of Digital Storytelling', *New Media Society*, 10: 373–91.

Couldry, N. (2012), *Media, Society, World: Social Theory and Digital Media Practice*, Cambridge: Polity Press.

Couldry, N. (2015), 'The Myth of "us": Digital Networks, Political Change and the Production of Collectivity', *Information Communication and Society*, 18 (6): 608–26.

Cramer, S. (2002), 'Review on *Helmet*', *Theatre Record*, 22 (10): 372.

Crimp, M. (2005), *Plays: 2 No One Sees the Video, The Misanthrope, Attempts on Her Life, The Country*, London: Faber and Faber.

Crockett, Z. (2019), 'The tragic data behind Black Friday deaths', *The Hustle*. Online, 23 November. Available online: https://thehustle.co/black-friday-deaths-injuries-data/

Croteau, D. and W. Hoynes (2003), *Media Society: Industries, Images, and Audiences*, Thousand Oaks: Pine Forge Press.

Crystal, D. (2001), *Language and the Internet*, Cambridge: Cambridge UP.

de Jongh, N. (2007), 'Review on *Attempts* in *The Evening Standard*', *Theatre Record*, 6 (27): 311.

Debord, G. (2010), *Society of the Spectacle*, Detroit: Black.

Deleuze, G. (1992), 'Postscript on the Societies of Control', *October*, 59: 3–7.

Delgado-Garcia, C. (2015), *Rethinking Character in Contemporary British Theatre: Aesthetics, Politics, Subjectivity*, Berlin/Boston: Walter de Gruyter.

Dibdin, T. (2014), 'The Yes/No Plays', 18 September. Available online: www.alledinburghtheatre.com/the-yesno-plays/

Dingli, A. and D. Seychell (2015), *The New Digital Natives: Cutting the Chord*, Berlin/Heidelberg: Springer.

Dixon, S. (2007), *Digital Performance: A History of New Media in Theater, Dance, Performance Art, and Installation*, Cambridge, MA: MIT Press.

Eagleton, T. (1996), *The Illusions of Postmodernity*, Oxford: Blackwell.

Eckersall, P. (2006), 'Towards an Expanded Dramaturgical Practice: A Report on "The Dramaturgy and Cultural Intervention Project"', *Theatre Research International*, 31 (3): 283–97.

Ellestrőm, L., ed. (2010), *Media Borders, Multimodality and Intermediality*, London: Palgrave Macmillan.

Elliott, A. (2007), *Concepts of the Self*, Cambridge: Polity.

Etchells, T. (1999), *Certain Fragments*, London: Routledge.

Fairclough, N. (1995), *Media Discourse*, London: Arnold/Hodder Headline Group.

Ferguson, B. (2014), 'Twitter Plays Fry Off the Screen and Onto Stage', *The Scotsman*, 4 September. Available online: https://www.pressreader.com/uk/the-scotsman/20140904/281732677673366

Fergusson, R. (1996), *Henrik Ibsen: A New Biography*, London: Richard Cohen Books.

Fisher, M. (2009), *Capitalist Realism: Is There No Alternative?*, Hampshire: Zero Books (Jhn Hunt Publishing).

Flusser, V. (2011), *Into the Universe of Technical Images*, trans. N. A. Roth, Minneapolis: Minnesota UP.

Foss, R. (1997), 'Review on Attempts on *What's On*', *Theatre Record*, 6 (17): 313.

Foucault, M. (1972), *The Archaeology of Knowledge and The Discourse on Language*, trans. A. M. Sheridan Smith, New York: Pantheon Books.

Foucault, M. (1978), *The History of Sexuality, Vol. 1: An Introduction*, trans. R. Hurley, Harmondsworth: Penguin.

Foucault, M. (1980), *Power/Knowledge*, ed. C. Gordon, New York: Pantheon Books.

Frasca, G. (2001), 'Videogames of the Oppressed: Videogames as a Means for Critical Thinking and Debate'. MA Thesis. Georgia Institute of Technology, Atlanta, Georgia. Available online: https://ludology.typepad.com/weblog/articles/thesis/FrascaThesisVideogames.pdf

Fried, R. K. (1985), 'The Cinematic Theatre of John Jesurun', *Drama Review*, 29 (1): 57–72.

Fromm, E. (2013), *Marx's Concept of Man*, London/New York: Bloomsbury.

Fuchs, E. (1996), *The Death of Character*, Bloomington: Indiana UP.

Furse, A. (2011), 'Introduction', in A. Furse (ed.), *Theatre in Pieces: Politics, Poetics and Interdisciplinary Collaboration*, v–ix, London: Methuen.

Gadamer, H. G. (2004), *Truth and Method*, London: Continuum.

Gardner, L. (1998), 'Sex in a Chilling Climate', *The Guardian*, 3 January.

Gardner, L. (2008), 'The Finger-Pointer', *The Guardian*, 4 August. Available online: https://www.theguardian.com/culture/2008/aug/04/edinburghfestival.festivals

Gergen, K. J. (1996), 'Technology and the Self: From the Essential to the Sublime', in D. Grodin and T. R. Lindlof (eds), *Constructing the Self in a Mediated World*, 127–41, London: SAGE.

Gergen, K. J. (1999), 'The Self: Death by Technology', *The Hedgehog Review*, 25–33. Available online: https://hedgehogreview.com/issues/identity/articles/the-self-death-by-technology

Giannachi, G. (2004), *Virtual Theatres: An Introduction*, London: Routledge.

Giddens, A. (1990), *The Consequences of Modernity*, Cambridge: Polity Press/Basil Blackwell.

Giddens, A. (1991), *Modernity and Self-Identity: Self and Society in the Late Modern Age*, Cambridge: Polity.

Graham, E. L. (2002), *Representation of the Post/Human*, Manchester: Manchester UP.

Hackman, R. (2015), 'Are You Beach Body Ready? Controversial Weight Loss Ad Sparks Varied Reactions', *The Guardian*, 27 June. Available online: https://www.theguardian.com/us-news/2015/jun/27/beach-body-ready-america-weight-loss-ad-instagram

Haley, J. (2014), *The Nether*, London: Faber & Faber.

Hamburger, M. (2008), 'Theatertreffen in Berlin, May 2008', *Contemporary Theatre Review*, 18 (4): 531–44.

Hansen, M. B. N. (2010), 'Introduction to Chapter 5 on Memory by Bernard Stiegler', in W. J. T. Mitchell and Mark B. N. Hansen (eds), *Critical Terms of Media Studies*, 64–88, Chicago and London: Chicago UP.

Haraway, D. (1991), 'A Cyborg Manifesto: Science, Technology, and Socialist-Feminism in the Late Twentieth Century', in *Simians, Cyborgs and Women: The Reinvention of Nature*, 149–81, New York: Routledge. Here it is accessed via https://gendermediatechnology.weebly.com/uploads/5/2/8/6/5286294/cyborg_manifesto.pdf

Haring-Smith, T. (2003), 'Dramaturging Non-Realism: Creating a New Vocabulary', *Theatre Topics*, 13(1): 45–54.

Harvey, D. (1990), *The Condition of Postmodernity: An Enquiry into the Origins of Cultural Change*, Oxford: Blackwell.

Hassan, I. (1977), 'Prometheus as Performer: Toward a Posthuman Culture? A University Masque in Five Scenes', *Georgia Review*, 31: 830–50.

Hayles, N. K. (1999), *How We Became Posthuman: Virtual Bodies in Cybernetics, Literature, and Informatics*, Chicago: Chicago UP.

Hayles, N. K. (2012), *How We Think: Digital Media and Contemporary Technogenesis*, Chicago and London: Chicago University Press.

Hemming, S. (1997), 'Review on *Faust is Dead* on *Financial Times*', *Theatre Record*, 17 (5): 235.

Hepp, A. (2012), 'Mediatization, Media Technologies and the "Moulding Forces" of the Media', *Communications*, 37 (1): 1–28.

Hjarvard, S. (2004), 'The Globalization of Language. How the Media Contribute to the Spread of English and the Emergence of Medialects', *Nordicom Review*, 1 (2), 75–97.

Hjarvard, S. (2009), 'Soft Individualism: Media and the Changing Social Character', in A. Strindberg (1998), '*Miss Julie*, Preface', in *Miss Julie and Other Plays*, trans. M. Robinson, Oxford: Oxford UP.

Hjarvard, S. (2013), *The Mediatization of Culture and Society*, London: Routledge.

Holborow, M. (2015), *Language and Neoliberalism*, New York: Routledge.

Hopkins, K. (2015), 'Rescue Boats? I'd Use Gunships to Stop Migrants', *The Sun*, 17 April. Available online: http://www.gc.soton.ac.uk/files/2015/01/hopkins-17april-2015.pdf

Horkheimer, M. and T. W. Adorno (2002), *Dialectic of Enlightenment: Philosophical Fragments*, trans. G. S. Noerr, Redwood City: Stanford UP.

Houlgate, S. (1986), *Hegel, Nietzsche and the Criticism of Metaphysics*, Cambridge: Cambridge UP.

Höyng, P. (2005), 'Lessing's Drama Theory: Discursive Writings on Drama, Performance, and Theater', in Barbara Fischer and Thomas C. Fox (eds), *A Companion to the Works of Gotthold Ephraim Lessing*, 211–31, New York: Camden House.

Hughes, H. (2001), (First Runner – poem in) 'The Message is the Medium', *The Guardian*, 3 May. Available online: https://www.theguardian.com/technology/2001/may/03/internet.poetry

Ilter, S. (2018), 'Blast Theory's *Karen*: Exploring the Ontology of Technotexts', *Performance Research*, 23 (2): 67–72.

Jackson, S. and M. Weems (2015), *The Builders Association: Performance and Media in Contemporary Theater*, Cambridge, MA: MIT Press.
Jameson, F. (1991), *Postmodernism or, The Cultural Logic of Late Capitalism*, London: Verso.
Jameson, F. and M. Miyoshi (2003), *The Cultures of Globalization*, Durham: Duke UP.
Jensen, A. P. (2007), *Theatre in a Media Culture: Production, Performance and Perception since 1970*, Jefferson: McFarland & Company Inc.
Jesurun, J. (2009), *Shatterhand Massacree and Other Media Texts*, New York: PAJ Publications.
Jesurun, J. (2012), 'Giving Voice to the Camera or How I Learned to Speak', *PAJ: A Journal of Performance and Art*, 34 (1): 121–3.
Jones, A. (2007), 'Review on *Attempts* in *The Independent*', *Theatre Record*, 6 (27): 309.
Jürs-Munby, K. (2006), 'Introduction', in H. Thies-Lehmann, *Postdramatic Theatre*, 1–15, London: Routledge.
Jürs-Munby, K. (2009), 'The Resistant Text in Postdramatic Theatre: Performing Elfriede Jelinek's Sprachflächen', *Performance Research*, 14 (1): 46–56.
Keegan, V. (2002), '160 Characters in Search of an Author', *The Guardian*, 7 November. Available online: http://www.guardian.co.uk/technology/2002/nov/07/textpoetrycompetition2002.poetry1
Kent, A. (1990), 'Medialization, Media Logic and Mediarchy', *Nordicom Review*, 11 (2): 47–50.
Kerbel, L. *National Theatre Education (Workpack): Attempts on Her Life*. Available online: https://www.nationaltheatre.org.uk/sites/default/files/attempts_bkpk.pdf
Kroker, A. (2001), *The Possessed Individual: Technology and the French Postmodern*, Montreal: CTHEORY Books.
Laurel, B. (1991), *Computers as Theatre*, Boston: Addison Wesley Longman, Inc.
Lavender, A. (2002), 'The Moment of Realized Actuality', in M. M. Delgado and C. Svich (eds), *Theatre in Crisis?: Performance Manifestos for a New Century*, 183–91, Manchester: Manchester UP.
Lehmann, H.-T. (2006), *Postdramatic Theatre*, trans. K. Jürs-Munby, London: Routledge.
Lifton, R. J. (1993), *The Protean Self: Human Resilience in an Age of Fragmentation*, New York: Basic Books.
Livingstone, S. (2009a), 'On the Mediation of Everything: ICA Presidential Address', *Journal of Communication*, 59: 1–18.
Livingstone, S. (2009b), 'Foreword: Coming to Terms with "Mediatization"', in K. Lundby (ed.), *Mediatization: Concept, Changes, Consequences*, ix–xi, New York: Peter Lang.
Lonergan, P. (2015), *Theatre and Social Media*, London: Palgrave.
Lundby, K. (2009), 'Media Logic: Looking for Social Interaction', in K. Lundby (ed.), *Mediatization: Concept, Changes, Consequences*, 101–22, New York: Peter Lang.

Lundin, R. (2005), *From Nature to Experience: The American Search for Cultural Authority*, Lanham and Plymouth: Rowman & Littlefield Publishers, Inc.

Macaulay, A. (1997), 'Review on *Attempts* in *Financial Times*', *Theatre Record*, 6 (17): 312.

Manovich, L. (2001), *The Language of New Media*, Cambridge, MA: MIT Press.

Manovich, L. (2008), 'Introduction to Info-Aesthetics', in O. Enwezor, N. Conde, and T. Smith (eds), *Antinomies of Art and Culture: Modernity, Postmodernity, Contemporaneity*, 333–45, Durham: Duke University Press.

Marber, P. (1999), *Closer*, New York: Grove Press/Atlantic Monthly Press.

Marranca, B. (2010), 'Performance as Design: The Mediaturgy of John Jesurun's *Firefall*', *PAJ*, 96: 16–24.

Martinson, S. D. (2005), 'Lessing and the European Enlightenment' in K. B. Fischer and Thomas C. F. (eds), *A Companion to Works of Gotthold Ephraim Lessing*, 41–67, New York: Boydell & Brewer, Inc.

Maxwell, D. (2002), *Helmet*, London: Oberon Books.

Mazzoleni, G. and W. Schulz (2010), '"Mediatization" of Politics: A Challenge for Democracy?', *Political Communication*, 16 (3): 247–61.

McLuhan, M. (2001), *Understanding Media: The Extensions of Man*, London: Routledge.

McMillan, J. (2008), 'Theatre Reviews: Fall / Pornography', *Scotsman*, 5 August. Available online: https://www.scotsman.com/news/theatre-reviews-fall-pornography-2477979

Mills, S. (2003), *Michel Foucault*, London: Routledge.

Mitchell, W. J. T. and M. B. Hansen, eds (2010), *Critical Terms for Media Studies*, Chicago and London: Chicago UP.

Muse, J. (2012), '140 Characters in Search of a Theater: Twitter Plays', *Theater*, 42 (2): 42–63.

Nyusztay, I. (2002), *Myth, Telos, Identity: The Tragic Schema in Greek and Shakespearean Drama*, Amsterdam: Rodopi.

O'Neill, S. (2015), 'Shakespeare and Social Media', *Literature Compass*, 12 (6): 274–85.

Pavis, P. (1998), *Dictionary of the Theatre: Terms, Concepts, and Analysis*, trans. C. Shantz, Toronto and Buffalo: University of Toronto Press.

Pavis, P. (2003), 'Afterword: Contemporary Dramatic Writings and the New Technologies', in Caridad Svich (ed.), *Trans-global Readings: Crossing Theatrical Boundaries*, 187–203, Manchester: Manchester UP.

Pavis, P. (2016), *Routledge Dictionary of Performance and Contemporary Theatre*, trans. A. Brown, London: Routledge.

Pfister, M. (1993), *The Theory and Analysis*, Cambridge: Cambridge UP.

Phelan, P. (1993), *Unmarked: The Politics of Performance*, London: Routledge.

Postman, N. (1992), *Technopoly: The Surrender of Culture to Technology*, New York: Vintage Books.

Radosavljevic, D. (2013), *Theatre-Making: Interplay Between Text and Performance in the 21st Century*, Hampshire and New York: Palgrave Macmillan.

Rancière, J. (2010), *Dissensus: On Politics and Aesthetics*, trans. S. Corcoran, London: Bloomsbury.
Rancière, J. (2013), *The Politics of Aesthetics: The Distribution of the Sensible*, trans G. Rockhill, London: Continuum.
Ravenhill, M. (1997), *Plays: 1 (Faust Is Dead)*, London: Methuen.
Ravenhill, M. (2003), 'A Touch of Evil', *The Guardian*, 22 March. Available online: http://www.guardian.co.uk/stage/2003/mar/22/theatre.artsfeatures
Ravenhill, M. (2006), 'Me, My iBook, and Writing in America', *Contemporary Theatre Review*, 16 (1): 131–8.
RT (2015), *Le Pen Compares Migrant Influx to Barbarian Invasion of Rome*. Available at: https://www.rt.com/news/315466-le-pen-migrant-barbarian-invasion/ (Accessed 5 July 2020).
Salen, K. and E. Zimmerman. (2004), *Rules of Play: Game Design Fundamentals*, Cambridge, MA and London: The MIT Press.
Saunders, G. (2008), *Patrick Marber's Closer*, New York: Continuum.
Schmidt, K. (2005), *The Theater of Transformation: Postmodernism in American Drama*, Amsterdam: Rodopi.
Schneier, B. (2015), *Data and Goliath: The Hidden Battles to Collect Your Data and Control Your World*, New York: W.W. Norton & Company.
Schradie, J. (2019), *The Revolution That Wasn't: How Digital Activism Favors Conservatives*, Cambridge, MA and London: Harvard UP.
Scott, R. D. (2002), 'Review on *Helmet*', *Theatre Record*, 22 (10): 626.
Seymour, R. (2019), *The Twittering Machine*, London: The Indigo Press.
Shepherd, S. and M. Wallis (2004), *Drama/Theatre/Performance*, London: Routledge.
Sierz, A. (2001), *In-Yer-Face Theatre: British Drama Today*, London: Faber and Faber.
Sierz, A. (2006), *The Theatre of Martin Crimp*, London: A & C Black Publishers.
States, B. O. (1985), 'The Anatomy of Dramatic Character', *Theatre Journal*, 37 (1): 87–101.
Stephens, S. (2009), *Plays: 2*, London: Methuen.
Stowell-Kaplan, I. (2015), 'In the Domain of The Nether: Theatre and Virtuality in a World without Consequence', *TDR*, 59 (2): 157–63.
Svich, C. (2003), 'Commerce and Morality in the Theatre of Mark Ravenhill', *Contemporary Theatre Review*, 13 (1): 81–95.
The Wooster Group (1981), 'The Wooster Group's *Route 1 and 9 (The Last Act)*', *Culture Shock*, Available online: https://www.pbs.org/wgbh/cultureshock/flashpoints/theater/woostert.html
Thompson, J. B. (1995), *The Media and Modernity*, Cambridge: Polity Press.
Thurlow, C. (2007), 'Fabricating Youth: New Media Discourse and The Technologization of Young People', in S. A. Johnson and A. Ensslin (eds), *Language in the Media: Representations, Identities, Ideologies*, 213–33, London: Continuum.

Tomlin, L. (2009), '"And their stories fell apart even as I was telling them": Poststructuralist Performance and the No-Longer-Dramatic Text', *Performance Research*, 14 (1): 57–64.

Trueman, Matt (2013), 'What Can Theatre Say about the Internet?', *The Guardian*, 21 January. Available online: http://www.guardian.co.uk/stage/2013/jan/21/theatre-say-about-internet

Turkle, S. (1995), *Life on the Screen: Identity in the Age of the Internet*, New York: Simon and Schuster.

Turkle, S. (2011), *Alone Together: Why We Expect More from Technology and Less from Each Other*, New York: Basic Books.

Turner, C. and S. K. Behrndt (2008), *Dramaturgy and Performance*, Basingstoke: Palgrave.

Wallace, C. (2005), 'Responsibility and Postmodernity: Mark Ravenhill and 1990s British Drama', *Theory and Practice in English Studies: Proceedings from the Eighth Conference of British, American and Canadian Studies*, 4: 269–75.

Wallace, C. (2016), 'Yes and No? Dissensus and David Greig's Recent Work', *Contemporary Theatre Review*, 26 (1): 31–8.

Worthen, W. B. (2010), *Drama: Between Poetry and Performance*, Chichester: Wiley-Blackwell.

Wotzko, R. (2012), 'Newspaper Twitter: Applied Drama and Microblogging', *Research in Drama Education: The Journal of Applied Theatre and Performance*, 17: 569–81.

Zimmermann, H. (2002), 'Martin Crimp, *Attempts on Her Life*: Postdramatic, Postmodern Satiric?', *Contemporary Drama in English*, 9: 105–25.

Index

Note: Page numbers followed by "n" refer to notes.

Actors' Touring Company (ATC) 49, 50, 56
Adorno, T. W. 103–5
aesthetic regime of art 35
Albery, T. 93–4, 201 n.11
Allen, R. 31, 200 n.10
Altheide, D. 16
Althusser, L. 104, 105
Anglophone theatre 3, 6, 7, 9, 11, 29, 37, 48, 60, 71, 93, 157, 194
Appadurai, A. 74
Aristotle 112
    Poetics 151
Aronson, A. 30
Artaud, A. 33
ATC, *see* Actors' Touring Company (ATC)
Auslander, P. 26–7, 199 nn.1, 2, 200 n.8
awareness with acceptance 49, 56

Bailey, C. B. 64
    This Is How We Die (*THWD*) 1, 10, 17, 63, 68, 162, 195
    consciousness 75–8
    invisible mediatization on stage 97–9
    mediatization and late capitalism, connection between 84, 87–90
    mediatized language 72–4
    mediatized subjectivity 79, 82–3
Baker, D. 58
Baudrillard, J. 41, 42, 53, 94, 107, 111

Bauman, Z. 13, 53, 70, 104, 106–7, 155, 165
Bay-Cheng, S. 60, 199 n.1
Beames, D. 59
Beck, U. 104, 105
Beckett, S. 114
    Act Without Words II 79
    Breath 79
    Not I 79, 83, 114, 131
Benjamin, W. 199 n.7
    'Work of Art in the Age of Mechanical Reproduction, The' 147
Bernard Shaw, G. 69, 113
Berry, D. M. 182
Between the Devil and the Deep Blue Sea 2
Birkbeck College 1
bite-size characterization 119
Blast Theory 28
    Can You See Me Now? 149
    I'd Hide You 23
    Karen 6, 197, 199 n.5
    Rider Spoke 2
Blinkist 201 n.5
Brecht, B. 21, 24, 114, 115, 190, 199 n.7
British theatre 6–7
Brueghel, P. 126, 141
Builders' Association 6, 22, 55, 200 n.8
    Continuous City 175
    Super Vision 14
Butler, J. 105

Cambridge Analytica 121, 194, 203 n.2

Cameron, D. 84
*Caucasian Chalk Circle,
The* 114
Causey, M. 27, 173–4, 183, 199 n.2,
200 n.7
Chapple, F. 199 n.1
characterization 1, 3, 5, 6, 8, 29, 41,
48, 55–7, 60, 73, 92, 94, 95,
102, 127–9, 131, 136, 138,
140, 147, 154, 161, 162,
176, 191, 196
bite-size 119
liberal-humanist approach
to 112, 113, 118, 121,
133, 136
mediatized subjectivity
and 111–17
mode of 10, 54, 101, 113, 119,
120, 122, 124, 133, 134,
137, 184
resistant aesthetics of 144–5
character presentation 6, 8, 10, 54,
101, 113, 114, 117, 125,
127, 129, 133, 137
Chekhov, A. 48, 69, 112
Churchill, C.
Heart's Desire 36
Love and Information 1, 3, 8,
10, 17, 28, 35, 68, 116, 122,
148, 149, 170, 183, 196
performing 167–9
shape of information
age 160–6
Clements, R. 189
cogito 103
Colvile, R. 201 n.4
commercialization 18, 19
Complicité 2
Encounter, The 14
computer games
definition of 150
dramatizing 149–58
computers 90–3
Coney 2, 198

consciousness, mediatized world
and 75–8
consumer capitalism 67, 84, 125,
154, 155, 157
Couldry, N. 16, 200 n.5
Crimp, M. 55, 64
Attempts on Her Life 5, 10, 17,
63, 68, 101, 118, 195
characterization 112, 116
consciousness 75–8
media-saturated stage, critical
aesthetics of 93–7
mediatization and late
capitalism, connection
between 84–7, 90
mediatized language 72–4
mediatized subjectivity 79–
81, 83
Treatment, The 39
Crouch, T. xiii, 1
I, Cinna (The Poet) xii, 198,
202–3 n.1
I, Shakespeare xii
Oak Tree, An 32, 59, 116
Crystal, D. 66
culinary theatre 59
Cuthbertson, C. 189

Darling, A. 182
dataveillance 13, 18, 19
Debord, G. 43
deindividuated posthuman
being 102–11
deindividuation/deindividuated 82,
101–11, 117–19, 121, 127,
129, 136, 140, 144
Delgado-Garcia, C. 112
Derrida, J. 115–16
Descartes, R. 103
desirable self 106
Devlin, E. 56
Dibdin, T. 189
Diderot, D. 113
Dieter, M. 182

Index

différance 116
Digital Humanities in Theatre Research 26
digital theatre 2, 26
discontinuity 25, 35, 120, 126–7
dissensus/dissident 25, 35, 40, 90, 99–100, 140, 157, 170, 190
distribution of the sensible 24, 35, 40, 59, 72, 106, 187
Dixon, S. 199 n.1
Digital Performance 28
dramatic dialogue 6
dramatic mediatized dramaturgy 9, 60–1, 72, 92
dramatic theatre 5, 9, 23, 24, 29, 33, 34, 40, 48, 50, 56, 59, 60, 73, 82, 92, 96, 115, 154, 157, 158, 160, 166, 169, 170, 174, 183, 188
dramatic writing xiii, 1, 3, 5, 6, 8, 14, 29–37, 60, 175, 179, 188, 191, 193, 196, 197
  for mediatized age and stage 32–4
dramaturgy, *see also individual entries*
  definition of 4–5
  of language 63–100
  mediatized (*see* mediatized dramaturgy)
  multi-lingual 87
Durif, E., *Via Negativa* 30

emancipation 104
embodiment xiii, 28, 42, 59, 102, 137, 143
Encounter, The 32
episodic plot structure 6
Etchells, T. 23, 26

Facebook 3, 6, 19, 20, 46, 106, 121, 124, 167, 176, 191
fate 112
Fisher, M. 200 n.6

Fleming, E. 58
Flusser, V. 200 n.4
Forced Entertainment 6, 22, 24, 198, 200 n.8
  Quizoola! 2
  Speak Bitterness 2
  Tomorrow's Parties 23
form, definition of 16
Foucault, M. 65, 104, 200 n.1
Fuchs, E. 115
Fuel Theatre, *Ring* 14

Gable, J., *15th Line, The* 7, 11, 174–6, 180, 184–7, 191, 194, 196
Gadamer, H-G. 64
Genet, J. 114
Gergen, K. J. 106, 201 n.1
Giannachi, G. 199 n.1
Giddens, A. 106, 121, 201 n.9
Ginsberg, A. 83
global capitalism 82, 85–7, 130, 136, 200 n.3
global capitalist culture industry 13
globalization 7, 18, 73, 84, 85, 87, 97
Gmail 167
Goode, C., *Hippo World Guest Book* 11, 175, 177, 178, 191, 197
Google 3, 19, 121
Greig, D. 177, 202 n.2
  Yes/No Plays, The 5, 11, 173–5, 177–91, 196, 197
Grusin, R. A. 158
Guardian, The 3, 66
Gutenberg, J. 17

Hadley, B., *Theatre, Social Media, and Meaning Making* 28, 176–7
Hale, A. 59
Haley, N., *Nether, The* 1, 7–9, 23–4, 29, 32, 37, 39–41, 46, 60, 92, 122, 157, 170, 189, 194

form 53–6
performance 56–9
thematics 50–3
Handke, P. 33, 79, 118
Hansen, M. 15
Haraway, D., 'Cyborg Manifesto, A' 109–10
Harvey, D. 201 n.8
Hassan, I. 109
Hayles, N. K. 109, 199 n.4
  How We Became Posthuman 110
Headlong 23, 56
Hegel, G. W. F. 112
Herrin, J. 56, 57
Hjarvard, S. 15–17, 107
homo media 145
  multidimensional reflections on 130–40
  on stage, performing 140–4
Horkheimer, M. 103
Husserl, E. 103

Ibsen, H. 48, 60, 69
  Doll's House, A 113
IFTR (International Federation for Theatre Research) 26
Ilter, S. 199 n.5, 203 n.3
Imitating the Dog 22, 198
individualization 18, 19, 96, 104–6, 108, 109, 117, 118, 120–2, 125, 136, 139, 155, 179
information and communication technologies 1, 200 n.3
information overload 161–4, 169
Instagram 14, 46, 106, 167
intermedial theatre 2
Intermediality in Theatre and Performance 26, 27
intertextuality 22, 25, 32
invisible mediatization on stage 97–9
Ionesco, E. 114

Jameson, F. 201 n.10

Jelinek, E. 33, 55, 79, 82
Jensen, A. P. 3, 29
Jesurun, J.
  Everything Rises Must Converge 68
  Firefall 1, 5, 7, 8, 10, 68, 102, 117, 175, 195
  multidimensional reflections on homo media 130–44
Joosr 201 n.5
Jouanneau, J., *Allegria* 30
Jürs-Munby, K. 23, 25

Kane, S. 33, 79
  Crave 112, 116, 118
  4.48 Psychosis 112
Kant, I. 103
Kattenbelt, C. 199 n.1
Kennedy, A., *Movie Star Has to Star in Black and White, A* 29
Kent, A. 199 n.1
Kirby, M. 21–2, 199 n.2
Kitt, T., *Next to Normal* 178
Kittler, F. 15
Koltès, B.-M., *Dans la solitude des champs de cotton* 30
Kroker, A. 111
Krotz, F. 16, 17
Kushner, T. 30
Kustow, M. 3, 29, 199 n.2, 200 n.8

language, mediatized dramaturgy of 63–100
  Attempts on Her Life 72–4
  Closer 69–72
  computers and online culture 90–3
  consciousness 75–8
  dissenting words 99–100
  invisible mediatization on stage 97–9
  media-saturated stage, critical aesthetics of 93–7

Index

mediatization and late capitalism, connection between 83–90
 in mediatized culture 64–7
 subjectivity 78–83
 THWD 72–4
language as protagonist 201 n.6
language surfaces (*Sprachflächen*) 82
Lascaux Caves 173
late capitalism 18, 19, 25, 40, 41, 70, 83–90, 121, 123, 140, 157, 170, 190
Laurel, B., *Computers as Theatre* 151
Le Pen, J.-M. 84
Lehmann, H.-T. 24, 34, 40, 82, 115
 Postdramatic Theatre 33
Lepage, R. 2, 22
 887, 23
Lessing, G. E. 113
Letterman, D. 49
liberal-humanist approach to characterization 112, 113, 118, 121, 133, 136
Life of Galileo, The 114
Lifton, R. J. 110–11
liquid love 53, 70, 165
liveness 2, 26, 27, 187–9, 191, 199 n.2
Livingstone, S. 15
Lloyd, E. B. 90
Lobel, B. 28
 Purge 177, 191
Lonergan, P.
 Social Media and Theatre 176
 Theatre & Social Media 28
Ludgate, L. 189
Lundby, K. 16
Lyceum Theatre-Traverse 23
Lynch, D. 83
Lyric Hammersmith Theatre 49

Macdonald, J. 8–9, 149, 167, 168
Macpherson, K. 189
Magruder, M. T. 58
Mamet, D., *Speed the Plow* 29
Manovich, L. 121
Mapping Intermediality in Performance 28
Marber, P., *Closer* 1, 5, 10, 23, 28, 39, 63, 67, 194
 computers and online culture 90–3
 consciousness 78
 medialect 69–72
Marranca, B. 11, 130, 131, 175, 176
Marx, K. 103
Maxwell, D. 202 n.1
 Helmet 10, 148, 169, 170
 computer games, dramatizing 149–58
 on stage 158–60
Mazzoleni, G. 15
McLuhan, M. 87
media, definition of 4
media ecology 13, 101
media language *versus* mediatized language 201 n.2
media logic 16–17
medialect 5, 10, 66, 69–72, 90, 92
mediasation 17
media-saturated stage, critical aesthetics of 93–7
mediascape 74, 78, 82
mediation 15–16, 47, 158
mediatization 3–5, 7–11, 22–6, 34–40, 61, 66–8, 72, 74, 102, 107, 136, 142, 144, 152, 174, 193, 195, 200 n.3, 201 n.2
 background of 14–17
 contemporary, theorizing 17–21
 definition of 199 n.2
 and late capitalism 83–90
 playtexts and 28–32
 on stage, invisible 97–9
 thematization of 41–59

mediatized age, theatre in   1–11
mediatized culture, language
    in   64–7
mediatized dramaturgy   3–5, 193–8,
    see also individual entries
    in action   8–9
    definition of   5
    dramatic, problematics of   60–1
    of language   67–8
    theorizing   13–38
mediatized subjectivity   78–83,
    101–45
    and characterization   111–17
    deindividuated posthuman
        being   102–11
    homo media, multidimensional
        reflections on   130–44
    pornography   117–30
    resistant aesthetics of
        characterization   144–5
mediatized theatre   6, 10, 11, 21–8,
    31, 32, 97, 193, 197
mediatized thematics   39–61
mediaturgical play   3, 5, 6, 11, 31,
    171, 173–92, 196, 197
    critical meanings and
        effects   187–92
    reflections on   191–2
    Twitter
        theatricality   179–80
        Yes/No Plays, The   180–6
mediaturgy   11, 131, 175–9, 185–91
Metis Arts   2
Miller, A.   22
    Crucible, The   21
Mills, S.   200 n.1
Mitchell, K.   2, 94, 95
    Fräulein Julie   22
Mitchell, W. J. T.   15
Miyoshi, M.   201 n.10
Müller, H.   33, 55, 79, 118
multi-lingual dramaturgy   87
multimedia theatre   2, 21
Murphy, J.   184

Murray, A.   182
Muse, J. H., '140 Characters in
    Search of a Theater: *Twitter
    Plays*'   31

National Collective Devolution
    Max   182
National Theatre   63
Nature Theater of Oklohoma
    Medea   2
    Rambo Solo   23
neoliberal capitalism   106
New Paradise Laboratories   197
    Fatebook   23
New York Futurists   197
New York Times   141
Nietzsche, F.   113
no-longer-dramatic theatre text   5–
    6, 10, 34–8, 64, 68, 72–4,
    78, 83, 100, 115, 144, 148,
    170, 174, 183, 190, 194
Nübling, S.   126–8, 141

objectification   32, 70, 84, 107, 108,
    117, 124, 129, 138
Öhrn, M., *Conte d'amour*   58
Old Vic Theatre   198
O'Neill, S.   31, 200 n.9
online culture   90–3
Ostermeier, T., *Richard III*   2
Owen, G., *Killology*   39

Parks, S.-L.   30
    365 Days / 365 Plays   68, 163
Pavis, P.   30, 116, 193, 199 n.2
Pelletier, A.   49
performance   21–8
    Faust Is Dead   49–50
    Nether, The   56–9
    postdigital   27, 174
    text-as-performance   191
Performance and New
    Technologies   26
Pfister, M.   201 n.2

Phelan, P. 26, 199 n.2, 200 n.8
Philippou, N. 49
physical reality 4, 47, 49, 52, 54, 57, 58, 183
Pinterest 167
Pirandello, L., *Six Characters in Search of an Author* 79
Piscator, E. 21, 199 n.7
Plaintext Players 197
Plato 103
playtext 2, 3, 9–11, 13, 14, 22, 33, 34, 36–8, 41, 48, 49, 56, 61, 63, 64, 68, 70, 73, 76, 81, 83, 90, 92, 94, 100, 102, 115, 126–8, 131, 133, 137, 140, 142, 145, 149, 152, 157, 167, 168, 171, 173, 174, 176–9, 181, 188, 189, 191, 193, 196–8, 199 n.6
  definition of 5–8
  and mediatization 28–32
plot structure 147–71
  shape 147–9
Plough, P. 149, 158
political correctness 83, 88
Pollesch, R. 33
Poschmann, G. 34, 133
  Textträger 73, 80, 115, 186
postdigital 27, 190
  culture 173, 183
  performance 27, 174
postdramatic 26, 33, 35, 116, 148–9, 202 n.2
  aesthetics 34, 60
  compositions 25
  theatre 5, 25, 33–7, 55, 115, 175
posthuman/posthumanism 10, 27, 101–11, 117, 122, 136–8, 140, 141, 143, 144
Postman, N. 13
Prebble, L., *Sugar Syndrome, The* 1, 39, 67, 70, 92
Price, T., *Teh Internet Is Serious Business* 39

Protokoll, R., *Best Before* 149
pseudo-individualism 104–5
Pulp Fiction 83
Racine
  Brace Up! 37
  Phèdre 37
Radosavljević, D. 166
Rancière, J. 24, 35, 40, 105–6, 190
Rau, M., *Five Easy Pieces* 58
Ravenhill, M.
  Faust Is Dead 3, 9, 29, 37, 39–41, 60, 69, 157, 200 n.1
    form 45–9
    performance 49–50
    thematics 41–5, 52, 53
  Shopping and Fucking 3, 29
Reed, L., 'Perfect Day' 134, 137
representative regime 35
representative regime of art 40
Robert Lepage/Ex Machina 22
Royal Court Theatre 9, 23, 56, 58, 167
  Bytes 1
Royal National Theatre 90
RSC, *Such Tweet Sorrow* 31
Ruhl, S., *Dead Man's Cell Phone* 1, 92

scenography 2, 8, 21, 23–5, 33, 99, 143, 144, 189
Schaubühne Berlin 198
Schaubühne theatre 22
Schmidt, K. 29
Schneier, B. 121
Schulz, W. 15
sensible, the 25, 29, 30, 37, 41, 56, 74, 100, 108, 125, 190
  distribution of 24, 35, 40, 59, 72, 106, 187
  reproduction of 35, 61
Sermon, P. 28
Seynaeve, P. 58
Shakespeare, W.

Julius Caesar xii
    Romeo and Juliet 31, 178
Simmel, G. 16
Sims: Superstar, The 150
Snow, R. 16
social apathy 106, 107, 123, 129, 165
social disintegration 5, 32, 71, 106–8, 117, 123, 124, 168, 169
social media xii, 2–4, 7, 8, 13, 15, 19, 20, 23, 27, 28, 31, 34, 43, 46, 51–3, 66, 67, 79, 89, 101, 102, 106, 107, 123, 124, 148, 160, 164, 173, 175–8, 180, 184, 185, 189, 191, 192, 194, 196, 197, 200 n.1, 202 n.1, 203 n.2
Sontag, S. 199 n.2
spectatorship 2, 28, 31, 197
Sprechtext 115
Stephens, S. 202 n.3
    Pornography 1–2, 10, 32, 102, 117–30, 145, 184, 196
Stiegler, B. 199 n.4
Strindberg, A. 22, 113
    Dream Play, A 31, 79
subversion 25, 59, 108, 136, 166
Such Tweet Sorrow 178
Sun, The 84
Suspect Culture 6
Svich, C. 41

TaPRA (Theatre and Performance Research Association) 26
technogenesis 17, 20, 101, 161, 173, 192, 197, 199 n.4
techno-texts 6, 199 n.5
text-as-performance 191
textscape 82
Theater Journal, The
    'Digital "Issues": Rethinking Media in/and/as Performance' 28
    'Digital Media and Performance' 28
    'Theatre, the Digital, and the Analysis and Documentation of Performance' 28
Theatre of the Absurd 114
Theatre@risk 29
theatre texts 6, 112, 169, 197
thematization of mediatization 41–59
    Faust 41–50
    Nether, The 50–9
Thompson, J. B. 17, 199–200 n.2
Thorpe, C., *I Wish I was Lonely* 1, 39
Tiffany, J. 158, 159, 202 n.2
Tolstoy, L., *Anna Karenina* 134
Tonnelgroep Amsterdam, *Roman Tragedies* 14
traditional dramatic form 39–61
transcendental ego 103
transparent immediacy 158
Traverse Theatre Company 149, 158, 188
Trueman, M., 'What Can Theatre Say about the Internet?' 3
Turkle, S. 107
    Alone Together: Why We Expect More from Technology and Less from Each Other 124
Twitter 3, 5, 6, 11, 14, 20, 31, 46, 55, 63, 66, 84, 89, 99, 109, 122, 124, 163, 167, 173–92, 196, 197
    theatricality 179–80
    Yes/No Plays, The 180–6

van Itallie, J.-C. 3, 7, 29
virtual proximity 106
virtual reality 4, 39, 50–2, 111, 154, 157, 159, 170, 182, 183, 194

Walker, H. J., *I Wish I was Lonely* 1, 39
Walsh, E., *Chatroom* 23, 39, 67, 70, 92
web 2.0 technology 177
weblogs 6
Weems, M. 175
Wellman, M. 30
   Bitter Bierce 116
   Jennie Ritchie 116
Wilson, R., *Einstein on the Beach* 2

Wooster Group 2, 7, 24, 55, 198, 200 n.8
   Brace Up! 23
   Hamlet 32
   L.S.D. (. . . Just the High Points . . .) 21–2, 25, 32, 37
   To You, the Birdie! (Phèdre) 37
Wotzko, R. 31, 200 n.11

Yorkey, B., *Next to Normal* 178

www.ingramcontent.com/pod-product-compliance
Lightning Source LLC
Chambersburg PA
CBHW062217300426
44115CB00012BA/2106